SAGE was founded in 1965 by Sara Miller McCune to support the dissemination of usable knowledge by publishing innovative and high-quality research and teaching content. Today, we publish over 900 journals, including those of more than 400 learned societies, more than 800 new books per year, and a growing range of library products including archives, data, case studies, reports, and video. SAGE remains majority-owned by our founder, and after Sara's lifetime will become owned by a charitable trust that secures our continued independence.

Los Angeles | London | New Delhi | Singapore | Washington DC | Melbourne

ADVANCE PRAISE

Battle-ready is a well-articulated account of how managers and companies should think about their businesses. It provides both the tools and critical thinking which is crucial to survive in today's hyper-competitive, complex and disruptive marketplace.

It urges you to be paranoid, rigorous and watchful about the competition. This is a classic book for 'all' managers, line and otherwise.

Ajit Sivadasan
President and Global Head of eCommerce, Lenovo, USA

For people in high-velocity industries such as mine (aviation), *Battle-ready* is an instructive read. It's a compelling text for strategy executives to seek a humbling reflection, and then question and revisit their plans, especially with an eye on the external world. There are lessons for both the Davids and the Goliaths here. Replete with real-world strategy examples, *Battle-ready* is a breezy affair!

Dr Anurag Jain
Chief Strategy and Planning Officer, Flynas, Saudi Arabia

The book is ambitious in scope, insightful and well researched. Competitive strategy is a fascinating topic, and adopting a lens of 'battle' is a very apt view but not emphasized enough, especially in industries with high intensity or rapidly evolving dynamics. Just like how a general must consider numerous factors, Sai has developed a comprehensive framework for CEOs to assess their competitive landscape. It is a must-read for competitive strategy and response!

Chris Yeo
Managing Director, Head of GrabPay and Grab Ventures, Singapore

Battle-ready has deftly navigated an intricate balance between theory and business practicality. It is an enjoyable read, where fierce business competitors square off in the game to appropriate higher business values. Business practitioners must pay heed to the writer's thesis, to focus systematically and consistently on the external drivers of performance as a critical lever to secure a long-term win in the business arena.

Eugene Teh
Chief Business Officer, Digi Telecommunications, Malaysia

This book focuses on building immunity in businesses through superior resources and relevant capabilities so that they can be battle-ready to face competition in all its avatars. It uniquely shows how business competitors can measure their battle-readiness and transform themselves to higher levels of battle-readiness. It is an essential reading for business students and managers seeking to be battle-ready at the highest level for a challenging career in leading businesses.

Professor Ganesh Prabhu
Professor of Strategy, Indian Institute of Management Bangalore, India

It is a well-written book by an author who understands business. It acknowledges the diversity of competitive situations and invites the reader to define their own relevant arena, players and moves. It stresses the importance of using know-how and innovation in a smart and strategic way and provides a lot of examples which make the reader think. Last but not least, it highlights the effective habits of several famous leaders and companies. If you are a business leader, you will get some good ideas out of this book!

Dr Jaap Kalkman
Chief Transformation Officer, ADQ, Abu Dhabi, UAE

Simply great! When I read Dr Iyer's masterpiece, I discovered a passionate storyteller that I consider an amalgamation of Jim Collins and Malcolm Gladwell. I loved the creative metaphors and anecdotes from different times, countries and professions—from Hindustan Machine Tools to Intel to Archilochus to Mike Tyson to Hans Rosling. Are you a David or a Goliath, a Level 0, 1 or 2, a fox or a hedgehog? Get your external trigger, read it and get battle-ready!

Petter Kilefors
Managing Partner, Arthur D. Little, Sweden

Battle-ready encapsulates Sai's deep insights into business strategy, market and competition analysis and business history. He has brought all these together in a very readable and useful book. It effortlessly takes the reader through difficult aspects and provides them with case studies and concepts which are easy to comprehend and use.

Rajesh Duneja
Partner, Arthur D. Little, Dubai, UAE

Sai has nailed it! *Battle-ready* is the 'boot camp' managers and practitioners have been looking for to stay ahead and on course to win wars, not just battles! The narrative provides tremendous insights to practising managers on how to systematically minimize the blind spots while they go about their daily grind to achieve targets!

Rajiv Sivaraman
Vice President—Global Alliances, Siemens
Digital Industry Software, USA

Battle-ready is a must-read for anyone looking to keep their business nimble, agile and competitive—which is all of us business leaders, really. Oftentimes, in our quest to keep our businesses competitive and ahead of the curve, we tend to look inwards. We pay little or no attention to what the author calls 'the competitive arena'.

This book is a comprehensive toolkit on how to take cognizance of the competitive arena and the players therein in order to stay 'battle-ready'.

S. V. Ramanan
CEO—India and South Asia, Intellect Design Arena, India

This is an eye-opener which gives us a comprehensive need to know how in a fast changing disruptive business era an outside approach can outsmart competition, leading to sustainable growth of businesses while defining strategy in both creating value and capturing value.

Battle-ready—a must-read book—aptly captures the fine prints of strategizing, executing and creating value in businesses. It captures the fine prints of where to play, what to adapt and how to win in an easy, enjoyable way.

Ravichandran Purushothaman
President, Danfoss India, and
President, Madras Management Association India

It came as no surprise to see Sai's most structured, rigorous and analytical framework to address the subject with very pragmatic approaches and solutions.

This book is a must-read for business managers across all levels to systematically develop, validate and implement a sound strategy based on a comprehensive understanding and prediction of the overall ecosystem, ensuring the best value captured from the 'job to be done' for potential customers.

Thomas Kuruvilla
Managing Partner and Member of Global Board,
Arthur D. Little, Dubai, UAE

Battle-ready is perhaps the most focused and comprehensive work on competitive strategy. Starting with defining the competitive arena and all the way to a battle-ready mindset, Sai has hit at the heart of critical gaps in strategic thinking facing most organizations. A must-read for Board members and CxOs.

Piyush Jain
Head of Strategy, Minda Industries Limited, Gurgaon, India

BATTLE READY

SAGE Response, our business books imprint, celebrates its silver jubilee this year. As we reflect on this transformational journey that began with a single title, we thank everyone who has helped us to produce content that is topical and relevant across a varied audience of aspiring managers, working professionals, practitioners and students. We feel privileged that eminent management and leadership experts, professionals and stalwarts from academia supported and trusted us with their work. Over the years, SAGE Response has built an enviable list of practice-based, reader-friendly books that provide creative strategies to keep pace with the rapidly changing global scenario. As we grow and evolve with the times, it is our endeavour to continue to publish books that offer innovative solutions, approaches and perspectives to the disciplines that we serve.

Sai Prakash R. Iyer

BATTLE READY

Crafting Strategy
to Beat Competition

Los Angeles I London I New Delhi
Singapore I Washington DC I Melbourne

First published in 2021 by

SAGE Publications India Pvt Ltd
B1/I-1 Mohan Cooperative Industrial Area
Mathura Road, New Delhi 110 044, India
www.sagepub.in

SAGE Publications Inc
2455 Teller Road
Thousand Oaks, California 91320, USA

SAGE Publications Ltd
1 Oliver's Yard, 55 City Road
London EC1Y 1SP, United Kingdom

SAGE Publications Asia-Pacific Pte Ltd
18 Cross Street #10-10/11/12
China Square Central
Singapore 048423

Published by Vivek Mehra for SAGE Publications India Pvt Ltd. Typeset in 11/13.5pt Bembo by Fidus Design Pvt Ltd, Chandigarh.

Library of Congress Control Number: 2021945634

ISBN: 978-93-5479-081-2 (PB)

SAGE Team: Neha Pal, Satvinder Kaur and Dally Verghese

To my guru
Professor Deepak Kumar Sinha

Thank you for choosing a SAGE product!
If you have any comment, observation or feedback,
I would like to personally hear from you.

Please write to me at **contactceo@sagepub.in**

Vivek Mehra, Managing Director and CEO, SAGE India.

CONTENTS

FOREWORD

As a student of business management, I have always wondered why some businesses and corporations perform consistently better than others. Several academicians and leading consultants have written quite a few books on this subject where usually focus has been on internal issues, that is, organization's leadership, culture, structure, etc., while in this book, Sai Prakash raises a provocative question to all organizations: 'Are you battle-ready', where the more significant focus is on external drivers of performance.

Sai Prakash uses the metaphor of battle for competition. In any business, you have to understand the arena and the players who would influence the outcome of sustained profit. It is essential to focus on value creation (increase the size of the pie), but it is equally important to focus on value appropriation. It is not uncommon in businesses to land up in a situation where the value appropriated by the firm is significantly lower than the value added by the firm. We need to understand how various participants in the arena, including competitors, suppliers and substitutors, affect how value is appropriated within participants in the value chain.

He has drawn on examples of some familiar companies and personalities to illustrate the strategies used by technology firms and consumer goods companies. The book incorporates several case studies on contemporary business strategies from HLL to Nirma and Apple to Nokia to help us understand how to implement the systems and ideas in a real-life context. It helps us understand how to operate at the strategic level to be competitive. It reminds us that just because we are successful, it does not mean we are battle-ready.

He draws on literature from strategy, economics, etc., but provides a unique way of looking at these issues. He, of course, provides frameworks and perspectives but goes beyond that. He has attempted to provide a toolkit which should help managers apply ideas in their context. He has suggestions for both Davids and Goliaths. Drawing from biblical times, Goliaths refer to market leaders and entrenched players, while Davids refer to new players in the business. He has discussed battle-readiness for both Davids and Goliaths. The book also challenges many underlying assumptions and beliefs about strategy and seeks to add clarity and context to the field.

I am delighted that Sai has written a book on this challenging subject. I remembered our conversation over lunch several months ago. It is lovely to see him bring this topic to life in an informative and engaging way. He weaves his deep understanding of strategy literature and his personal experiences of several consulting assignments where he has tried out several ideas in the book. I read practically everything written on this subject of competition, and I must say that Sai has been able to address issues in a more comprehensive way than one has found in the most popular books on this subject. He is uniquely qualified to write this book. He explains complex concepts lucidly without sacrificing rigour.

I have known Sai Prakash for 20 odd years. My first interaction with him was as a doctoral student of strategy at IIM Bangalore. I was impressed with his razor-sharp mind and voracious reading, and curiosity about various business issues. Now, for a decade, he has been teaching a popular course titled 'Industry and Competitor Analysis' at IIM Udaipur. The book is an outcome of this course which he kept refining at every iteration. I am pleased that through this book, his insights would be made available to larger audiences.

I would highly recommend this book to anyone interested in business; whether you are a David or Goliath, you would find very detailed actionable insights. Overall, this is a concise volume with well-thought-out tie-ins to theory and practice in the real world, which would give you a proper understanding of an often-difficult topic. After reading this book, you would develop better understanding of the external drivers of the business performance and in the process be better battle-ready. Like me, I am sure you are going to enjoy the book.

Janat Shah
Director, IIM Udaipur

PREFACE

On a windy afternoon in early 2012, my friend Professor Thomas Joseph asked if I could offer a strategy elective for the first batch of MBA students at IIM Udaipur (IIMU). What started with that has gone on to become an annual fixture in my calendar, even as I moved from Kolkata to the Middle East and then to Chennai. The course goes by the dull title of 'Industry and Competitor Analysis' and is about gaining deep understanding of how the business landscape impacts business performance and how to factor this into strategy making. It's about crafting a competitive strategy which will improve the chances of beating competition. That's the origin story of this book.

Over the years, as a strategy advisor as well as a facilitator of learning, I have seen managers and soon-to-be managers focus a lot on what is within the organization—leadership, culture, organization, innovation and so on. What about competitors? Business partners? Players in other arenas? Providers of new technologies? More often, the attention to external drivers of performance is fleeting. The course which I offer at IIMU tries to correct for that—get the soon-to-be managers to give more emphasis on what's outside. In consulting engagements, I have tried to get managers to look outside more and gain deeper insights. The results have been quite satisfying. Having refined the ideas—most of those received from giants in the academic disciplines of strategy, economics, sociology, etc., over years of discussing and applying in real-life settings—I realized that a larger audience might benefit from it. That's the motivation for this book.

It's not that managers do not appreciate the importance of looking outside. Right from the C-level executives to the front-line warriors, we struggle every day to find time to do that 'sit back and think about the game that's going on'. Caught in an unending stream of urgent tasks, the only time when we look outside is during the annual ritual called business planning. There, we are lulled into false comfort by templates which help us get over the task of looking outside with minimum effort. As much as we would like to look outside, we don't seem to have, ready at hand, the tools and instruments which will make the task of looking outside easier to do, insightful and useful.

Ask yourself: Am I battle-ready? Without looking outside carefully, without drawing deep insights about what's going on out there, we are not likely to be battle-ready. If we have been winning, it's probably because our rivals aren't battle-ready either. Maybe they are in a worse shape. If we have been slipping recently, it's because some of our rivals are getting more battle-ready than us. Either case, there is no excuse for us not to get battle-ready. That's the pitch to get you to read this book.

ACKNOWLEDGEMENTS

As I was in the last lap of my doctoral dissertation, my guru, Professor Deepak Sinha, suggested that I might want to look at industry and competitor analysis as a potential elective when I enter academia. That suggestion was backed by more than four years of intense learning under him in diverse academic specializations within social sciences, management and strategy. All that has come of use immensely in advising corporates, teaching the course and writing this book, which I dedicate to him. I am indebted to Professor Janat Shah, director at IIMU, who guided and facilitated my journey as an adjunct professor with the institute and provided the opportunity for great learning experience from teaching MBA students for a decade now.

My debt of gratitude to Professor Thomas Joseph, who triggered my affiliation with IIMU and my former employer Arthur D. Little. I wouldn't have travelled the path I did in the last 15 or so years but for him. V. K. Sasi Nair, Uday Bhaskar, P. Shrinath and the Programmes Office team at IIMU ensured that I can focus on delivering the course. Abhishek Kumar Gupta of IIMU library has all along helped me access tough-to-get content with a smile. My sincere thanks to all of them. My thanks to Vengat Krishnaraj for his valuable inputs in getting the companion website up and running.

If what comes next page on is somewhat readable and clear, it's thanks to the generous help by Rajiv Sivaraman, Mathew P. Joseph, Chalasani Srinivasa Rao, Madhavi Srinivas, Rajesh Duneja and Ashok Namboodiri, for sharing their thoughts after reviewing various parts of early drafts. Rajiv patiently read every word of the first draft and shared incisive comments—on emails as well as over calls. I don't know how I can express my gratitude to all these kind souls other than saying a big 'thank you'. My thanks to Professor Anirvan Pant who pointed me to recent developments in academic literature on identity and its links with competitive dynamics, which helped immensely. The usual caveat applies. Special thanks to the fantastic team at SAGE—Neha Pal and Manisha Mathews, who have been there since the start, always understanding and patient as I took an extra year to complete what I had to do; Satvinder Kaur Sandhu and her editorial team, who converted my manuscript into a book.

The journey which started sometime before the COVID-19 lock-down went on through the lockdown and till I am about to get my second dose of vaccine. During this journey, the two ladies in my life—Meenakshi and Anjana—made sure that I stay on track. They sometimes nudged me along, sometimes poked fun, sometimes left me alone, on one occasion got me a mouse pad which read, 'finish what you start', but never gave up. But for their support, I wouldn't have gotten to this. Finally, to all my students—the countless discussions and debates we have had in and outside classrooms have gone on to shape what appears in the following pages—a big thanks for helping me stay young at heart.

CHAPTER ONE

The Game

Of every seven smartphones sold in 2017, only one was an iPhone. Yet of every seven dollars of profit made by smartphone makers, Apple, the maker of iPhones, pocketed four dollars. Samsung and Huawei together sold twice the number of smartphones as Apple. But their combined profit was less than half of Apple's.[1] The easy explanation is that iPhones are pricey. But that's nowhere near the complete picture on why Apple has been the leader in profit share among smartphone makers. It has been capturing more than 60 per cent of industry profits for several years. In addition to smartphones, Apple rakes in a decent sum through profits on its other products such as personal computers (PCs), laptops and wearables. It generates profits through subscription services such as iCloud and Apple Music and platform offerings such as App Store and Apple Pay.

The smartphone ecosystem creates tremendous value for all participants involved—the competing smartphone makers, their suppliers, complementors, the supply chain and retail partners, and the

---

[1] Data on shipments for 2017 from https://www.forbes.com/sites/chuckjones/2018/03/02/apple-continues-to-dominate-the-smartphone-profit-pool/#14e1d6e161bb (accessed 2 June 2021). Data on profit share from handsets from https://www.statista.com/statistics/780367/global-mobile-handset-profit-share-by-vendor/ (accessed 2 June 2021).

end customers. Apple leads the pack when it comes to 'value appropriation'—capturing a high share of profits made in the ecosystem. It is not alone in being good at value appropriation. Firms from diverse businesses and geographic regions fill up the leader board of top value appropriators. These positions however change over time. Thirty years ago, General Electric (GE) would have been among the top value appropriators, and 70–80 years ago, DuPont and Sears, Roebuck and Co. would have been. Not anymore! Making profits, making more profits than your competitors and doing it consistently over time are awfully tricky. And this has been the focus of managers, especially the C-levels, strategy consultants and scholars.

There have been several excellent expositions on why some businesses and corporations perform consistently better than others, that discuss a wide range of drivers of corporate and business performance such as leadership, innovation, culture, and distinctive resources and capabilities possessed by the firm.[2] Most of these explanations of superior firm performance focus on drivers which are internal to the firm and the business—factors which lie within organizational boundaries and over which managers can exert influence and even control. These internal drivers do play a critical role in every example of superior value appropriation such as Apple now, or GE, DuPont or Sears in yesteryears. Yet is this the complete story?

MANAGING EXTERNAL DRIVERS

All these great firms appropriated value, often more than any of their rivals, while conducting their affairs in a business landscape consisting of their competitors, wannabe competitors, customers, suppliers,

---

[2] See, for instance, Jim Collins, *Good to Great* (Manhattan, NY: Harper Business, 2001); Jim Collins and Jerry I. Porras, *Built to Last: Successful Habits of Visionary Companies* (Manhattan, NY: Harper Business, 1994); Jim Collins and Morten T. Hansen, *Great by Choice* (Manhattan, NY: Harper Business, 2011).

business partners, governments and their regulatory framework, investors, analysts and so on—the external environment. It is not possible for a firm to succeed in value appropriation by just focusing on the internal drivers of business performance such as leadership, innovation and culture. Equally important is the ability of the firm to manage the external drivers of business performance. There's the view that focus on external environment is needed only if the business is operating in uncertain environments such as intense competitive rivalry, regulatory uncertainty and rapid changes in customer preferences or technology. Research shows that attention to external environment by top managers has a positive influence on business performance irrespective of whether the business operates in a turbulent or placid external environment.[3] Looking outside helps improve performance, whether the outside is kind or wicked.

External drivers are many, and they impact business performance in many ways. There is no excuse not to pay attention to external drivers. To start with, there are the customers. What we know about them is inferred from data we have of them which may or may not be a rich picture of who they are, what problems they are trying to solve and why they buy from us or others. We may or may not update the data periodically. Then there are the competitors who are vying for the same customers, same suppliers, same employees or same sources of funding. There are always a few wannabe competitors waiting on the wings wanting to come in. There are the suppliers—providers of inputs, human capital, financial capital, ideas and what not. The governments of countries in which we operate our business put in place regulations. Then there are the analysts, the media and a good share of the public at large. All these affect our business and its performance.

The external environment provides opportunities and at the same time puts in place constraints and challenges. It imposes uncertainties,

---

[3] Vinay K. Garg, Bruce A. Walters, and Richard L. Priem, 'Chief Executive Scanning Emphases, Environmental Dynamism, and Manufacturing Firm Performance', *Strategic Management Journal* 24 (2003): 725–744.

some that are knowable and many that we only come to know after the event. The external environment changes its very nature over time. Often, even when we are aware of some of these changes, we do not appreciate their significance until our business performance is impacted.

A monopolist is surprised by the entry of a formidable rival. In the 1980s, British Satellite Broadcasting (BSB) obtained a monopoly licence from the British government for direct satellite broadcasting (DSB) of television programmes. It went on a sedate pace to launch its service and was blindsided to Sky and Rupert Murdoch who came in late but launched a rival service even before BSB went on air.[4]

While we think that we know what the customer wants and doesn't want, the customer ditches us for something we thought was just a passing fad. That's what happened to Nokia and Blackberry when Apple launched a phone with touch interface.

Our competitors can play havoc by spoiling the market for us. They can make it difficult, if not impossible, for us to profit from unique resources or capabilities we toiled to acquire. Procter & Gamble (P&G) launched a patented new product for teeth whitening in the early 2000s which practically locked out Colgate-Palmolive (C-P) from this high-growth category. C-P responded by launching a product which significantly lowered the profits that P&G could earn in this new category.[5]

BSB shareholders, after locking horns with Sky in a war of attrition, capitulated to takeover by Sky. Could BSB have guarded its monopoly against Sky's aggression? Blackberry, which was king of the hill in smartphones, fell from its perch and eventually faded into irrelevance in a matter of few years. Could it have averted the fall?

---

[4] Pankaj Ghemawat, 'British Satellite Broadcasting versus Sky Television' (Harvard Business School Case 9-794-031, 2007).

[5] Felix Oberholzer-Gee and Dennis Yao, 'Brighter Smiles for the Masses: Colgate vs. P&G' (Harvard Business School Case 9-706-435, 2007).

P&G had a patent on teeth-whitening strips which it could have milked for several years. Yet it had to get into a street fight with C-P just three years after launch. Could it have protected its ability to appropriate the value of its patent?

The answer is, yes. If only they had paid more attention to the external drivers of business performance. One always looks wiser with hindsight. Unfortunately, hindsight can only make us look wise after the event. Hindsight is not available to guide decisions and actions before the event. However, we can learn from hindsight. We can learn from our own past as well as that of other businesses.

Time and again, we see around us business failures which are triggered by lack of attention to external environment. Yet not much learning seems to take place from these episodes. Reality is that many CEOs and managers do not pay enough attention to the external environment. Findings from a research study in 2017 involving activities of 1,114 CEOs from 6 countries[6] show that two-thirds of CEOs' time spent focused on interactions with insiders (employees), while only one-third of their interaction time was with those from outside the organization.[7]

Top management's focus is often inward-looking. It is on driving innovation, building a strong leadership team and succession pipeline, instilling culture and values which will make the organization a utopia, coming up with great new products, patenting technologies which they have invested in and so on. On all these, considerable

---

[6] 282 CEOs in Brazil, 115 in France, 125 in Germany, 356 in India, 87 in the UK and 149 in the USA. See Oriana Bandiera et al., 'CEO Behavior and Firm Performance' (Harvard Business School Working Paper 17-083, 2017), 6.

[7] See Table B3 (page 45) in ibid. One can argue that a CEO's time spent with internal constituents could be on topics about external environment. Equally likely is the possibility that time spent with external constituents focuses on internal issues, for instance, time spent with a consultant to figure out how to address internal challenges. The CEO is ultimately responsible for business performance. The premise here is that relative time spent between internal and external constituents is indicative of the relative emphasis by the CEO on internal vs external factors which influence business performance.

effort and resources are spent. Teams are deployed, consultants are engaged, advice is sought, and trainings and workshops are held. Organizations often carefully plan and put in dedicated effort to influence the internal drivers of business performance. All these are critical and essential, and top management has to be engaged in all this.

On the other hand, understanding of external environment and gaining insights on how it is likely to influence business performance often take a back seat. Managers do not pay enough attention to gaining actionable insights about the external environment. There is limited effort which goes into understanding what's going on outside the business and its implications for performance. Whatever passes for external assessment is often weaved into business planning and strategic planning exercises and tends more to be lip service as part of corporate rituals.

What passes for understanding the external environment is often done based on information gathered from business press as well as chance conversations with other business leaders and managers in management conclaves and airport lounges. Information thus gathered is likely to be partial at best, random in most cases and often too late to know. It's based on our perceptions of what customers want, not based on a systematic exploration and insights on why our competitors' customers do not come to us. Sometimes, it's based on a packaged report from a consulting firm or the opinion of a trusted advisor or a blue-eyed boy.

More often, our insights on how the external environment influences our business performance is partial, poorly informed and too late in coming. Our insights are skewed by gaps in information as well as biases in interpreting available information, which are built into our organization's culture and processes. To drive business performance better, we need to pay more attention to external drivers.

PLAY TO WIN

The Indian cricket team pays a lot of attention to select cricketers with great skills. It ensures diversity of skills which can be configured to deploy distinctive game plans against opponents. It spends considerable effort and resources in training the team, honing their skills and building a positive team culture. Imagine that with just these and nothing else, how would the team face the opponent in their home turf? Our team would enter the game without any knowledge of the line-up of players in the opponent team. They will be clueless about the opponent's distinctive skills and their most favoured techniques. Our team would have no idea about the likely game plan of the opponent team. Our team wouldn't have factored in how the weather might affect their game play, or their opponent's. Our team would have ignored how supportive the crowd is likely to be for the opponent. They would have forgotten that their opponent team members won't suffer from fatigue due to recent long-distance travel. The result of the game is not that difficult to guess. Most businesses compete like this.

We compete to gain customers. We compete to secure better prices and higher market share. We compete to get the best inputs at the most favourable terms from our suppliers. We compete to achieve best efficiencies in our operations. We compete for top-quality human capital. We compete to source capital at the lowest possible cost. We compete to own and control the next breakthrough technology. We compete to be regarded as the most reputed company and the best workplace. We compete to make more profits, today and in future.

To play this game and win, we need to be 'battle-ready'. We should have a clear focus on what we bring to the game. We need to have a keen eye for what our opponents bring to the game, what the rules of the game are, how we can shape these rules, what other factors affect the game and how we can leverage all these to drive outcomes favourable to us. The end goal is a higher tally than competition. Just like the top-scoring team becomes the champion, the winner of the competition game is the firm which takes home most profits— the one that's best in 'value appropriation'.

We are good at understanding, influencing and leveraging internal drivers of business performance—what we bring to the game. Same can't be said about the external drivers of business performance. In general, managers pay less attention to the external drivers compared to the internal drivers of business performance.

This book is about how to get battle-ready. It's about paying more attention to the external drivers of business performance—attention which is systematic, replicable and can provide actionable insights well in time to act and gain an upper hand in the competitive battle. It's about spotting and acting on potential opportunities to improve our business performance when compared to competitors. It's about anticipating and guarding against pitfalls and potential threats from external drivers which can drag down our business performance. It's about better understanding of emerging risks in a timely manner so that we can take mitigating actions. It's about making all these part of how we do things in our organizations.

It's about gaining actionable insights which will enable us to improve our ability to appropriate more value, protect our value appropriation and sustain our value appropriated over time. Combined with what we already know and practise in terms of leveraging internal drivers of business performance, this book is about gaining deeper and actionable insights on how to get battle-ready to beat competition.

KEEPING SCORES

Every game has a well-defined way of keeping scores. In cricket, it is the tally of runs; in football or soccer, it is the number of goals. Highest score wins in these cases. We also have games and sports where lowest score wins such as golf (number of strokes) or a race (time to finishing line). In the game of business, we keep scores by counting the value appropriated in the currencies in which we buy and sell. The winner is the most profitable player over time—the top value appropriator.

Whenever I use the term 'profits' henceforth, I use it as an easy-to-relate synonym for 'value appropriated', though what we mean by 'value' is different from accounting profit. To get a better understanding of value—'value created' and 'value appropriated'—let's do a simple thought experiment.[8]

Let's consider Biju's Salad Bar. Biju, the incumbent player, makes and sells salads. He buys veggies and dressing from Sonu. Biju makes one salad which is bought by Cindy, who will pay a maximum of ₹100 for the salad, nothing more. If Biju asks for a higher price, Cindy would not buy the salad at all. Let's say that this is Cindy's willingness to pay (WtP) for the salad. If Sonu is not able to sell the inputs—veggies and dressing—to Biju, he could sell these for ₹20 to a nearby restaurant. That becomes the opportunity cost for supplier (OCS) of Sonu for the inputs. Sonu will not sell the inputs to Biju at a price less than ₹20.

Value is created when Cindy buys a salad from Biju, for which Biju buys the inputs from Sonu. The 'value created' can be quantified as ₹100 less ₹20 (WtP less OCS), which is ₹80. In this simple thought experiment, the three participants—the supplier, the incumbent and the customer—have come together to create the value of ₹80. We can think of 'value created' as a pie which the three have jointly made. If any of the three doesn't participate, there's no pie—value created becomes zero.

So far, we haven't mentioned the price which Cindy pays Biju for the salad or the cost which Biju incurs to source the inputs from Sonu. First insight is that the value created depends not on transaction prices and costs but on the monetary value of benefits derived from the exchange by participants in the value chain. Any of the three participants can influence the value created positively or negatively.

Let's say that Sonu finds that restaurants are willing to pay ₹25 for the inputs he wants to sell. Unless Biju pays him at least ₹25, Sonu would prefer to sell the inputs to a restaurant. The value created by the salad value chain shrinks to ₹75 (₹100 less ₹25). The opposite is also possible wherein the value created by the salad value chain goes up.

---

[8] Adam M. Brandenburger and Harborne W. Stuart Jr. 'Value-based Business Strategy', *Journal of Economics & Management Strategy* 5, no. 1 (1996): 5–24.

Let's say that Cindy finds that a new falafel stand has come up which offers a falafel at ₹80. Cindy finds that the falafel is comparable to the salad in terms of nutrition and gratification. She realizes that she is really not that keen to part with an additional ₹20 for the salad. Her WtP drops and as a result the value created shrinks.

Let's say that Biju's grandmother gives him a magic ingredient—a taste enhancer. To keep this simple, let's say that his grandmother gives him the taste enhancer for free, which means no cost to Biju. With that, the taste of the salad vastly improves and a totally impressed Cindy is now willing to pay ₹115 for the salad with enhanced taste. The value created increases in this case.

So far, our thought experiment has looked only at value creation—what's the size of the pie that's created by the participants in the value chain and how this can change. Now, let's get to 'value appropriation'—how the pie is shared among the participants. Reverting to the first scenario of WtP of Cindy at ₹100 and OCS of Sonu at ₹20, the value that's available to be divided up is ₹80. Sonu and Biju will bargain on the price of inputs. Sonu will not sell the inputs at less than ₹20, as he has a restaurant ready to buy the inputs at that price. Biju will not buy the inputs at a cost that's more than the price that Cindy is going to pay for the salad, so as to avoid a loss. Likewise, Cindy will not pay more than ₹100 for the salad. The cost of inputs to Biju and the price of salad to Cindy have to lie between ₹20 and ₹100, and the price of salad has to be more than the cost of inputs.

There are several feasible answers. Let's say that Biju and Cindy agree on the price of salad as ₹70, and Biju and Sonu agree on the cost of inputs as ₹30. Now, we can look at how the value pie of ₹80 has been shared by the three participants (see Figure 1.1). Cindy the customer, appropriates ₹30. Sonu the supplier of inputs, appropriates ₹10. Biju, the incumbent, appropriates ₹40. Value appropriation is the share of the value pie which we are able to take and depends on the prices and costs at which the participants in the value chain engage in exchanges.

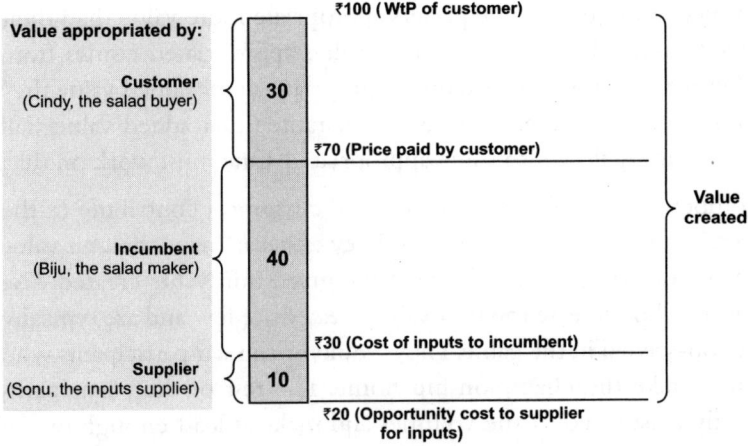

Source: Adapted from *Value-based Business Strategy* by Adam M. Brandenburger and Harborne W. Stuart Jr.

Figure 1.1. Value Creation and Value Appropriation

Value creation is the outcome of the joint effort by all participants in the value chain, and it happens when customers derive the benefit from buying the product. The amount of value created in an arena consisting of several suppliers, incumbents and customers will be the sum of value created per unit of product over the volume of products bought. In the case of differentiated products or inputs, the highest WtP or the lowest OCS will drive the value created per unit. The sum of value created for the volume of products consumed will give the measure of 'value created' in the arena by all the participants. This is the value pie, over which all participants who contributed to value creation—the suppliers, incumbent players and the customers—have a claim. Each participant will take a slice off the pie—their 'value appropriated'.

'Added value' for a participant is the contribution which a player makes to the overall value created. We can view this as the value created with the participant in the arena less the value created if the participant is not present. In an ideal world, each participant's value appropriated will equal their added value. But in the real world, this need not be so. Some players appropriate more value than their added value.[9] The excess of their value appropriated comes from other participants who couldn't appropriate all the added value they brought to the game. There is no guarantee that added value will automatically flow into value appropriated. One must work on that.

Competing incumbents, suppliers and customers contribute to the overall value created in two ways. They either increase the unit value created or bring more volume at the given unit value created. The players who increase the unit value created are few and are typically the top-seeded in the game. They would be the star participants who usually take the championship home. The rest of the participants mostly exist to cover the volumes and make at least enough out of the game to stay on and possibly invest in trying to improve their position for future. Thus, it is not easy or commonplace for a firm to become the top value appropriator in any competitive arena.

The bottom line for a business competing in an arena is that it must bring positive and substantial added value, and its value appropriated must at least be its added value. This has to be done while every competitor and every other participant are trying to bring new added value and increase their share of value appropriated. Battle-ready players take a keen interest in value creation, added value and value appropriation.

LEVELS OF BATTLE-READINESS

An important question we ought to ask ourselves would be: How battle-ready am I? We may be tempted to answer this question by turning to the scores kept—our past profits. With that approach, we would believe that we need to capture the highest score to claim that 'I am playing the best.' However, that's a circular inference

---

[9] If we assume that all participants 'seek any and all profitable opportunities' (ibid., 13), no participant can appropriate more value than their added value. But this assumption is not tenable under conditions of bounded rationality and time-bound decision-making under imperfect and incomplete information.

and doesn't help us understand how to improve our performance over time, which really is a result of getting better at battle-readiness.

To understand how we can improve our battle-readiness, we need to ask: Why am I where I am vis-à-vis competitors, and why are they where they are? This question is relevant in two scenarios. First, some of our rivals seem to be better than us. In this case, how are my competitors more battle-ready than I am, and how can I bridge the gap? Second, we are the leader of the pack. In this case, how can I make myself more battle-ready than before, putting more distance between the rivals and me?

The answers to these questions would come from an assessment of how we are playing the game, when compared to competitors. For that, we need to reflect and understand at what level we are competing. To improve our chances of winning, we need to compete at a level more sophisticated than our rivals.

There are several ways in which we can view the level of sophistication of how we compete. We can view this in terms of what the focus of our business is. Are we focused on a narrow product definition to draw the boundaries of our game, or are we taking a broad view of the customer function we meet or an even broader view by considering the problems our customers are trying to solve? Theodore Levitt urged managers to take a broader view of the business in which they are competing.[10] More than half a century later, his call to broaden how we view competition is still relevant in defining the scope of business and competition. However, the view does not provide a holistic view of how well we compete.

Another way to view levels of competition is about how fiercely we engage in rivalry. This can range from collusion (illegal in most countries) on the one end to death matches such as a war of

---

[10] Theodore Levitt, 'Marketing Myopia', *Harvard Business Review* (Best of 1960) 38 (July–August 2004): 45–56.

attrition[11] at the other extreme. The types of competition articulated in economics literature[12] are closer to this view, with benign competitive landscape under a monopolist (or a few colluding oligopolists) at the one end of the spectrum and fierce rivalry among perfectly competitive players at the other end. This view doesn't provide useful insights on how to compete to win.

We view levels of competition in terms of how well we understand the arena, its participants and their game plans, the evolving nature of the arena, and how well-prepared we are in playing the game to win (see Table 1.1). We view levels of competition in terms of how 'battle-ready' we are.

Level 0

At the bottom of the pile are the Level 0 competitors. They are mostly inward-focused and do not spend much effort or resources in understanding what's going on outside their organization. They define their competitive arena as per their historical and current product line-up and often tend to ignore underlying customer functions. They have a narrow view about external drivers of performance, if at all.

Most often, they continue to do what they have been doing, even when significant events and changes affecting their industry and market are common public knowledge. At best, they react with a delay to competitor actions and other developments which deeply impact their business performance. Typically, they are too late in responding. They do not pay enough attention to value appropriation, letting other participants take away value that they should have appropriated.

---

[11] War of attrition refers to a specific competitive strategy where the player aims to win by wearing down the rival(s) in terms of resources. It's essentially a death match where the last player alive (not necessarily standing) wins the game.

[12] Monopoly, oligopoly, monopolistic competition and perfect competition, often referred to as market structures.

Table 1.1. Levels of Battle-readiness

	Level 0	Level 1	Level 2
Definition of competitive arena	Narrow: focus on current products/ services	Broader: focus on utility derived by customers	Broadest: focus on problems customers are trying to solve
Attention to external environment	Minimal: inward-focused	Selective: external attention triggered by specific events or contingencies	Exhaustive: systematic approach to understanding external environment and its impact on business
Focus on external drivers of performance	Narrow	Selective: few drivers based on managers' worldview	Broad-based: covers a wide range of drivers
Engagement with stakeholders in external environment	Restricted: primarily engages with transaction partners (customers/ suppliers)	Ad hoc: engages opportunistically with participants in the arena other than transaction partners	Broad: engages with a wide range of participants in the arena periodically and systematically to better understand trends and impact on business
Time horizon and breadth of attention to understand and engage with external environment	Short term: focus mainly on factors which have immediate impact on business	Short to medium term: considers factors which go beyond immediate impact on business but restricted to current industry/product/customer context	Short to long term: views a wide range of developments, ranging from short-term impact on business performance to long-term impact from trends in technology, market and customer preferences

(Continued)

	Level 0	Level 1	Level 2
Definition of and attention to competitors	Restricted to current and direct rivals	Focus on current rivals with selective attention to potential rivals and substitutors	Clear view of broad competitive arena: identifies current and potential rivals, substitutors and emerging rivals using disruptive technologies
Emphasis on understanding competitors	Minimal and mostly anecdotal understanding: often taken aback/ surprised by competitor actions	Selective analysis of competitors based on perception of competitive threats: limited systematic analysis of competitors' strategies and capabilities	Extensive under-standing based on periodic and systematic analy-sis of current and potential competitors, their strategies and capabili-ties, their likely moves, as well as good under-standing of tech-nologies which can change the industry
Ability to predict/ identify and initiate timely response to competitive actions	Limited: mostly reacts to competitor actions, often with considerable delay	Selective: will respond to or even pre-empt some competitor actions but can completely miss some critical competitor moves	Accurate and swift: will most often predict competitor actions before the event and pre-empt these with a good degree of success; limited instances of failing to predict/pre-empt competitor moves

(Continued)

(Continued)

	Level 0	Level 1	Level 2
Ability to thwart competitive threats	Low to none	Moderate	High
Emphasis on value appropriation	Low: weak in sensing loss of appropriation	Moderate: able to appropriate only in straightforward scenarios	High: able to ensure appropriation even in complex scenarios

Source: The author.

Hindustan Machine Tools (HMT) of India was a government-owned monopoly watchmaker, among other things. For decades since the 1950s, their competition was from Japanese and Swiss watches which were imported into the country legally or otherwise. In 1986–1987, about 18 years after Japanese watchmakers introduced the new and better technology of quartz movement (lower cost and more accurate) in the global watch market, just 4 per cent of HMT's production of 5 million watches had quartz movement. The remaining were with mechanical movement and in limited number of models.[13] Ironically, HMT had access to quartz movement technology early on through its collaboration with Citizen of Japan, and after a brief experiment with quartz, it decided to focus on mechanical watches.[14] In 1989, Titan—a joint venture led by the

[13] M. Rahman, 'New Watch Companies Try to Capture a Lucrative Market', *India Today*, 31 August 1987. Available at: https://www.indiatoday.in/magazine/economy/story/19870831-new-watch-companies-try-to-capture-a-lucrative-market-799211-1987-08-31 (accessed 27 November 2019).

[14] Mahesh Kulkarni, 'Why Time Ran Out on HMT', *Business Standard*, 14 September 2014. Available at: https://www.business-standard.com/article/management/why-time-ran-out-for-hmt-114091400691_1.html (accessed 27 November 2019).

Tata business house—entered the market with a large variety of quartz watches, a nationwide network of swanky exclusive retail stores and service centres and made themselves visible through multicoloured centerspread advertisements in leading national and regional dailies. Although HMT knew for close to two decades that Tatas were entering watches in India, it did nothing to counter their entry.[15] In just about a decade after the launch of Titan, HMT became yet another yesteryear iconic brand. HMT eventually shut shop on watchmaking a few years on.

HMT did not bother to build on the cost advantage of quartz movement technology to grow and retain the market, though it had a 20-year lead over Titan. After the launch of Titan, HMT reacted in a sedate pace to beef up its range of watches with quartz movement. By then, it was too late. The market went over to Titan.

Level 1

Britannia and Parle dominated the biscuits industry in India with more than 80 per cent share of the market. This was during the early 2000s. ITC, the Indian tobacco major and commodities to hotels conglomerate, entered biscuits with its Sunfeast brand in 2003. Sunfeast was able to leverage the extensive distribution network ITC already had through its tobacco business, and it grabbed 7 per cent market share from the well-entrenched incumbents in three years.

During 2000–2005, neither Britannia nor Parle released any new products. Picking up chatter from the market about ITC's entry even before it happened and following ITC's launch, Britannia went about relaunching key brands as well as bringing out new products such as additional flavours and assorted biscuit boxes for festival gifting.[16]

---

[15] Vinay Kamath, *TITAN: Inside India's Most Successful Consumer Brand* (Gurugram, Hachette India, 2018).

[16] Govindakrishna Seshan, 'Coming Up from Behind', *Business Standard*, 27 June 2006. Available at: https://www.business-standard.com/article/management/coming-up-from-behind-106062701008_1.html (accessed 24 November 2019).

Although Britannia lost share to the new entrant, it was still able to respond quickly to stave off the challenge by ITC's Sunfeast. Britannia, back in the early 2000s, would be a Level 1 competitor.

Level 1 competitors are inward-focused. But they opportunistically spend effort or resources in understanding what's going on outside their organization based on triggers from specific events, such as talk about potential entry. They define their markets as per their current product line-up as well as underlying customer functions. They take a selective view of external drivers of performance, limited by the experience and worldview of their managers.

More often, they continue to do what they have been doing, and pause and change course, sometimes with a delay, only when significant events and changes affect their market. Typically, they respond quickly to competitor actions and other developments which deeply impact their business performance but do not excel in forestalling potential competitor actions. They would be able to ensure value appropriation in straightforward business scenarios, but once a while, a smarter rival will pip them and take away the value which is theirs to appropriate.

Level 2

Level 2 competitors are more battle-ready than Levels 1 and 0. They are outward-focused without losing sight of the internal drivers of business performance. They systematically and periodically channel effort and resources to understand what's going on outside their organization. They define their markets by paying close attention to the problems which their customers are trying to solve. They use these insights from their customers to drive their innovation agenda.

More often, they keep looking for new ways of doing things in both customer-facing activities and backend operations. Typically, they anticipate competitor actions and other developments which deeply impact their business performance and excel in pre-empting potential competitor actions. They are often the first to bring emerging technology trends into their business. They are focused on ensuring value appropriation, whatever be the business scenario.

For more than two decades, Jeff Bezos has been reminding folks at Amazon that it's 'Day 1'. According to him, 'Day 2 is stasis. Followed by irrelevance. Followed by excruciating painful decline. Followed by death. And *that* is why it is always Day 1.' Bezos suggests 'embracing external trends' as one of the four essentials to fend off Day 2. 'The outside world can push you into Day 2 if you won't or can't embrace powerful trends quickly. If you fight them, you're probably fighting the future. Embrace them and you have a tailwind'.[17] For Bezos, the Day 2 mindset is the thin end of the wedge.

Back in Amazon's early days, Bezos reminded his employees 'to wake up every morning terrified … not of our competitors, but of our customers'. That's possible and makes sense only when we are couple of steps ahead of our rivals. That doesn't happen by chance. It has to be deliberately engineered. Talking about customer–driven proactivity, Bezos says, 'We lower prices and increase value for customers before we have to. We invent before we have to.'[18] A less-battle-ready player might end up being compelled to do these, if at all.

THE GAME PLAN

Playing the competition game at a higher level than your rivals will greatly improve your chance of success. However, rivals too will make progress. So it makes sense to periodically assess ourselves and our rivals on what level we are currently playing the competition game.

You can use the tool 'Are You Battle-ready?' on the companion website[19] to assess your business from your perspective (see Appendix A). You can also use the tool to assess the level at which your key rivals

---

[17] Jeffrey P. Bezos, *Invent & Wander* (Boston, MA: Harvard Business Review Press and PublicAffairs, 2021).

[18] Ibid.

[19] https://www.battle-ready.co

are competing. If any of your competitors are playing at a level better than yours, you are feeling the heat already and there is a clear need to up your game. If none of your competitors are playing better than you, moving up in battle-readiness provides a great opportunity for you to put some more distance between you and your rivals. Improving the level at which you compete would always be beneficial. Who would not want to play the competition game like a pro? But that requires an astute game plan and a clear prioritization of our action agenda.

A good game plan starts with an understanding of the 'arena'. Most golf courses have 18 holes, but there ends the similarity. Each course will have its own unique configuration of fairways, greens, roughs and hazards. A prudent golfer would try and understand the structure and distinctive features of a course and also think about how these would impact her game play, before teeing off. Likewise, in the game of business competition, the prudent manager ought to figure out the landscape of the arena in which competition unfolds. We start with understanding what the arena is in Chapter 2 'The Arena' and figure out how the arena impacts our business strategy in Chapter 3 'Understanding the Arena'.

While understanding the arena is a good starting point, it is often essential to clarify who we are fighting with and gauge how these rivals are likely to play the game. In Chapter 4 'The Players', we focus on how to spot our competitors, identify their game plan and also figure out the behavioural traits of competitors. We look at distinctive types of competitors and the typical approaches each of these types adopt in the battle.

Gaining a deep understanding of specific opponents in the game— 'sizing up opponents'—is critical. We focus on this in Chapter 5 'What's Your Move?' Sizing up specific competitors will provide key insights with which we can 'predict competitor's potential actions/ reactions' to a reasonable degree of certainty. With the insights on what the competitor is likely to do (or not do), it is possible to take 'pre-emptive actions' which would constrain the competitors from putting their best foot forward—all to our advantage. Figuring out whether we should make a competitive move proactively or in response to a predicted or actual competitor move, and if so, how, are the focus of Chapter 6 'What's Our Next Move?'

Competition rarely takes place between equals. Often, the Goliath is challenged by a seemingly weaker player. What the Goliath does to hold on to the throne would be quite different from what the David would do to dethrone the Goliath. How the challenger can beat the dominant player is what we discuss in Chapter 7 'Beating the Goliaths'. Likewise, the dominant player can, with adequate attention to the challenger's game play, potentially thwart any challenge and retain the throne. Chapter 8 'Chest Thumping, Moats and Forts' provides insights on how challengers dethrone dominant players, and how dominant players deter challengers. Deterrence doesn't work always. Chapter 9 'Guarding against Davids', discusses the dominant player's repertoire of competitive actions which are aimed at protecting their turf against attacks from challengers.

Often, we find ourselves in a situation where the fruits of our hard work are enjoyed by someone else. Remember that our value appropriated need not be corresponding to the added value we bring to the game. When that happens, some of the participants in the arena—competitors, suppliers, substitutors, complementors and even customers—would have appropriated value which we should have captured. Avoiding this, and taking what's rightfully ours, calls for understanding what drives our ability to appropriate value and how to ensure that we do so. That's what we deal with in Chapter 10 'The Pursuit of Profits'. The final chapter (Chapter 11 'Towards Battle-readiness') looks at the mindset of 'battle-ready managers'.

NOTE TO THE READER

During much of 2020 and now in early 2021, the expectation has been that anything which is written has to have a view on the 'post-pandemic new world order'. Whatever the upshot of the pandemic in the business world—accelerating adoption of digital, emphasizing the importance of agility, ability to weather the unknown unknowns, and so on—that pundits have been talking about would impact businesses through participants in the competitive arena and the external environment, which is the focus of this book.

The last two decades have seen convergence of general-purpose technologies in computing, communication and mobility, which is reshaping the way we do things. It's similar to how electric energy transformed the world a hundred years ago, or how coal, steam and steel ushered in the first Industrial Revolution before that. The impact of 'digital' on businesses is in reshaping the entire value chain of activities within companies and across the global economy. Again, the mechanisms through which digital will impact businesses will be through participants in the competitive arena—some of them new and from totally unexpected spaces, and the external environment. Both of these are the primary focus of this book. I have omitted a separate discussion on both the impact of the pandemic and of digital, as these have to be discerned through the actions of participants in the emerging competitive arena.

It might seem that my interchangeable use of the metaphors of games and battles is a sign of confused mind. That might very well be so. My choice of using the two metaphors to describe the business context is driven by the high congruence I see in the three settings. In all three, rivals face off. There is a clear prize to be won. The winner gets more than the loser. The players take deliberate actions based on their view of what a winning game plan ought to be. In coming up with their game plan, they speculate on how rivals are likely to play and how the external environment will impact the game play and outcomes.

There is the contention that business as a battle is passé. The argument is that nowadays we talk of win–win strategies and cooperating. Take any win–win scenario, scratch the surface and you will find that there is at least one participant who has been left out in defining win–win. And that participant would have lost. It's true that today's business ecosystems are facilitating far more cooperation among participants than a few decades ago. Participants who cooperate do so out of self-interest, not altruism. This makes business competitive, like a game or a battle.

There are several real-life examples which I have narrated—all backed by proper sources—to highlight and drive home concepts. Not all of them are about victories. Many of them are about businesses that faltered or got it outright wrong. These are not a reflection of the capabilities of the managers who were involved in those situations. Some of the examples might seem dated, but they find a place here because they eminently suit the context. If you think of examples which would be a great fit for some of the topics discussed, please write to me.

I have generally used first person plural in my discussion of concepts, as though we are having a conversation. First person singular is used only when I am talking about something done specifically related to this book, like now. Second person is used in two occasions—in thought experiments where I want you to think about a hypothetical scenario and when I want you to focus on prescriptive statements. Where it improves readability, I have resorted to third person, like the managers. When I say 'managers', I am not referring to someone who is at the paygrade which carries the designation, Manager. I am referring to everyone who 'manages', from the frontline warriors to the CEO. When I say 'products', I mean 'products or services', and when I say 'resources', I mean 'resources and capabilities'.

The contents of this book, including the results from the tool to assess battle-readiness, are meant as guides to shape the thought process of managers. At the end of the day, it's the ingenuity of managers in coming up with new ways of doing things, it's the tenacity of managers in getting things done, and it's the ability of managers to learn from missteps—their own and that of others—which advance business ecosystems on their evolutionary paths. I am a believer of evolution—be it individuals or social systems such as organizations and business ecosystems. I also believe that evolution does not happen by luck or chance. It happens as a result of the initiative and astute actions of a few players in the ecosystem. As long as we remember that the future can be made better than the present, and we can do something about it, we have a great future.

CHAPTER TWO

The Arena

Uber Eats started in 2014 as an experiment by Uber in local food delivery in Los Angeles.[1] Unlike the ride-hailing business, Uber's key partners for Uber Eats were restaurants. Ordering a food delivery is different from hailing a ride for the customers. Uber Eats has to compete with businesses which provide local food delivery. It also has to compete with other ways for customers to get food at their dining table such as takeaways and food cooked by a housekeeper. Managers at Uber responsible for the performance of Uber Eats would have to understand how to serve customers for food delivery, manage the ecosystem of partners and vendors, and compete with other options for customers to obtain food at their doorstep, including other food delivery businesses. Regulatory environment for food delivery would be different from that for ride hailing. Uber Eats had to get battle-ready to succeed in local food delivery.

SoftBank-backed Indian ride-hailing start-up Ola entered Australia, its first foray outside India, in January 2018.[2] Managers at Ola had

---

[1] Mike Isaac, 'One Surprise Standout for Uber: Food Delivery', *The New York Times*, 23 September 2017. Available at: https://www.nytimes.com/2017/09/23/technology/ubereats-food-delivery.html (accessed 2 June 2021).

[2] https://en.wikipedia.org/wiki/Ola_Cabs (accessed 2 June 2021).

been managing the ride-hailing business in India since 2010. They had a three-year lead over Uber in India. Yet Ola's managers would have had limited understanding of how to manage a ride-hailing business in Australia before their entry. Ride-hailing customers in Australia would have preferences different from their Indian counterparts. Alternate options for customers to commute would be different in Australia, some of which might be totally unfamiliar to Ola's managers. Partners and vendors to Ola in Australia would not be like those in India. The regulatory environment would be quite different in the two country contexts. For Ola to succeed in Australia, they had to get battle-ready.

Getting battle-ready is a necessity not only when our business is entering a new arena, as in the cases of Uber Eats or Ola Australia, but also an everyday necessity for our business. As the Ionian philosopher Heraclitus is supposed to have said, 'You never enter the same river twice.'[3] Step into a river and then step in again a few seconds later, and we are stepping into water we haven't been in before. That's change happening in real time. Our customers, their preferences, our rivals, our business partners, other players, technologies, the regulatory regime, everything evolves. Some of these would change quickly, while others would change slowly. The pace of change itself changes over time. Some changes are triggered by other changes which are triggered by yet other changes. We may not even be fully aware of the causal chain. Every morning, we wake up to a business landscape which is different from the one we saw the previous night. There is no guarantee that what worked yesterday would work today. There is a good chance that it won't.

To win in the competition game, it is essential that we bring our best weapons to the battle. But that alone won't give us a win. We need to understand how our rivals are going to compete. We need to understand how other relevant players will act. We need a keen understanding of the evolving arena where the game unfolds.

---

[3] https://en.wikipedia.org/wiki/Heraclitus#Panta_rhei (accessed 2 June 2021).

Getting battle-ready includes a deep understanding of the business landscape and, with that, gaining insights relevant for our game plan. Without the understanding and insights about the arena, our game plan will be incomplete. We can't get battle-ready.

Before we can get to gaining insights about the arena, which we will do in the next chapter, we need to get clarity on what we mean by arena. For that, we first need to clarify what we mean by industry and market.

INDUSTRY AND MARKET

We often use the terms 'competitive arena', 'industry' and 'market' interchangeably. We say, 'We are a key player in this industry' or 'Our plan is to enter that market.' Yet again, we say, 'The competitive arena has become tougher.' Do these three terms mean the same? If so, why are we preferring one term over the others in specific contexts? What do we mean by industry, market and competitive arena?

Let's start with 'industry' and 'market'. The common view is that 'We belong to this "industry"' and 'We compete in that "market".' The implications are that industry is a collection of players similar in certain ways. Market is where the battle for customers and profits takes place. But then, don't players in an industry compete? So what's the difference between industry and market?

Industry

The concept of industry comes from the configuration of resources and capabilities which are needed to produce a specific product or service. Here, 'configuration' means the distinctive way in which resources and capabilities are interlinked—resource configuration, in short. A commercial passenger airline will possess a configuration of resources and capabilities which would be similar to that of other airlines. Airlines produce and offer scheduled air travel service and air cargo service for their customers. An automaker's configuration of resources and capabilities produce a set of products and services such as automobiles, auto-financing and after-sales service of automobiles. Both the configuration of resources and capabilities, as well as the output—the products or services—are quite similar among airlines or automakers but are quite different between an airline and an automaker.

'Industry' is a collective of players who possess similar resource configurations with which they produce products or services which are close substitutes. Just like the automobile or airline industry, we can think of the steel industry, the oil and gas industry or the white-goods industry. The defining characteristics of an industry are the 'product or service' and the way the players transform their inputs to create and deliver their products or services—the 'production technology' embodied in their resources and capabilities.

Observe players in an industry and we will see that most, if not all, of them use similar technologies in their value chain of activities such as planning and management, procurement, production and supply chain, marketing, sales and customer service. Here, we take a broad view of 'technology' as ways of doing things. For instance, in delivering this book into your hands, my publisher has used a certain way of doing things like the work of commissioning editors engaging with potential authors—a technology to obtain content. Business magazines which get us news and views about businesses, corporations and the economy use a different way of doing things like hiring correspondents working with an editorial team—a different technology to obtain content.

Some of these technologies are specific to an industry. Oil and gas industry uses industry-specific technologies in exploration, extraction and refining of crude oil. Some technologies are not so specific to a particular industry and are deployed in multiple industries. Both the automobile and the white-goods industries use assembly line production as the way of putting together their product. They employ similar methods for quality assurance. Some technologies are even more widely adopted across a diverse range of industries. Generic technologies such as those underlying customer care operations are used across a large number of industries. And then there are general-purpose technologies like the steam engine, electricity or digital which become the foundation of economic activities across all industries during their era. Technologies—ranging from industry-specific to generic and general-purpose—possess characteristics such as economies of scale and scope which impact the competitive behaviour of players. Before we get to that, let's look at what we mean by market.

Market

Economists define a market as the space within which the price of a product is the same—they call it the 'law of one price'. This assumes that the market has no frictions including absence of transportation costs. The more practical definition of a market relevant for business managers is that of a 'strategic market'. John Kay defines a strategic market as 'the smallest area within which it is possible to be a viable competitor'.[4] Anything smaller, and a business will invariably not make enough money. Although Kay talks about area, a general definition of a strategic market should be in terms of the number of units of the product or the currency value of the product—the 'market size'. Boundaries of the market become critical, as moving the boundaries tighter or wider will change the market size and, along with that, the possibility of competing viably.

Another way to look at a market is to describe who's in it and who's not. Here, the primary focus is on the participants. A market essentially brings together two sets of players. There are those who are on the lookout for folks who would buy what they have to offer. Then there are folks who derive utility through purchase and use of products or services offered by the first set of players. Everyone calls these folks the 'customers', so we will call the first set as 'players'. According to Derek Abell, 'The way various competitors define their scope of [business] activities determine market boundaries.'[5]

---

[4] John A. Kay, 'Identifying the Strategic Market', *Business Strategy Review* 1, no. 1 (Spring issue, 1990): 2–24.
[5] Derek F. Abell, *Defining the Business* (Hoboken, NJ: Prentice Hall, 1980), 191.

By making choices on what products or services to produce and offer, businesses and their managers decide who all become their customers and in turn decide who's included in the 'market'.

Markets can be seen as the intersection of three dimensions—customer functions, technology and geography. Customer functions (or functions) are the purpose for which customers use the products. Technology is a certain way of fulfilling the customer function. Thus, we get a product or service when a customer function is combined with a specific technology. There could be multiple ways—technologies—to fulfil a particular function, each of which will be a distinct product. A product offered to customers who belong to a geography gives us a 'market'.

Take for instance the function of washing clothes. A washing machine is a product which gives this utility using the technology of mechanized washing of clothes. A laundry service would provide washing and pressing of garments as a service using technologies such as customer-facing capabilities to collect and deliver clothes and backend capabilities such as mechanized bulk washing of clothes and logistics. A housekeeper would wash and press clothes as service rendered at customer's premises. Although the underlying function of washing clothes is the same, the customers are looking at three different products or services. The market for washing machines is distinct from the market for laundry service or housekeeper service.

The businesses which provide these products or services may also provide other products to deliver other functions, but employing more or less the same technologies. Take for instance the maker of washing machines. Using a similar technology for product design, production, testing, logistics, marketing, sales and service, the maker of washing machines also produces and offers refrigerators and air conditioners. The player would belong to the 'white-goods' industry and would be active in the markets for washing machines, refrigerators and air conditioners in one or more geographic regions.

The business which provides housekeepers would belong to the industry which may be called 'housekeeping and janitorial services' and might also provide the services of janitors, gardeners, plumbers and electricians to their customers. Across the different markets, the housekeeping services business would use the same technology—hiring semi-skilled and skilled workers and offering their services to customers on a time basis. The business would be active in multiple markets as it caters to different customer functions such as housekeeping, gardening and plumbing and may or may not operate in multiple geographic regions.

Size of Market

The size of a market is typically given in terms of the number of units of product exchanged or, more generally, the dollar value of products exchanged. It is an important factor, as it indicates the quantum of business opportunity which players in the market can hope to tap into. Bigger the market size, bigger will be the size of the value pie and more the profits which can be made by the players. The size of a market is driven by factors relating to the three dimensions we used to define the market (see Figure 2.1)—function, technology and geography. Of these, factors relating to technology—economies of scale and scope—arise from industry characteristics. Factors relating to geography relate to logistical constraints relevant for the product or service and the institutional landscape of the geography. Factors relating to function arise from characteristics of the product or service and how these relate to markets for other products or services.

Technology: Economies of Scale

Wistron, the Taiwanese contract manufacturer for Apple, announced in November 2020 that it will augment its production capacity in India by 200,000 units per year with fresh investments of ₹13 billion.[6] Assuming that this investment is to be depreciated over

---

[6] ET Telecom, 'Apple Supplier Wistron to Expand Its Bangalore Facility: Report', 9 November 2020. Available at: https://telecom.economictimes.indiatimes.com/news/apple-supplier-wistron-to-expand-its-bangalore-facility-report/79124299 (accessed 2 June 2021).

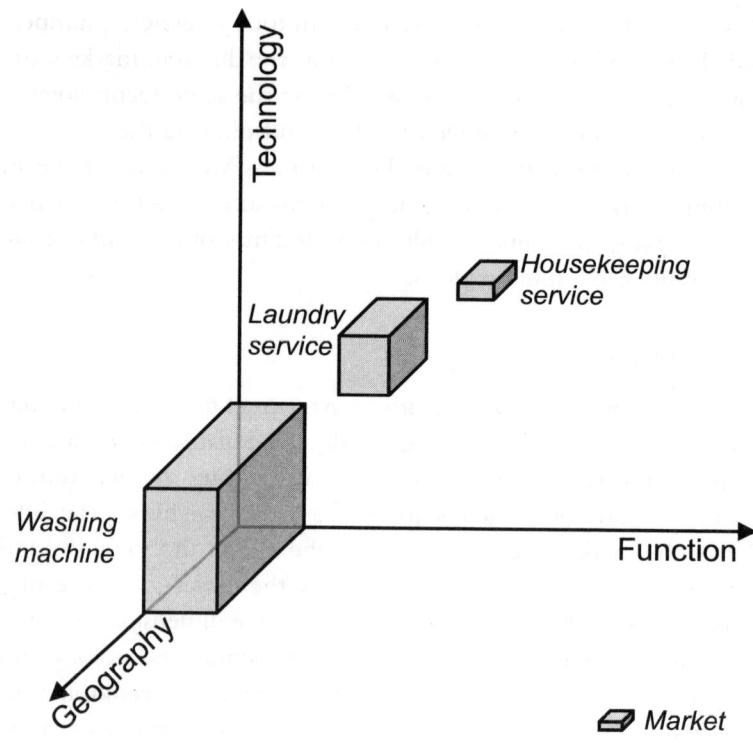

Source: Adapted from the definition of business by Derek F. Abell and J. S. Hammond, *Strategic Market Planning* (Hoboken, NJ: Prentice Hall, 1979), 9.

Figure 2.1. Defining the Market

10 years, this translates to a fixed cost of ₹6,500 per phone if the added capacity runs at full utilization. However, if the added capacity runs only at three-fourths utilization, the fixed cost per phone would rise to ₹9,750. In contrast, the cost of components used per phone[7] would be fixed for a model.

---

[7] Let's assume that Wistron buys these from the suppliers and charges back its customer, Apple.

Fixed costs, including depreciation/amortization of capital expenses, need to be allocated over the actual number of units of activity which eventually get monetized as products for which customers pay. As the number of units produced increases, the fixed cost per unit reduces. As we operate close to capacity in any business activity, we achieve close to lowest possible per-unit fixed cost. Since variable cost is fixed per unit, the total unit cost is lowest when we operate close to the full capacity. We know this concept as 'economies of scale', and the size of activity at which lowest per-unit cost is achieved is called the 'minimum efficient scale' (MES). MES depends on the technology which is employed in the activity.

Economies of scale impacts the minimum size of market in which we can viably compete—our strategic market. MES is driven by the technology which underlies an activity. Larger the MES, bigger has to be the minimum market which the business needs to target so that it can operate at lowest possible cost. If it doesn't, its competitors will likely do that, making the business less profitable, as it will now end up with higher unit cost than its competitors. Take the case of carbonated soft drinks. This market has been a global duopoly for many decades now. Before that, regional and local soft drinks makers profitably catered to a good proportion of the market demand. This was because making concentrates, bottling drinks and distributing those to retail outlets are activities which do not involve high MES. One can operate at a sub-national level and still make good profits. The two global players Coca-Cola and Pepsi upped the game in the 1980s by increasing the fixed cost of brand—and product management. They did this by running national ad campaigns, engaging celebrities for high-budget creatives, aired on prime time and expensive media slots such as Super Bowl. To be viable at the high fixed cost, a soft drink maker is forced to target a much larger market—national or bigger. Most of the local and sub-national drink makers who couldn't do that sold out or shut shop.

Economies of scale exists for every activity which the business carries out in transforming its inputs into a finished product in the hands of its customers. Often, the activity which involves the largest MES will dictate the minimum size of the market that the business should target so as to viably compete, as we saw in the case of soft drinks. Economies of scale, and specifically MES, sets minimum size for the strategic market, below which it will be difficult to compete viably. MES is a descriptive concept which looks at the relationship between scale and cost. From a strategic perspective, it's critical to understand the minimum viable market share (MVM) for a product and market. This is the minimum market share that a player should secure to operate at the lowest cost, for the relevant MES (see Appendix B).

Technology: Economies of Scope

Eli Lilly, an American pharma major, has several lines of products catering to nine broad therapeutic areas including diabetes.[8] Novo Nordisk, a Danish pharma company, focuses primarily on diabetes.[9] Sales teams of both Eli Lilly and Novo Nordisk call on doctors to share information about their products and therapeutic benefits. In a region where diabetes treatment is given mostly by general practitioners, the sales teams of Eli Lilly and Novo Nordisk would end up meeting the same set of doctors. However, Eli Lilly's sales team talks to doctors about drugs and treatments for many therapeutic areas, compared to Novo's sales team. The unit cost of calling a doctor per therapeutic area turns out to be much lower for Eli Lilly in comparison with Novo Nordisk. When the joint cost of two or more activities is lower than the sum of standalone costs of doing the same activities, there is benefit from 'economies of scope' for the business.

The presence of economies of scope makes it more cost effective for a business to manage a portfolio of products. Consumer packaged products companies such as P&G derive significant economies of scope in value chain stages such as logistics, distribution and media

---

[8] https://www.lilly.com/our-medicines/current-medicines (accessed 2 June 2021).
[9] https://www.novonordisk.com/products.html (accessed 2 June 2021).

buying. With economies of scope, it is possible for a company to configure an activity to utilize its capacity over multiple businesses. This brings down the minimum size of market to be addressed for each of the businesses. However, without significant benefits from economies of scale for an activity, benefits from economies of scope would not matter much. In general, benefits from economies of scope, if available and can be leveraged, have the effect of lowering the MVM, given a certain MES.

Geography: Logistical Constraints

Market size gets constrained through factors such as shipping costs, perishability and logistics infrastructure, all driven by the nature of the product. Try shipping cement beyond a few thousand kilometres, and the cost of shipping would be about the same as the cost of cement being shipped. Instead of shipping cement over long distances, it would be more cost effective to locate cement plants closer to the locations of consumption. This is what cement companies do. On the other hand, crude oil gets shipped around the globe and doesn't make the business any less viable. The value-to-weight ratio—cost of product as a multiple of cost of shipping over a given distance—drives the maximum viable distance between the place of production and place of consumption for a product. Lower the value-to-weight ratio, smaller will be the viable distance the finished product can travel to reach the customer, and smaller will have to be the strategic market. It is no surprise that cement has been a sub-national–national market (depending on the size of the country). Over time, new technologies like shipping bulk cement on barges has increased the geographic scope of cement market marginally. It is another matter that the same set of players operate across most of the markets, but these players compete within the geographic boundaries not across. Italcementi in Europe competes with Lafarge in Europe, but not with Lafarge in Brazil. Higher value-to-weight ratio for a product enables businesses to compete viably in larger markets.

Growers of grapes can sell their produce as fresh grapes or convert it to a product with longer shelf life such as wine or raisins. Fresh grapes have to reach the end consumer before they perish. Freshness of grapes can be maintained through climate-controlled shipping and storage. With this, the speed of shipping will then determine the distance which can be covered to reach the end consumer. Given the price that the end consumer will be willing to pay, the distance that can be viably covered will be driven by the cost of shipping for various means of shipping such as by road, rail, sea or air. It generally costs more to ship faster. Lesser the shelf life, in other words faster the product will perish, smaller will be the strategic market.[10]

Logistics infrastructure plays a critical role in determining both shipping cost and perishability. Better roads, rail networks and air/sea shipping infrastructure result in lower unit cost of shipping. Improvements in technologies for climate-controlled storage and shipping can result in lengthening of time to perish. Logistical constraints operate along two dimensions—distance and time. Logistical constraints put an upper limit on the size of the strategic market.

Geography: Institutional Landscape

Institutional influences on the boundaries and size of market can come in various forms. Explicit restrictions on trade are the most direct way that institutions and policies can influence market size. In both Canada and India, beer brewed in one state cannot be sold in other states. Thus, the strategic market for beer in these countries is limited to the size of the state where it is produced, irrespective of how other factors stack up.

Regulations relating to product sale, exports/imports as well as investments are other ways in which market size gets influenced by government policies. For certain sectors, access to market itself is

---

[10] Michael J. Enright, 'Note on the Geographic Scope of Competition & Strategy' (Harvard Business School Background Note 9-793-135, 1993).

regulated. Drug regulators have to approve drugs before they can be sold in a market. They also impose statutory labelling requirements in terms of content and languages. Regulations on automotive safety as well as emissions vary across countries. Many countries impose local value–addition requirements for businesses to be able to access their markets. Often, this requirement is imposed in the form of high import duty for fully assembled products, making it unviable to import and sell. Players need to set up shop within the country to access the market.

Most countries have policies which influence foreign direct investment into various sectors. These policies could focus on restricting foreign investments either for strategic reasons or to protect local players, which will lead to restricting the market to the national level. Policies aimed at promotion of exports will allow location of production in a geography to cater to markets outside the geography. These policies operate on the industry side and will not have a direct impact on the market size.

Customer Function

The customer function drives the market size through linkages among different markets and industries. Consider customers' need for petrol as an energy source to run their automobiles. More number of automobiles sold and in use, larger will be the market size for petrol. As adoption of electric vehicles picks up, growth in the market size for petrol is likely to reduce. More the use of tablet computers for storing and reading books and taking notes, less the need for paper books, notebooks and pens.

The size of one market is driven by the change in market size in other markets, positively or negatively. Economists label these as complements and substitutes. If the demand for a complementary product goes up, the demand for the product goes up as well—car and petrol. And if the demand for a substitute goes up, the demand for the product comes down—electric car and car that uses petrol. While all these are neat ways of explaining how market size changes, it just makes the life of a business manager more complex.

The manager could define the market size for her business along the function served by its product and merrily ignore substitutes and complements. When the demand for her product falls because a substitute takes the fancy of customers or a key complement plummets in demand, our manager is suddenly in trouble. It turns out that it's not prudent to ignore the linkages that our market has with other markets.

But then, there are strong and weak substitutes. Same is with complements. So where do we draw the line? Michael Porter acknowledges this problem, 'There is often a great deal of controversy over the appropriate definition [of market], centering around how close substitutability needs to be in terms of products, process or geographic market boundaries.'[11]

Focusing on their own (strategic) market is what managers do most often. Our attention is on those players who also belong to the same industry as us, and who are vying with us to get the attention of a common group of customers. This focus on immediate rivals is much needed. But as a result, we do not realize that the competitive game is going on in a broader arena, where actions by other players have a direct impact on our market and business performance. By ignoring the broader arena, we seriously handicap ourselves with limited insights about opportunities and challenges from outside our current market. That weakens our battle-readiness.

FROM FUNCTION TO 'JOB TO BE DONE'

To move to a broader view of where we compete, we need to understand 'why' customers buy from us, in addition to 'what'—the function that our product or service provides—and 'who'— the characteristics of our customers. 'Customers don't buy products or services … they "hire" [a] product or service to solve [a] "job" they are trying to get done,' according to Clayton Christensen and

---

[11] Michael E. Porter, *Competitive Strategy* (New York, NY: Free Press, 1980), 5.

colleagues.[12] The idea is that by using a product or service, customers 'make progress in their circumstance'.

When we buy a pair of shoes, we are not buying a product, but trying to achieve an improvement in our circumstance compared to some other product or not having one of the products at all. With a pair of industrial safety boots, the progress is protection of feet. With a pair of patent leather tuxedo shoes, the progress is being ready for an event with formal dress code. With a pair of trekking shoes, the progress is comfort during long periods of walk. The tux shoe may provide only limited protection in an industrial environment and would start hurting during a long trek. The trekking shoe would attract unsavoury attention in a social setting which calls for formal dress code. Being barefoot would definitely be a problem in any of these circumstances. If the product performs a poor job of making progress, we fire the product and hire another product which can do a better job. That's how we think about the pair of shoes to pick up for a particular circumstance.

Products or services are 'what' we buy and consume. How we use the product and why we use it is not captured in the product description. Job to be done focuses on the outcome for a customer in consuming a product. Christensen and colleagues propose the concept of jobs to be done to come up with new products which would more likely succeed in the market. Closely related to this is the idea of a competitive arena where customers look for alternate ways to solve their jobs to be done and choose some ways—products or services—over others. That in essence is the broadened view of how we compete for customers and profits, beyond the narrow confines of markets defined along functions, technologies and geographies.

---

[12] Clayton M. Christensen et al., *Competing against Luck* (New York, NY: HarperCollins Publishers, 2016).

COMPETITIVE ARENA

Players in an industry compete with each other to secure inputs for their value chain of activities. They compete to acquire human capital and financial capital. They compete to become the leader in the dominant technology of their industry by investing in research and development (R&D). In the market, players compete for customers and profits. The way we have viewed markets as the intersection of customer function, technology and geography, competitors in a market are likely to belong to the same industry and their products or services are likely to be highly similar in terms of features, attributes and the function they will provide to the customer. If we restrict our view of the competition arena to this, we miss two key insights.

Blinders On

First, we miss out on other products and services which can potentially address the jobs to be done for our customers but do not belong to our industry or market. Take for instance an occasion where you want to compliment a friend on an achievement. A box of chocolates, a book appealing to your friend's taste, a bunch of flowers or even a handwritten congratulatory note could do the job. Which one will you choose? Most likely it will depend on what the friend would appreciate and the nature of your relationship with the friend. Now put yourself in the place of a producer of chocolates or books or flower bouquets or craft writing pads. Whom are you competing with? Other players in the same industry and market you are in who sell the same product? Or other players who offer potential solutions to your customer's job to be done?

Second, we miss out on other products and services which are typically part of how our customers make progress in their circumstances. We are talking about complementary products or services. Back in 2004, Sony launched the first ever e-book reader using E-Ink display which gives the feel of reading print on paper, Sony Librie. Weighing 300 g, the product came with onboard memory of

10 MB (megabytes) which could store about 10–20 books.[13] Three decades earlier, Sony had lost a vicious battle to JVC and others over video cassette recorders. Sony's Betamax lost out to the VHS format primarily due to lack of availability of titles in its format—a key complementary product.[14] The lesson from that episode was not forgotten, and Sony launched an e-book store so that customers could get access to the key complementary product—e-books. Customers would require both the e-reader and e-books to fulfil the job to be done of reading a book. Good for Sony that it thought of the key complementary product. By 2006, when Sony launched Librie in the USA, its store carried 45,000 titles.

Then Kindle happened. Amazon, the fast-growing online retailer who started with books, launched its e-reader along with Kindle Store which carried 145,000 titles. And Amazon didn't stop there. It thought of yet another complementary service to the e-reader and e-books—wireless connectivity and automated delivery of content into the e-reader. Sony's customers could purchase books from the company's e-book store through a computer and had to transfer the book to the e-reader by connecting the device to the computer. This was the solution that Apple provided to its early iPod customers who wanted to buy and load music onto their portable music player. Sony followed Apple, but Amazon went one step ahead. It partnered with AT&T to put a mobile SIM inside Kindle e-readers so that books could be purchased right from the device and the content would load almost immediately. Amazon offered its customers newspaper subscriptions, and the day's newspaper would get updated even as customers wake up.[15] No need for a computer, no need to hunt for a cable, connect, figure out how to transfer and

---

[13] https://en.wikipedia.org/wiki/Sony_Reader#2004_Model (accessed 2 June 2021).

[14] Length of recording/play was a critical technical difference between VHS and Betamax, but Sony lost when movie studios decided to adopt the VHS format. https://en.wikipedia.org/wiki/Videotape_format_war#Competing_technologies (accessed 2 June 2021).

[15] John Gapper, 'Why Sony Lost the Battle of the e-book', *Financial Times*, 7 August 2008.

so on. The complementary service that Amazon layered on top of the e-reader and e-book store was wireless connectivity with automated content delivery. The progress that Amazon offered its customers by combining complementary products and services—the reader, content, connectivity and automated delivery—was far superior to what Sony offered with Librie and its e-book store. By 2014, Sony shut its e-book store.[16]

Blinders Off

I am driving on a highway. My eyes are glued to the traffic up ahead in the lane I am driving on. That should be fine for a normal day when nothing interesting happens. What if someone cuts me off? What if there's a broken-down car and the driver is trying to get help? What if a cop is gesturing me to pull over? What if from the opposite direction an out-of-control super-sized truck is ploughing into my side of the highway? What if a camel is trying to cross the highway at a sedate pace without looking hither or thither? If I am just focused on my lane, there is not going to be much difference between me and the camel.

The concept of industry and market comes from microeconomic theory, specifically of the neoclassical orientation. Products are treated in isolation and the only place two products come together is in an indifference curve, used to figure out how much of each I will buy and at what price. That's like one-lane focus while driving. That should be enough on a normal day.

On interesting days, we still keep our focus on the lane ahead—no distractions from that. In addition, we keep in our peripheral view what's going on in adjacent lanes, the shoulder, the lanes on the other side and so on. We keep half an eye on the rear-view mirror to make sure that nothing is there that shouldn't be there. We keep the music a tad below blaring so that we can pick up audio cues on

---

[16] https://www.sony.com/electronics/support/articles/00070056 (accessed 2 June 2021).

what's going on around us, not just the lane ahead. As we wade through the competitive battle, such mindfulness is essential. Blinders off is the only way to fight the battle of competition. And we are fighting not just rivals from our industry and market but also with other players who can mar our chances of success by snatching from us our customers and our profits. Sometimes we can join hands with some of the other players to get an upper hand. Sometime later, the same partners may turn against us. Unless we get the blinders off, we won't see anything beyond the direct rivals from our own industry and market. That's a 'dangerous way to think about competition', according to Rita Gunther McGrath.[17]

Defining the Arena

Think of a group of customers with similar jobs to be done. Around them, think of groups of players who offer products or services which contribute to fulfilling the customers' jobs to be done. The players will likely belong to multiple industries. It will look like the players are competing in different markets, the way we viewed market earlier. When customers look at the offerings from various players, they would see some offerings which can do more or less the same 'job'. Some offerings will have to be taken along with some others to fulfil a 'job'. The customer brings resources and capabilities to consume some of the offerings and seek improvement in their circumstance. When they do that, value is created. And the value thus created gets distributed among the players who contributed to creating value. This is the arena in which offerings compete with offerings to deliver improvement to customers' circumstances. Offerings are mixed and matched with other offerings to deliver improvement. Often the customers figure out such mixing and matching. Sometimes, one of the players figures this out and provides the mixed-and-matched offering ready-made. This is how

---

[17] Rita Gunther McGrath, *The End of Competitive Advantage: How to Keep Your Strategy Moving as Fast as Your Business* (Boston, MA: Harvard Business Review Press, 2013).

competition among players—to deliver improvement to their customers' circumstances—evolves in the arena.

Arenas differ from our conception of market (and industry) in two important ways. First, it enables us a more nuanced view of the competitive process, going beyond product attributes and customer characteristics. As Rita Gunther McGrath says, arena gives us a 'new level of analysis … characterized by particular connections between customers and solutions'.[18] Second, it brings to focus the importance of other players, beyond our direct rivals, who are critical to the competitive process—substitutors and complementors. Ronald Burt highlights the social structure of competitive arena as 'players trusting certain others, obligated to support certain others, dependent on exchange with certain others, and so on'.[19] The competitive game unfolds in this broader competitive arena as a complex multi-player game involving the customers, our business and its direct rivals, and other players who seek to substitute us or complement us.

Whirlpool Corporation of America entered several new markets in Europe and Asia during the 1980s with its range of white goods such as washing machines, refrigerators and cooking ranges. They were present only in North and South Americas prior to that. Whirlpool's managers at that time believed that the market for white goods was becoming global and were focused on building global competence centres and developing global products such as a 'world washer'. With this assumption of global market, their product portfolio for the European market naturally consisted of products which weren't specifically designed for any European customer group. However, significant differences existed in what various European customer groups wanted from white goods.

One account of what Europeans looked for in washing machines went thus, 'Swedes preferred galvanized washing machines to

---

[18] Ibid.
[19] Ronald S. Burt, *Structural Holes* (Cambridge, MA: Harvard University Press, 1992), 11.

withstand the damp salty air. The British washed their clothes more often than the Italians did, who wanted quieter machines.'[20] It is no surprise that Whirlpool struggled in its first attempt to make inroads into European white-goods markets. It focused on the function of washing clothes and believed that a single product concept could meet the requirements of all Europeans. However, the various European customer groups were trying to solve different problems. The Swedes wanted to mechanize the task of washing clothes and also wanted machines which do not rust away in a few months. Galvanized washing machine was what solved their problem. Brits or Germans didn't worry that much about the machine rusting, so they didn't value or pay for galvanization. Brits preferred smaller washing machines but didn't value quieter ones, while the Italians valued quieter and larger machines. The world washer did not meet the job to be done for any one of the customer groups.

Galvanized or quiet washing machine might look like product features or attributes. We might be tempted to conclude that these are after all additional functions that customers of specific groups need. Focusing on 'function' of a product won't give us the opportunity to understand which additional functions or features are relevant for which customer group. That's where jobs to be done come handy. By defining the competitive arena on the basis of the job to be done, two shifts in paradigm come about in how we understand competition. First, we are viewing competition as a process by which multiple players vie to fulfil a specific customer's job to be done. This is in contrast to the product- and production-centric view that we would espouse if we viewed competition as among players in an industry. Second, we are viewing technology as a means to the end of fulfilling the customer's job to be done. This is in contrast to the view that characteristics of technology such as economies of scale and scope define competition among players in a market (Figure 2.2).

---

[20] Andrew C. Inkpen, 'Whirlpool Corporation's Global Strategy' (Thunderbird School of Global Management case study TB0175, 2001), 3.

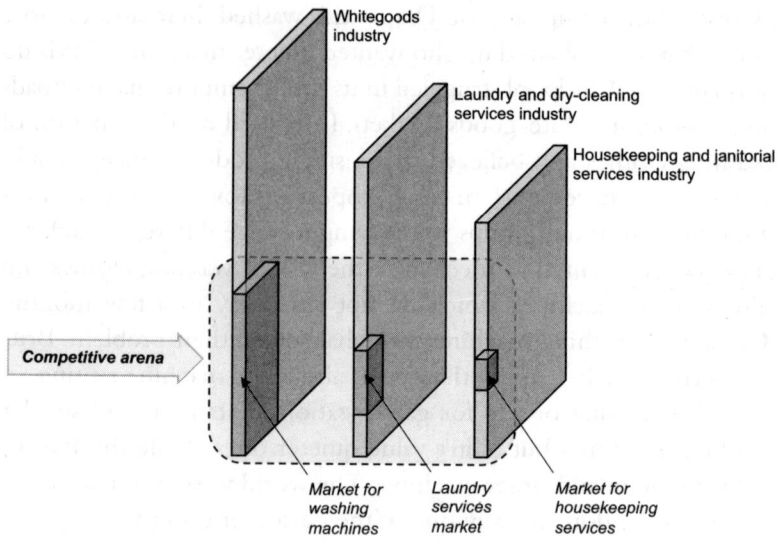

Source: The author.

Figure 2.2. Industry, Market and Competitive Arena

Arena cuts across industries and markets. It spans multiple and rival technologies which can fulfil a given job to be done. Arena covers multiple markets and would straddle parts of multiple industries. The meaningful boundary for an arena is defined by two dimensions. First is the job to be done, wherein multiple markets compete with one another. Second is geographic, where the boundary is dictated by the ability of the players to interact and transact with one another. In the digital era, this is tending to be global.

Competition takes place at three levels. First among players within a market where rivalry is among products. Second among players within the industry where rivalry is for inputs, production technology and cost efficiency. Third in the competitive arena for customers and profits.

The geographic boundaries of different markets are not necessarily in sync. Thus, the notion of geographically relevant rivals works only within markets, not with players in the same competitive arena. The views about industry and market are relevant and useful, but not at the expense of ignoring the vantage that competitive arena provides. The battle-ready player views the battle as unfolding across all three levels—market, industry and competitive arena.

« LONG STORY » « SHORT »

Understanding the competitive arena is the starting point of getting battle-ready. An industry is a collection of players using similar technologies to produce products which are close substitutes. A market is where customers and players engage in exchange and is defined along three dimensions—customer function, technology and geography. A strategic market is the smallest market in which a business can compete viably. A competitive arena encompasses multiple markets which meet a specific job to be done for customers. Managers typically focus on markets and industries. Competition takes place at three levels: at the level of market where rivalry is among products; at the level of industry where rivalry is on inputs, production technology and efficiency; and at the level of competitive arena where rivalry is about customers and profits. Battle-ready players focus on all three, especially the competitive arena.

CHAPTER THREE

Understanding the Arena

The arena critically influences the chances of success in a competitive battle. Ask Xerxes I, the Persian emperor who brought a vastly larger and superior fighting force against the Greeks to the Battle of Thermopylae.[1] Ask Cao Cao, the Chinese northern warlord who pinned the alliance force of southern warlords Liu Bei and Sun Quan in a naval blockade with an army 16 times bigger than the opposing side during the Battle of Red Cliffs.[2] Xerxes was denied an early victory by the 300 Spartans led by Leonidas I, which allowed the remaining Greek contingent to withdraw to fight another day. Cao Cao's blockade went up in flames, and his army was forced to beat a hasty retreat.

The Greeks chose the passes of Thermopylae and Artemisium to face the Persian army, as a narrow pass is best suited for smaller number of soldiers defending in tight formation—that's how the Greeks wanted to fight. The larger numbers as well as superior resources such as chariots and elephants which the Persians brought to battle turned out to be useless in the narrow pass defended by a phalanx of Spartans.

---

[1] Paul Cartledge, *Thermopylae* (New York, NY: The Overlook Press, 2006).
[2] Rafe de Crespigny, 'Generals of the South' (Asian Studies Monograph No. 16, Australian National University, 1990).

The southern warlords denied Cao Cao the opportunity to fight them in land and in open plains, forcing Cao Cao to mount a naval blockade. The northern warlord ended up putting his cavalry and infantry on ships—not the best use of a land-based army. The result was that Cao Cao's vastly superior army was forced to retreat, as ships in the blockade were put to fire by the weaker opponents.

Having a superior and larger base of resources and capabilities does not guarantee success in a competitive battle. Both Xerxes and Cao Cao relied on superior numbers and ignored warnings about an unfavourable arena. The battle-ready player's game plan would ensure that their best weapons are most relevant, and their worst weapons are least relevant for the battle. At the same time, the game plan would also strive to blunt, deflect or make irrelevant the best weapons of their rival. The game plan of a battle-ready player would include an astute understanding of the competitive arena—the participants and how they influence value creation and appropriation, and how these insights matter for our business.

PARTICIPANTS IN THE ARENA

The competitive arena consists of six types of participants.[3] There are our business and our rivals—we call them the incumbents. There are our customers and our suppliers. These three sets of players— the suppliers, incumbents and customers—belong to the industry value chain, and each set of participants is a stage in the value chain (Figure 3.1). Most industries will have mile-long value chains consisting of hundreds of stages.

---

[3] Five of the participants are identified in Porter's industry analysis framework. See Michael E. Porter, *Competitive Strategy* (New York, NY: The Free Press, 1980), 3–33. Nalebuff and Brandenburger identify five participants, but one of their participants—complementors—do not appear in Porter's framework. They leave out potential entrants though. See Barry J. Nalebuff and Adam M. Brandenburger, *Co-opetition* (Great Britain: HarperCollins Publishers, 1996), 70–74. I have added complementors to Porter's list of five participants. The discussion on participants draws from these two sources.

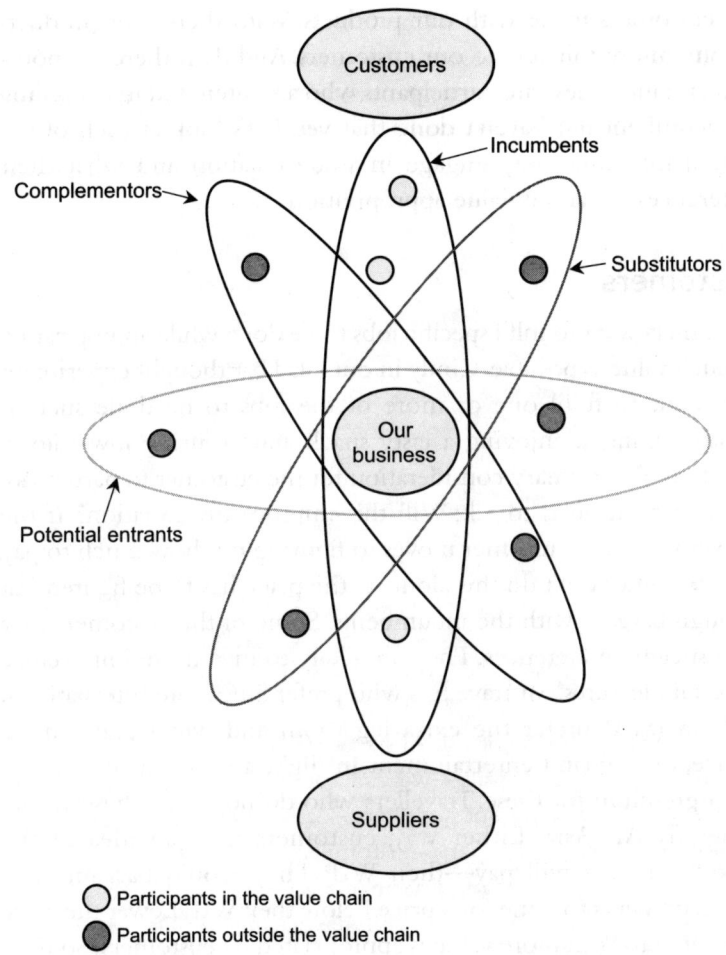

Source: The author.

Figure 3.1. Participants in the Competitive Arena

There are the substitutors who fulfil our customers' jobs to be done but using different technologies. They would belong to a different industry and its corresponding industry value chain. Complementors are participants who provide our customers with products and services which enhance the improvement in circumstance which our customers make with our products. With them, our products become more valuable to our customers. And then there are potential entrants. These are participants who are interested in becoming an incumbent but haven't done that yet. Let's look at each of the participants, how they engage in value creation and what their preferences are about value appropriation.

Customers

Customers want to fulfil specific jobs to be done while appropriating as much value as possible. Cindy in our salad bar thought experiment may want to fulfil one or more of the jobs to be done such as satiating hunger, enjoying a tasty snack and ensuring low-calorie nutrition. The primary consideration for the customer to participate in value creation is to ask: Will this improve my situation? If the answer is yes, the customer moves to figuring out how much to pay. The customer can't do this alone, as the price has to be figured out through bargain with the incumbents. Some of the customers may have specific preferences. They are likely to give more importance to certain features. Air travellers who prefer Singapore International Airlines (SIA) prefer the extra leg room and wider seats, menu choice, on-demand entertainment in flight and so on, and would pay a premium for these. Travellers who do not value these would rather fly Air Asia. Either way, customers have an idea of the maximum they will pay—their WtP. They would bargain with the incumbents to settle for a price below their WtP. Lower the price compared to WtP, more value is appropriated by customers. So their preference is to buy at as low a price as possible, given a certain level of quality and features.

Customers contribute to value creation by engaging in exchange with incumbents to fulfil their job to be done. They impact value appropriation through their bargaining with incumbents. Their inclination to drive a hard bargain depends on their circumstances and preferences. If there are many incumbents vying to sell to them, customers are likely to bargain more and drive prices lower. If they prefer a certain type or quality of offering, like the comfortable air travel that SIA offers, their options are limited, compared to if they don't have such preferences. This reduces the number of incumbents they will consider and bargain with, reducing their ability to drive a hard bargain. If the price is likely to nearly empty their wallet, customers are more likely to drive a tough bargain. If the price is small change for them, they won't.

Tougher the bargain by customers, lower will be the price and higher will be the value appropriated by the customers. The higher value appropriated by customers eats into the value appropriated by incumbents, lowering it to a similar extent. The opposite will happen, resulting in an increase in value appropriated by incumbents if the customers' ability to bargain goes down. What the customer gains in value appropriation, the incumbent loses, and vice versa.

Suppliers

Suppliers are businesses who are into selling inputs to the incumbents. Incumbents may pursue different game plans. Biju might be making salads that boast of several premium features such as superior-quality raw materials, variety of ingredients, consistent size, appealing container, high quality and choice of dressings. One of the other incumbents might be focusing on lowering the cost of salads and might churn out a standard salad with minimal features. The suppliers naturally find a fit between their offerings and demand from incumbents. Once the suppliers figure out who all could buy from them, the bargaining for the cost of inputs comes up. Here, as we have discussed earlier, each supplier will have a floor price—the opportunity cost to supplier (OCS)—below which they won't sell to the salad bars. Higher the cost in excess of OCS which suppliers get from the incumbent, higher is their value appropriated. Suppliers focus on getting as high a value appropriated as possible for a given quality of inputs.

Suppliers impact value creation by bringing inputs which allow the incumbents to create more value for their customers. They also impact value appropriation through their bargaining with incumbents. Again, the bargain with incumbents depends on the context. If only few suppliers are offering premium inputs (such as high quality), the suppliers are able to drive a hard bargain with the incumbents. If many suppliers are offering similar inputs, they have limited ability to bargain with incumbents. The suppliers of inputs which are critical for the overall quality of incumbent's offering, such as a premium dressing, are able to drive tougher bargain compared to the suppliers whose inputs do not critically impact quality. Some suppliers might make it difficult for the incumbents to switch to other suppliers, which makes it difficult for the incumbents to drive a hard bargain. On the other hand, if an incumbent makes her own inputs or even threatens to do so, they would likely be able to bargain harder.

Overall, harder the bargain which suppliers can drive with the incumbents, more value will the suppliers appropriate. The higher value appropriated by the suppliers eats into the value appropriated by incumbents, lowering it to similar extent. If the ability of the suppliers to drive hard bargain weakens, their value appropriated will go down, resulting in a corresponding increase in value appropriated by the incumbents.

Incumbents

Incumbents exist to facilitate customers to make progress. They create and deliver the means through which customers fulfil their jobs to be done. They manage a wide range of activities to convert a set of inputs into products or services. Michael Porter calls these the value chain[4]—we will call it 'firm-level value chain' to distinguish it from the industry value chain we discussed earlier. The firm-level value chain captures the perspective of activities which an incumbent's business performs with its configuration of resources and capabilities. The transformation of inputs to output adds a substantial

---

[4] Michael E. Porter, *Competitive Advantage* (New York, NY: The Free Press, 1985), 33–61.

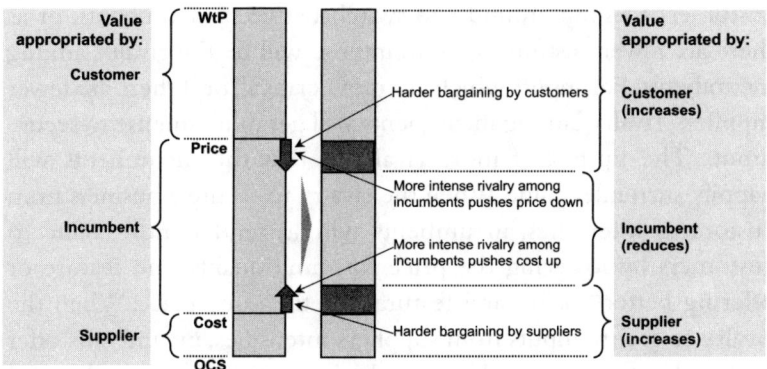

Source: The author.

Note: The direction of change in value appropriation will flip for the opposite cases of reduced bargaining or less intense rivalry.

Figure 3.2. Value Appropriation by Customers, Suppliers and Incumbents

value. Vegetables properly cleaned and cut, mixed in the right proportion, garnished with salt, spices and dressing, go to make a salad. Some incumbents bring more added value by providing features which are valued by customers. We have discussed that already. The incumbent bargains with both the customers and suppliers to jointly decide the price and cost, which impacts value appropriation (Figure 3.2). We have discussed this as well.

In bargaining with customers and suppliers, incumbents compete with one another. For instance, SIA completes with several international airlines such as Emirates, Lufthansa and British Airways in vying for passengers who want to travel between Southeast Asia and Europe. These airlines compete with each other to hire pilots and cabin crew. They compete to source airframes and aircraft engines and obtain the services of partners such as those who provide cabin fit-out, maintenance and overhaul. There is rivalry in both the customer and supplier sides.

As the offerings of incumbents get more similar, more intense will be their rivalry to secure customers. As it becomes easier for customers to shop around and switch between incumbents, or as there are fewer customers, more intense will be the rivalry among incumbents. For inputs which are more critical, or if there are fewer suppliers, rivalry among incumbents will get more intense to secure inputs. The upshot of more rivalry is that the incumbents will happily surrender value. When the rivalry to secure a business from customers intensifies, incumbents will surrender more value to customers by lowering the price for same quality and feature or offering better quality and features for the same price. When the rivalry to secure inputs from suppliers intensifies, incumbents offer more value to suppliers through a higher cost for same quality and features or same cost for lower quality and features. The opposite dynamic will be the case when rivalry becomes less intense. As rivalry intensifies, value appropriation by incumbents goes down, and as rivalry becomes less intense, value appropriation by incumbents goes up.

Value appropriation—how the value pie is shared by customers, incumbents and suppliers—is intricately linked to how these three participants interact with each other. We will get to 'how this matters' after we also take a look at other participants in the arena.

Complementors

Complementors are the unsung heroes in the competitive arena. They positively impact the size of the value pie—the overall value created in two ways. First, complements have the effect of enhancing the benefit which our customers derive from our products. The improvement our customers achieve by consuming our product along with a complementary product is likely to be more than the sum of parts. Nintendo, Sony and Microsoft understand that this is a key driver of success in their video game console business. While they produce and sell the game consoles, most of the game titles are produced and sold by third-party game studios. All the console makers also have in-house game studios, just in case. With every new console generation, major console makers ensure that a large variety of titles are released or slated to release, compatible with their console. The effect of complements is so strong in this case that video gamers decide to buy (or delay) the console of one console maker or the other based on titles available and expected—the complementary products. This results in increased WtP for our product, and the extra value created typically gets shared among relevant participants.

Second, the availability of complementary products spurs demand, as more customers find the overall solution to their job to be done attractive. Take Tesla and other electric vehicle makers, for example. One of the key complementary products for electric vehicles is availability of charging infrastructure, especially in the highways. We take for granted the petroleum-based fuel retail network which dots our highways. Think of how the demand for electric vehicles will be impacted if a similar charging network is available (assuming that the time to charge is not significantly more than the time to fill the tank). Thus, complementary products enhance the size of the value pie by increasing the volume of exchange (Figure 3.3).

Complementors enhance both the value created per exchange and the volume of exchange. So this is a double bonus for the incumbents. More established the businesses of incumbents and complementors, less dependent will the two sets of players be, as customers will drive the joint purchase and consumption—how we buy cars and fuel. Less established the businesses, more likely the incumbents and complementors are to engage in formal alliances to ensure joint production and delivery in a coordinated manner. That's what game console makers and game studios have been doing. These alliance agreements often specify how value is appropriated between the incumbents and complementors. For instance, game console makers take a fixed royalty per copy of every game title which game studios release for a console, while automakers and fuel retail networks operate independently.

In some cases, the complementary product can become more important and valuable in fulfilling customers' job to be done, which can change the value appropriation mix between incumbents and complementors. Till about the mid-2000s, most of the mobile

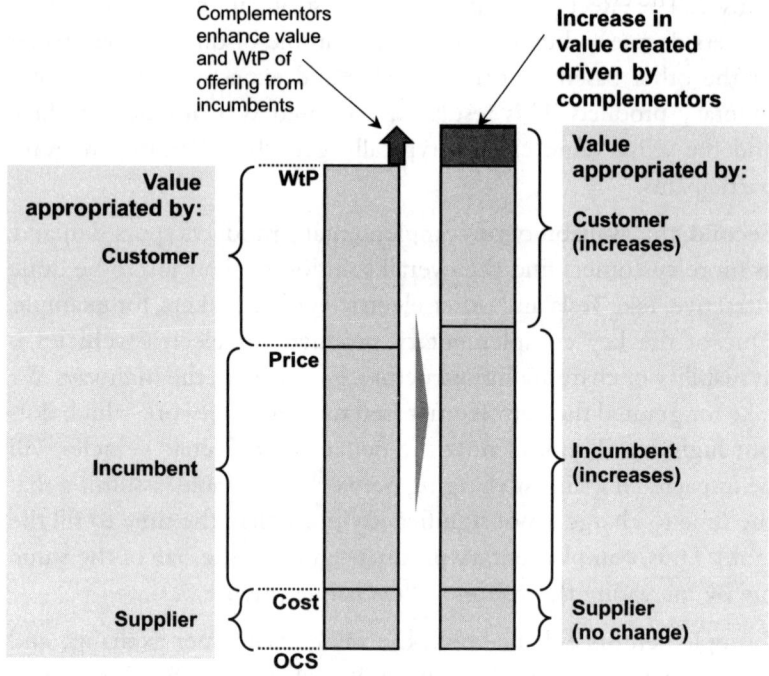

Figure 3.3. How Complementors Impact Value Creation

Source: The author.

Note: The figure shows the impact on value creation per unit of the incumbents' product. Complementors also spur the demand for the incumbents' product, which is not shown.

telecom operators used to appropriate more value by bundling their connectivity offering with high-priced mobile handsets—a key complement—through medium-term contracts with customers. As Apple's iPhone and a large variety of Android-based smartphones became more popular, customers preferred the freedom to choose handsets. Mobile operators were forced to offer plans for connectivity alone, reducing their value appropriated compared to the earlier contract era. How value is appropriated by participants critically depends on the evolving dynamics of value offered by incumbents and complementors, and value perceived by customers.

Substitutors

Substitutors are competitors who do not belong to our industry. They fulfil highly similar jobs to be done, using technologies different from what we use in our industry. Think of the washing machine as a substitutor for a housekeeper offering washing services at our home. Or the other way around. Generally, the term 'substitutes' carries a value judgement that these are inferior to the originals—the products offered by our industry. As a result, incumbents tend to underestimate substitutors more often at their own peril. Some of the substitutors are harbingers of change which is likely to hit our industry soon (Figure 3.4).

The clear sign that a substitutor is becoming a serious competitor is when our customers start comparing the substitutors' offerings with our products while making purchase decisions. If substitutors offer similar or better benefits at a lower or comparable price, our customers will likely choose their offerings. What happens is that customers downsize their WtP for our products once the substitutes

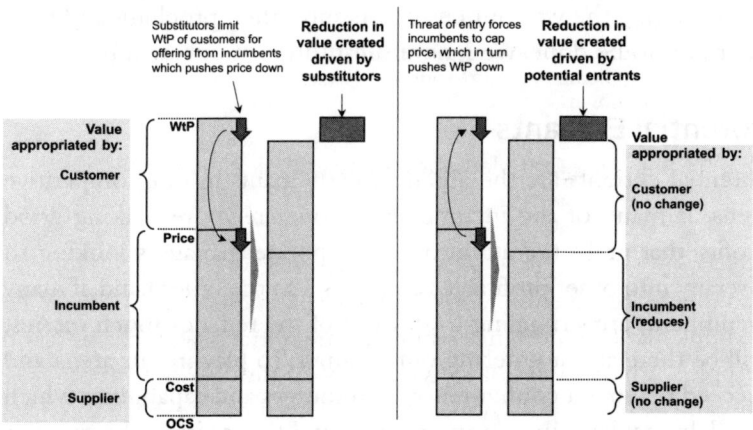

Source: The author.
Note: Substitutors shrink the size of the value pie by taking away the demand from the incumbents, which is not shown.

Figure 3.4. How Substitutors and Potential Entrants Impact Value Creation

enter the comparison set. This puts a downward pressure on our price as well, lowering our value appropriated. In addition, by taking away some of the demand for our products, substitutors reduce the volume of business for all incumbents. The way substitutors impact value creation is just the opposite of how complementors do. They lower per–unit value created and reduce the overall size of the value pie.

During the 1980s, *Encyclopædia Britannica* (EB) was the undisputed leader in reference books, selling a 23–volume set of its eponymous product for close to US$2,000. Customers would take a loan to buy it so that their kids have a veritable reference source to see them through school. As PCs became popular in homes, Microsoft launched Encarta in 1993, an encyclopaedia in a CD–ROM which sold for US$50. In no time, customers embraced the easier–to–use and far cheaper Encarta.[5] EB didn't realize that its substitute was the PC, which could run an encyclopaedia like Encarta along with hundreds of other applications. The PC, with Windows operating system, could fulfil many jobs to be done, whereas the EB served mostly one job to be done. What we see as a substitutor might be the tip of the iceberg of a larger ecosystem of participants coming and changing the way our customers solve their problems and fulfil their jobs to be done. We ignore substitutors at our own peril.

Potential Entrants

Potential entrants are the absentee participants in our competitive arena. If many of the incumbents in our arena are making good profits, that grabs the attention of corporate managers looking to diversify into other profitable businesses. On the other hand, if many incumbents are struggling to stay out of the red, not much interest will be there about entering our business. To play in our arena and succeed requires a configuration of resources and capabilities which can deliver what our customers want, and that reduces the number of potential candidates who are likely to consider entering our arena.

---

[5] Shane Greenstein and Michelle Devereux, 'The Crisis at Encyclopedia Britannica' (Kellogg case KEL251, 2008), 18.

Threat of potential entry is often a robust deterrent which restrains incumbents from abusing their dominant position. The most common outcome of abuse of market power is higher prices for customers resulting in higher profitability for dominant incumbents. However, the high profitability heightens interest among potential entrants to enter the arena. Potential entrants are likely to enter with new or different business models (see Appendix C) as well as with new capacity. Additional capacity will depress the price for a given level of demand. The entrants might play the game differently, adding to the dynamics of the competition. The new entrants will take away customers from practically all incumbents without enhancing the size of the value pie. Entry is not good news for incumbent players as it reduces the value appropriated for all incumbents.

Entry makes it more difficult for incumbents to make same levels of profits as before. Anticipating this, incumbents are likely to set prices at levels which make the business case for entry less attractive to potential entrants. Lowered price level from incumbents when sustained over time would be viewed by customers as a structural change. Accordingly, they adjust their WtP downwards. Potential entrants, without even entering, can shrink the value pie by constraining the pricing ability of incumbents.

HOW THE ARENA MATTERS

To get actionable insights from our understanding of participants in the competitive arena, we need go one step further and ask: What does this mean for my game plan for this arena? Incumbents who are already in the game need to think differently compared to potential entrants who would like to enter the game.

How Arena Matters for Incumbents

The incumbent player's focus is on understanding how to protect and enhance value appropriation and figuring out how to enhance as well as lessen the constraints on value creation. We are interested in a larger pie for the arena and a larger share of the pie for ourselves.

Enhancing Value Appropriation

We can enhance our value appropriation by reducing that of the customers or suppliers. For that, we need to shift the balance of bargaining power towards us. Recall the factors which drive the bargaining power of customers as well as suppliers. We need to focus on factors which are against us the most and ask: What can we do to turn these in our favour?

During the years NutraSweet had patent protection for the artificial sweetener aspartame, it enjoyed tremendous bargaining power over Coca-Cola and Pepsi, its key customers. This was evident in long-term contracts, high price (US$70 per lb) and branded ingredient strategy that NutraSweet was able to impose on the cola majors who featured the NutraSweet swirl prominently in their cola cans and bottles. As the patent was about to expire, the cola majors actively engaged with Holland Sweetener, a rival who was building aspartame production capacity in Europe. Through the branded ingredient strategy, NutraSweet had already gained visibility and acceptance among consumers, and the cola majors risked loss of market share if either of them switched to Holland Sweetener and the other didn't. It was a tough call—achieve reduction in cost or forego sales volumes. What ensued was a bargaining game which ended in both cola majors continuing with NutraSweet as their primary aspartame vendor but at far lower prices (about US$20 per lb) while keeping Holland Sweetener as a second vendor. The cola majors now pocketed the difference of US$50 per lb of inputs—more value appropriated.[6] What the cola majors did was to lessen the bargaining power of a key supplier—NutraSweet—reducing the value appropriated by NutraSweet. Recall Figure 1.1—with NutraSweet's value appropriated going down, the cola majors appropriated more value.

Higher rivalry weakens the strength of bonds which associate us with our customers, resulting in customers shopping around resulting in lower profits for us. We can enhance our value appropriated by

---

[6] Nalebuff and Brandenburger, *Co-opetition*, 70–74.

ensuring that we face lesser rivalry from other incumbents. For that, we need to look at factors which influence rivalry among incumbents and figure out ways to lessen the impact of rivalry on our relationship with our customers. Airline markets are notorious for high rivalry among airlines and high bargaining power of both channels and end customers.[7] Travellers shopping around for the cheapest flights is the norm, and airline seats perish the moment the gate is closed. SIA overcame the consequences of high rivalry by building superior services as its customer value proposition (CVP), thereby becoming consistently profitable. It then reinforced this for frequent travellers by offering additional services such as lounge access, complimentary upgrades and priority baggage delivery for members of its frequent flyer programme. Business travellers highly valued the package of services and were willing to pay fares higher than other airlines, creating a virtuous loop of superior services, differentiation, customer lock-in, higher prices and profitability. Others such as Emirates Airlines and Qatar Airways have since then tried to emulate SIA's strategy to lessen the impact of rivalry on their value appropriation.[8]

Enhancing Value Creation

Complementors are great allies in enhancing value creation. Microsoft figured this out early on in the context of their Windows operating system business. Its customers—PC makers such as IBM, Compaq and HP—were focusing on manufacturing and retail. That could only push so many new PCs into homes. Microsoft figured out that complementary products—applications that run on Windows PCs—are the way to drive adoption of PCs in homes. During the 1990s, it systematically explored and invested in several applications which expanded the range of jobs to be done that a PC

---

[7] Michael E. Porter, 'International Air Transport Association Vision 2050', 2011, 31. Available at: https://www.hbs.edu/faculty/Pages/item.aspx?num=46944 (accessed 3 June 2021).

[8] Kannan Ramaswamy, 'Singapore International Airlines: Strategy with a Smile' (Thunderbird case TB0173, 2001).

can fulfil in homes, by adding spreadsheets, word processors, present-ation tools, media players, home finance software and even an encyclopaedia. To support the large number of application devel-opers, Microsoft released its software development kits (SDKs) free, enticing more application developers to prefer Windows. Apple, during this time, used to charge US$10,000 from application developers for the Mac SDKs. Such deliberate actions by Microsoft drove up adoption of Windows PCs by families and were one of the many reasons that cemented its eventual dominance in the arena for PC operating systems.[9]

Partnerships between incumbents and complementors have become more prevalent in recent decades. Such partnerships allow joint development of offerings and joint go-to-market initiatives which vastly improve our chance of not only enhancing value created but also gaining a lead over other incumbents. Game console makers have been doing this over the past three decades successfully. The only cautionary note about partnerships with complementors is the need to keep in mind that the nature of partnership and the benefits to the parties will evolve over time.

It is also possible to loop in customers into such arrangements in situations where customers can self-produce the complements. This is the underlying logic of letting customers personalize our offerings.

Lessening Constraints on Value Creation

As an incumbent facing constraints on value creation, we ought to focus on understanding what factors are driving up threats from potential entrants and substitutes. Heightening the barriers to entry is a terrific way to keep entrants at bay, but that takes time and money. Trade secrets, patent protection and copyrights are some ways of ensuring that new entrants cannot come in and spoil our game. If we are able to maintain such protections, even our rivals can't

---

[9] Walter Isaacson, *The Innovators* (London: Simon & Schuster, 2015).

challenge us easily. But it's not always that we can protect the value we have created.

Investing in new technologies or innovation which increase the MES can discourage many potential entrants. Commitment to capacity in excess of demand can signal to potential entrants that we will aggressively defend our turf if challenged. Market leaders often adopt tactical posturing through aggressive promotion and pricing to signal both their rivals and potential entrants about their intent not to concede ground. Creating lock-in for customers and distribution channels, as well as locking in suppliers, will make the entry tougher for potential entrants who will be locked out of access to these participants in the arena. Unrelenting focus on improving organizational efficiency and effectiveness, even if not under pressure to do so, will keep the business ready to respond to entry aggressively, if and when needed.

A substitute which attracts customers away from us clearly indicates that we are slipping in our understanding of customers' jobs to be done. If we are unable to provide customers with great products which they don't want to live without, while some other player is doing that, we can't blame the customers for deserting us. We need to go back to our customers to really understand what problem they are trying to solve and what improvement in circumstances they are aspiring to make, and then come up with offerings which continue to remain relevant for them while being profitable for our business.

How Arena Matters for Potential Entrants

As a potential entrant, the key insights from understanding the arena would be to solve an additional challenge which incumbents do not face—the problem of overcoming entry barriers. Our ability to do that will depend on the resources and capabilities which we can readily bring to the business or can build in the short term.

The first scenario is that we possess all the resources and capabilities, and maybe more, to play in the arena we want to enter. Here's a straightforward case of entry by taking on the entry barriers head on. Britannia and Parle had dominant national presence in India's biscuit market for decades. One of the key entry barriers in this business was access to distribution channels. In the early 2000s, any new entrant into biscuits could not hope to win in the game unless they could reach about one million traditional retail outlets which carried more than 95 per cent of food and beverages retail. ITC, the Indian tobacco major, was exploring opportunities to diversify their businesses, and biscuits looked promising. For them, overcoming the barrier of access to distribution was already solved due to channel presence they had in their tobacco business. In 2003, they made a successful 'full-scale entry' into biscuits through the Sunfeast brand. At the time of entry, Sunfeast featured the entire range of products from the low-cost glucose biscuits to premium cookies. They were the first to introduce centre-filled cookies, pipping the market leader in launching this category. ITC could overcome the entry barrier of access to distribution, as it had unfettered access to the million retail outlets in the country.

In the second scenario, our resources and capabilities will allow us to overcome the entry barriers only partially, say for a specific segment in the arena. Just a year after ITC's entry, Unibic Australia entered the Indian market through a joint venture. Lacking the access to distribution channels that ITC possessed, Unibic's game plan focused on a part of the retail network it could access—modern retail. Modern retail was taking off in India, growing from less than 5 per cent in the early 2000s to about 12 per cent by 2017.[10] Unibic's game plan was a 'limited entry' focused on a narrow range of products—cookies primarily—retailed only through modern retail outlets. Although it had a rough ride during its early years, it has survived and is growing in the Indian biscuit market, turning

---

[10] Report by Deloitte Touche Tohmatsu Limited, *Unravelling the Indian Consumer* (February 2019). Available at: https://www2.deloitte.com/content/dam/Deloitte/in/Documents/consumer-business/Unravelling%20the%20Indian%20Consumer_web.pdf (accessed 3 June 2021).

profitable in 2016.[11] What you bring to the game influences how you can play it.

In the third scenario, our resources and capabilities aren't much, and taking on the entry barriers directly is just not feasible. Overcoming such odds requires ingenuity. Most often, it would involve business model innovation. It would involve making redundant the resources and capabilities which provide the incumbents with an unassailable advantage. It would involve turning the incumbents' most valuable resources and capabilities into millstones around their neck. That's what Michael Dell did with his entry into PC market in the USA in the mid-1980s. PC makers of that day—IBM, Compaq, Packard Bell and so on—relied on the retail network to reach customers. This meant that they had to produce to stock and maintain as well as finance inventory to feed the distribution network. This also meant that product offerings were based on a catalogue—a limited number of PC configurations which would meet the needs of most customers. Dell turned the business model upside down. He saw an opportunity to cater to customization needs of IT managers who wanted to tailor the configuration of PCs for their users' specific needs and ensure that money spent on computers is spent on features their users needed. Customized PC configuration went along with two other features of Dell's business model—direct sales to customers and advance payments while placing orders. Soon, Dell had built a PC business which was based on a business model that bypassed two key aspects of high-entry barriers—access to retail network and the need to finance inventory. Dell's 'bypassing entry' into the PC market did not focus on the home PC segment due to low profits in selling to households through direct sales, until growth of the internet made it viable during the late 1990s.[12]

---

[11] Rishabh Mansur, 'Cash Strapped for 3 Years', YourStory, 1 January 2019. Available at: https://yourstory.com/smbstory/cash-strapped-for-three-years-read-how-nikhil-sen-turned-unibic-into-indias-fastest-growing-cookie-brand (accessed 3 June 2021).

[12] https://en.wikipedia.org/wiki/Dell (accessed 3 June 2021).

Once we have solved the problem of overcoming entry barriers—full-scale, limited or bypassing entry—the previous discussion on how to enhance value appropriation and how to lessen pressures which constrain value creation, meant for incumbents, would be relevant. Afterall, we are now in the game!

SHAPING THE ARENA

Boundaries and size of the arena evolve over time. Government policies which facilitate bilateral and multilateral trade have the effect of enlarging the arena, while trade restrictions at national or sub-national levels have the opposite effect. Customer preferences change over time, and drive changes in the industry and market. Business innovations—new ways of doing things, including adoption of innovative technologies—shape the boundaries and size of the arena. These drivers operate through one or more of the factors which determine the size of the arena, discussed in the previous chapter, resulting in reshaping of the arena in terms of boundaries, size and participants. This in turn drives changes to the size of the pie—value creation—and how the pie is shared—value appropriation. Battle-ready managers look for opportunities to shape the arena—make the value pie bigger and make their share bigger.

Take the beer industry in the USA for example. Up to the early 1990s, the industry was dominated by large brewers. During the 1980s, large brewing consolidated into the hands of two corporate players—Anheuser-Busch InBev and MillerCoors. That's when the rebellion started, 'Born from the frustration of mass-produced beer made from cheap ingredients, entrepreneurs went head-to-head with global brewery giants to showcase local and independent craftsmanship.'[13]

---

[13] Katie Jones, 'Craft Beer Boom: The Numbers behind the Industry's Explosive Growth', Visual Capitalist, 1 August 2019). Available at: https://www.visualcapitalist.com/numbers-craft-beer-industry-u-s/ (accessed 3 June 2021).

Table 3.1. Number of Breweries and Growth in the USA

Year	# of Breweries in the USA	Growth during Decade (CAGR in %)	Key Driver
1948	403	–	–
1958	198	–6.9	–
1968	148	–2.9	–
1978	89	–5.0	–
1988	199	8.4	–
1998	1,514	22.5	Change in consumer preferences
2008	1,574	0.4	–
2018	7,450	16.8	New technology (digital advertising)

Source: https://www.brewersassociation.org/statistics–and–data/national–beer–stats/ (accessed 3 June 2021).

Niches in consumer tastes, long ignored by the large brewers, provided an opportunity for entrepreneurs to set up craft breweries and viably compete in the beer markets. Discerning customers lapped up the broader variety and distinctive flavours offered by craft breweries. This primarily led to the 22 per cent compounded annual growth rate (CAGR) in number of breweries during 1988–1998. The rise of craft beer changed the boundaries of beer market in the USA (Table 3.1). Craft beer, with its much smaller MES in production, would target a smaller geographic market such as a city. Yet craft breweries had to fight a tough battle against the huge MES in advertising that large brewers relied on. Although craft beer did not wither off, it also did not create a credible challenge for the large brewers yet.

For the next decade—1998–2008—the number of breweries did not change much. From 2008 on, the number of breweries again grew at 17 per cent (CAGR) for a decade, primarily driven by new craft breweries. During 2007–2016, beer shipments from top five large brewers fell by 14 per cent.[14] In 2018 alone, beer consumption in America went down by 1.6 million barrels compared to the previous year, a 0.8 per cent fall. Craft beer sales volume, however, grew by a million barrels. Beer made by large breweries fell by 2.6 million barrels.[15] The phenomenal increase in the number of breweries and the growing market share of craft beer during the decade of 2008–2018 seem to be primarily driven by a new way of doing things—digital marketing. Craft breweries could now advertise in digital platforms and social networks with small budgets. New tools made available by Google, Facebook and others meant that the craft brewers could create and deploy advertising campaigns which were highly targeted to consumers' tastes and relevant geographies. The blunt weapon of television advertising wielded by the large brewers met its match in the scalpel of digital advertising. It was now even more viable for craft brewers to compete with large brewers while targeting a much smaller market. Large brewers now had to come up with different game plans to compete with craft brewers in smaller markets such as Vermont, Montana, Maine, Oregon and Colorado which came to have the highest number of craft breweries per capita.[16]

The three broad drivers of change of arena—policies, customer preferences and innovation—can be shaped by managers. It is often the challengers who seek to proactively shape the arena, as they have little to lose in maintaining the status quo. The dominant incumbents

---

[14] Derek Thompson, 'Craft Beer Is the Strangest, Happiest Economic Story in America', *The Atlantic*, 29 January 2018. Available at: https://www.theatlantic.com/business/archive/2018/01/craft-beer-industry/550850/ (accessed 3 June 2021).

[15] https://www.brewersassociation.org/statistics-and-data/national-beer-stats/ (accessed 3 June 2021).

[16] Katie Jones, 'Craft Beer Boom'.

would rather prefer to maintain the status quo. The battle-ready incumbent would rather not wait for an upstart challenger to come along and shape the arena. They would seek to do it themselves. At the very least, the battle-ready incumbent would anticipate and thwart any move by challengers seeking to shape the arena. For that, the incumbent needs to know who its rivals are. That's what we look at next.

«LONG STORY» «SHORT»

The competitive arena consists of six participants—customers, rival incumbents, suppliers, substitutors, complementors and potential entrants. Understanding the arena involves insights on how participants influence value creation and appropriation, and how that matters for our business. Understanding how the arena matters for incumbents will help enhance value creation and appropriation for our business. If we are a potential entrant, we face the additional challenge of overcoming entry barriers. That too requires understanding of how the arena matters. Understanding the arena and how it matters for our business is the starting point of looking outside.

CHAPTER FOUR

The Players

During the early 1920s, Ford Motor Company was the leader in the American automobile industry with a 55 per cent market share. General Motors (GM), then a 12-year-old company, was struggling to stay afloat. Ford's game plan was to produce cars at a low cost, price them low and sell them in large volumes. Model T was the only car model available from Ford's cutting-edge production facilities. Ford treated its dealers as though they didn't matter, which is to say shabbily.[1] Customers bought Model Ts because these were the most affordable. Against the advantages that Ford enjoyed—low cost, high-volume production facility, huge market share and the by-then established reputation—rivals couldn't do much. The low price of Model Ts had triggered a massive spurt in demand—car became an affordable product. Ford made modest margins in each car sold, but the massive volumes drove up its profits.

About this time when Ford was at its peak, a new CEO took over the reins at GM. Alfred P. Sloan came up with a different game plan for GM. Several models were launched to meet diverse customer

---

[1] Richard S. Tedlow, 'The Struggle for Dominance in the Automobile Market: The Early Years of Ford and General Motors', *Business and Economic History* 17 (1988): 49–62.

needs in terms of features and price points. GM started offering its cars in different colours, compared to the only-black policy of Ford. Sloan brought 'annual model change', which remains the de facto product policy in the industry to date. Sloan rounded off his game plan with financing for both dealers and car buyers.[2] In about a decade, GM rose to leadership position. GM's offerings provided many new attributes and features which customers valued and were willing to pay for. Ford just didn't provide customers any choice. By offering choice to customers and an easier way to own a car, GM was able to charge its customers a premium in price, which increased its per-car profits. As more customers started going to GM, its overall profits went up.

Players in an arena should have a game plan which is consistent internally and over time, and externally viable. Thanks to Michael Porter,[3] we know that there are broadly two main viable ways to compete—'differentiation' and 'cost leadership'. A differentiator, like GM of the 1920s, seeks to provide distinctive customer benefits for which customers are willing to pay extra—a premium. The benefits are valuable, at least to a section of the customers. If the differentiator can produce and deliver these valuable benefits at a cost which is less than the premium that customers are willing to pay, two things will happen. Those customers who value the benefits will prefer the differentiator over other players, meaning more business volume for the differentiator. The difference between premium and additional cost will result in additional profits from differentiation, meaning overall higher profits. That's how successful differentiators make more money than other players.

The cost leader, like Ford of the 1900s, runs a tight ship, resulting in cost position vastly superior to other players. For comparable customer benefits, their unit cost would be the lowest among rivals. With that, the cost leader can set their price below the lowest priced rival, resulting in two things. The lowest price in the market attracts

---

[2] Ibid.
[3] Porter, *Competitive Strategy*, 34–46.

more customers, meaning more business volume, possibly lot more if the price is low enough to spur growth in demand. Being the lowest in cost, the cost leader will still make profits, while their rivals would be scrambling to stay above water. The cost leader will go for high volume of business at low but positive margins. This is how successful cost leaders make more money than other players.

KNOWING YOUR COMPETITORS' GAME PLAN

Rivals' game plans are often apparent from observing their product positioning, marketing as well as visible choices in terms of how they manage their business. What we often are not sure just by observation is how good the rivals are at their game plan. A straightforward way to validate the game plans and relative success of competitors is to compare their return on assets (RoA).[4]

First, we can figure out who's doing well and who's not. Higher the RoA, better is the player's performance on profitability. Second, we can identify whether a player is a differentiator or cost leader. Asset turnover (or asset velocity), a measure of efficiency, will be best among rivals for the successful cost leader. Their sales margin, though positive, is likely not the best. On the other hand, the successful differentiator will have the best sales margin with somewhat lower asset turnover.

What these two measures indicate is the relative focus of a player, given their game plan. The differentiator's focus in strategic decisions and actions would be to deliver distinctive and premium-fetching customer benefits, which, if successful, will translate into high sales margins. The differentiator would give lower priority to efficiency

---

[4] RoA = Profits for the year/Average assets for the year, which can be split into two terms: R/S = Profits for the year/Sales for the year and S/A = Sales for the year/Average assets for the year. This is two-thirds of DuPont analysis, in which we multiply the two terms with leverage (measured as average assets/average equity) to get the return on equity. Since we would like to compare the operational performance of the business without the influence of leverage, we will stop with RoA.

of its assets and operations. Rather, they would end up deploying more assets per dollar of sales to support their differentiation, resulting in lower-than-best asset turnover. Sales margin is the key driver of RoA for a differentiator.

The cost leader lives by the code of efficiency. Their strategic decisions and actions focus on cost-efficient technologies, processes, systems and capabilities. They squeeze assets to earn as much revenue as is legally possible. Thus, their asset turnover turns out to be best among rivals. With their superior cost position, they gun for volumes, lowering prices below competition, running rivals into the red and sometimes even out of the game. This leads to sales margins that are not worth bragging about. Asset turnover is the key driver of RoA for the cost leader.

The two game plans—differentiation and cost leadership—are two distinct paths to winning the game. In the illustration in Figure 4.1, both the differentiator and the cost leader end up with the same RoA, implying that both are performing equally well in terms of profitability, though the source of profitability is different. Players who fall in a given curved line in the chart would have same RoA. Players who perform better are located towards the right and top.

The sales margin vs asset turnover scatter plot (Figure 4.1) reveals the realized strategy of players, not their intended strategy.[5] Identifying the competitive strategy of successful players is easier. The different-iators cluster to the bottom right, and the cost leaders bunch up towards the top left in the plot. Porter labels those who aren't (yet) successful as 'stuck in the middle'.

These players cluster below the curved lines where successful players sit, and towards the origin. Sometimes, it's a bit of challenge to identify the intended competitive strategy of stuck-in-the-middle players, but tendencies—attempts at differentiation or cost leadership—could be discerned.

---

[5] Henry H. Mintzberg and J. A. Waters, 'Of Strategies: Deliberate and Emergent', *Strategic Management Journal* 25, no. 3 (1982): 465–499.

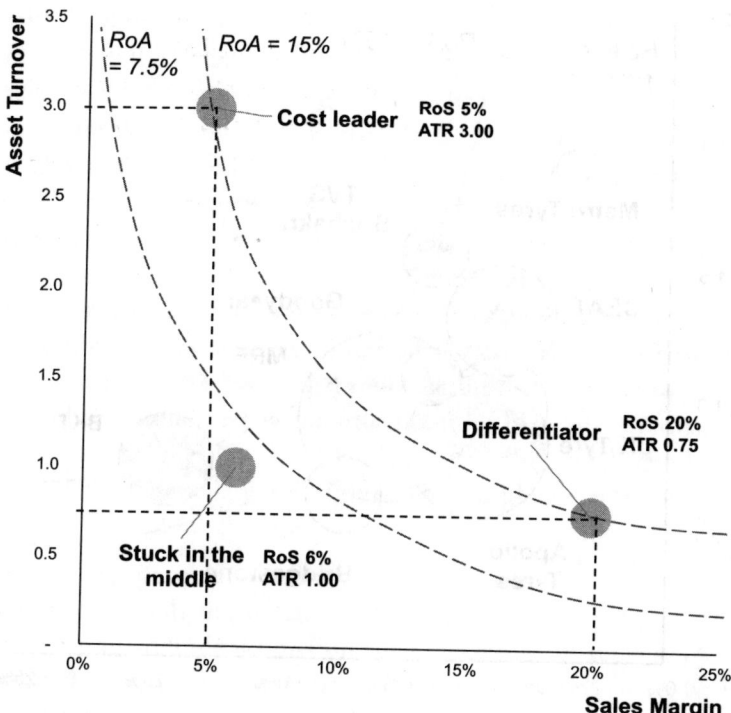

Source: The author.

Figure 4.1. Rivals and Their Game Plans

I have illustrated this analysis with data on tyre makers in India (see Figure 4.2). The largest player by revenue is MRF followed by Apollo Tyres. However, neither are best performers in terms of RoA for the years considered. BKT can be seen as the best-performing differentiator and TVS Srichakra as the best-performing cost leader. Among the others, tendencies towards differentiation or cost leadership can be discerned from their relative positions.

This analysis provides us with a first glimpse of competitor game plan, the starting point for understanding each of our competitors. In the preceding discussion, we assumed that we know who we are battling with. That's not always the case. Battle-ready players seek

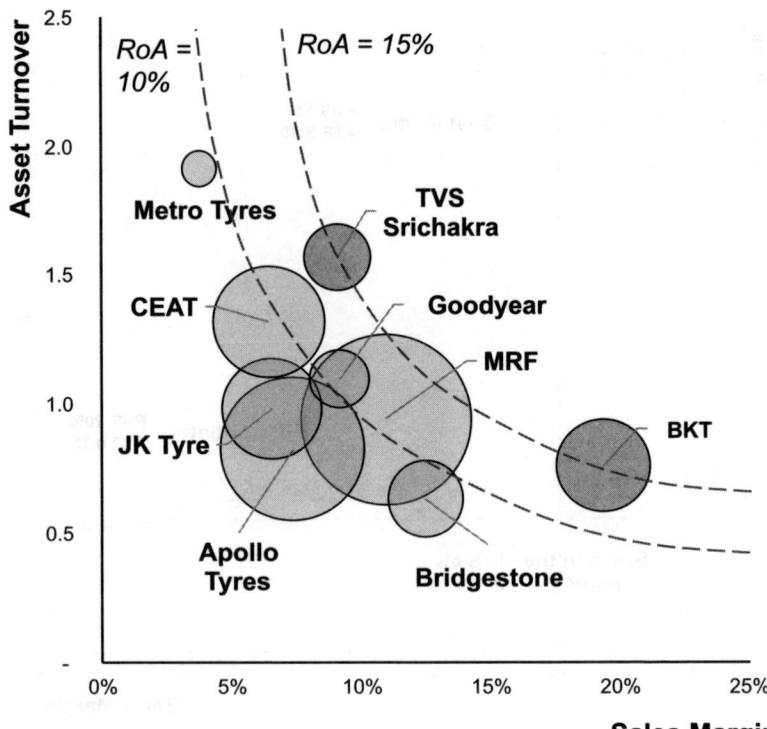

Source: Data from CMIE Industry IQ database; author's analysis.
Notes:
1. Assets at the start and end of a year averaged to estimate asset for each year.
2. Three-year average of sales, profits and assets used to estimate sales margin, asset turnover and RoA (2016–2017 to 2018–2019).
3. Bubble size represents relative size of sales—larger the bubble, higher is the player's sales of tyres in INR.

Figure 4.2. Game Plans of Tyre Makers in India

answers to the questions: Who are the competitors in the game? Who are the other participants? And what type of players are they?

SPOTTING RIVALS AND OTHER PLAYERS

Ask a group of managers from the same business in a company who their main competitors are. There is good chance that their responses do not fully match. More often, the top competitor or two would be the same. After that, the list is likely to vary. Consider two questions asked to managers from rival players in a competitive arena. First, 'who are the players in your arena', and second, 'who all are competing with you?' Answer to the first question by different players in the market is more likely similar. Answer to the second would depend on the player answering the question.

Competitors come in various shapes and forms. They can broadly be understood and categorized along two characteristics—the arenas they compete in and the strategic endowments they bring to the game in the form of resource configurations. On a standalone basis, these characteristics about a player do not provide meaningful insights. We need to compare the market presence and resource configuration of our business with that of each of the competitors. Based on how this pair-wise comparison stacks up, we can gain insights on what each of them mean for us. Ming-Jer Chen's research on competitive dynamics[6] provides us with the framework of market commonality vs resource similarity, with which we can gain useful insights on the competitive landscape for our business. To avoid the risk of being pedantic, we will use arena and market interchangeably, going forward.

Market Commonality

'Market commonality' of a particular competitor with our business would be 'the degree of presence the competitor manifests in the markets it overlaps'[7] with our business. If both competitor and we are present in only one market, and that too the same one, then market commonality between the two of us is 100 per cent. If both are present in only one market, but not the same one, then market commonality is 0 per cent. This is often seen only in textbook examples. Most companies would be present in more than one

[6] Ming-Jer Chen, 'Competitor Analysis and Interfirm Rivalry: Toward a Theoretical Integration', *Academy of Management Review* 21, no. 1 (1996): 100–134.
[7] Ibid.

market and would be involved in multiple businesses. Market commonality of our business with a particular competitor could be high or low or somewhere in between. Market commonality with a competitor is a function of the importance of the market for our business and the presence of the competitor in that market.

Market Importance

Importance of a market for our business can be assessed using quantitative measures as relevant data is likely available in our database of business transactions. The most straightforward measure of 'market importance' is an estimate of business from that market as a proportion of our overall business.[8] Take, for instance, Tata Motors, which plays in the markets for passenger and commercial vehicles including in a specific market called medium and heavy commercial vehicles (MHCVs). Tata Motors sells MHCVs in several markets in India, each delineated by state boundaries. Out of the total sales of 184,789 MHCVs during 2018–2019, it sold 19,265 vehicles in Uttar Pradesh, followed by 17,357 vehicles in Maharashtra.[9] The importance of Uttar Pradesh MHCV market is estimated as 10.4 per cent and that of Maharashtra MHCV market as 9.4 per cent, from the above data. Here, we took the number of vehicles sold as the basis for estimating market importance. More markets a player is operating in, less will be the importance of any one market for its overall business. A player operating in fewer markets will be dependent more on each of these markets.

Taking the number of units sold may not lead to meaningful estimates in all contexts. Take, for instance, Siemens, which sells electric motors of different power ratings (given in kilowatts or kW). The product range for low–tension motors would start from less than a kW and go all the way up to 1,000 kW. Adding up the number of motors sold would be meaningless because of the massive difference between the smallest and largest power rating of motors

---

[8] Ibid.

[9] Data from CMIE Industry Outlook database for commercial vehicles.

in their product range. Instead, sum of motors sold weighted by power rating would give the total kW of motors sold, which would be more appropriate. The ratio of total kW sold in one market upon total kW sold in all markets would provide a better estimate of importance of that market for Siemens.

If volume-based measures are not meaningful, revenue share from the market as a proportion of overall revenue of business in currency units can be used to estimate market importance. As the required data relates to our business transactions, it should be possible to estimate market importance using either a volume-based or revenue-based measure.

Competitor Presence

'Competitor presence' in a market can be estimated as the market share which a competitor has in the market.[10] Market share estimates are typically volume-based or revenue-based. Estimates of market share, especially for competitors, suffer from shortcomings such as overestimation of own share (for instance, underestimation of competitor business volume or value), incorrect estimate of overall market size (for instance, missing out smaller competitors in bottom-up market sizing or incorrect assumptions about relation between drivers of market growth and market size in top-down market sizing) and low reliability of information about competitors and customers. In certain market contexts, information would be hard to come by. Measures of activities which proxy business volume reasonably well can be used to estimate competitor presence.

For instance, for a retail business, presence of a competitor can be proxied through retail space the competitor has (square meters) in the market as a proportion of total retail space across all retailers in the market. For a professional services business such as auditing, the number of auditors that the competitor employs in the market

---

[10] Chen, 'Competitor Analysis and Interfirm Rivalry'.

as a proportion of auditors across all audit firms catering to the market would capture competitor presence.

There may be situations where even such measures of activities are hard to come by. Expert opinion—from those who have been tracking the market for years—could be used to rank players in the order of competitor presence. Although this would be ordinal and subjective, using rankings from a few experts to come up with a rank order of competitor presence for a market would be tenable in contexts where other methods are not feasible.

Assessing and Understanding Market Commonality

Market commonality between us and a particular rival can be estimated by multiplying estimates for our market importance and competitor's market presence for that market. This pair-wise analysis needs to be done for all competitors that you think are relevant in the first cut. You can always add more rivals or other participants in later iterations as needed. The estimates for market commonality within a market are normalized for comparability and 'one' indicates highest score, and all market commonality scores range between zero and one.

I have analysed the market commonality among key players for two markets in the commercial vehicles industry in India—buses and passenger carriers[11] (see Table 4.1). The analysis used data on the number of vehicles sold for the year 2018–2019 across 23 state markets for buses and 24 state (provincial) markets for passenger carriers. In the market for passenger carriers, the top players are Tata Motors and Force Motors, each with about 35 per cent share. Their market commonality scores with the other are high—1.00 and 0.99—and almost symmetrical. Consider Ashok Leyland in the same market with a market share of 2.8 per cent. From Ashok Leyland's perspective, Tata Motors is an important rival—market commonality

---

[11] Passenger carriers are smaller vehicles compared to buses. The primary difference is capacity.

Table 4.1. Market Commonality: Commercial Vehicle Makers in India (2018–2019)

Market Commonality of … with →	Market Share (%)	Ashok Leyland	Force Motors	Mahindra & Mahindra	SML Isuzu	Tata Motors	Volvo-Eicher
Passenger Carriers							
Ashok Leyland	2.8	–	0.62	0.10	0.15	0.69	0.20
Force Motors	34.4	0.07	–	0.17	0.26	0.99	0.26
Mahindra & Mahindra	4.9	0.05	0.62	–	0.21	0.69	0.19
SML Isuzu	9.6	0.05	0.66	0.11	–	0.73	0.20
Tata Motors	35.0	0.07	1.00	0.12	0.26	–	0.30
Volvo-Eicher	13.3	0.05	0.64	0.09	0.18	0.80	–
Buses							
Ashok Leyland	42.0	–	0	0.11	0.20	1.00	0.25
Force Motors	0	0	–	0	0	0	0
Mahindra & Mahindra	3.1	0.58	0	–	0.18	0.67	0.14
SML Isuzu	7.2	0.61	0	0.14	0	–	0.15
Tata Motors	37.1	0.98	0	0.13	0.21	–	0.25
Volvo-Eicher	9.7	0.67	0	0.08	0.13	0.69	–

Source: Data from CMIE Industry IQ database; author's analysis.

Note: Market commonality was estimated as the sum of products of importance of market for focal player and presence of competitor in that market for all state markets in India (23 states for passenger carriers and 22 states for buses). Market importance for a market was estimated as the share of the business from the market upon total business from all the markets. Competitor presence for a market was estimated as the market share of the competitor in that market.

of 0.69 (more than moderate). But Tata Motors does not see Ashok Leyland as a rival due to low market commonality of 0.07. Rivalry is not always mutual and symmetrical.

Now look at the market for buses, and a similar picture unfolds, but the players are different. Here, Tata Motors and Ashok Leyland see each other with high market commonality. They are direct rivals and big ones at that. Force Motors has market commonality of zero with all players here as they don't make and sell buses. Small players such as Volvo-Eicher and SML Isuzu in both markets see large players as key rivals due to high market commonality. But these won't see other smaller players as key rivals due to lower market commonality.

The market commonality score reflects how prominent as a rival a player is to another player in the market. The largest players are visible as rivals to all, including other large players who compete head on with them in multiple markets. Small players are usually ignored as rivals by larger players. But ask the small players, and they will point to the largest players as their key rivals. This asymmetry in identifying who your rivals are is a defining characteristic of how players in a market selectively focus on some rivals to the exclusion of others, leading to blind spots, especially for larger players, that can at time be costly. We will discuss more on how to spot and correct for this later.

Resource Similarity

'Resource similarity' between a particular competitor and our business captures the 'extent to which the strategic endowments of the competitor are similar in type and amount'[12] to those of our business. 'Strategic endowments' of a competitor relevant to the market are the configuration of resources and capabilities that the competitor has and can bring to the game. It's not merely the laundry list of resources and capabilities the competitor has but how these are interlinked and

---

[12] Chen, 'Competitor Analysis and Interfirm Rivalry'.

deployed in their value chain of activities. If we and our competitor are following different games plans, say we are pursuing differentiation while the competitor is trying to be cost leader, resource similarity between us and the rival cannot be high. It ought to be low because we and the rival are pursuing different competitive strategies. Worst case, resource similarity could be medium.[13] If we and the rival are both pursuing similar game plans and are of comparable size, resource similarity between us ought to be high.[14]

Comparing Strategic Endowments

Resource similarity can be assessed through direct comparison of the strategic endowments of our business with that of the rival in question. Businesses source inputs from their suppliers, transform these inputs into products and deliver to their customers. Michael Porter's concept of firm-level value chain[15] elegantly captures this in the form of a sequence of activities performed within the business as well as at its interface with external stakeholders. It captures the flow of value through the business and enables us to understand the linkages between resource configurations in various parts of the value chain and the value these add to the end result of the value chain—the product in customer's hands. Two businesses pursuing similar competitive strategies will have a high degree of congruence in the configurations of their resource base. This allows us to assess their relative resource position by mapping their resources and linkages along each part of the value chain and check for three things—presence of specific resource types, quantity of the resource and the linkages among resource types. Relative resource position reveals how a player's strategic endowments compare with that of a competitor—superior, at par or inferior. This is how we can use the value chains to assess the relative resource position between two

---

[13] If it is high, it means that at least one of the pair has goofed up on strategy execution!

[14] If not, again one of the pair has goofed up on strategy execution.

[15] Porter, *Competitive Advantage*, 33–61.

businesses. From the relative resource position, we can infer whether the resource similarity between the two players is high. If not, the extent of differences would drive the conclusion about resource similarity (low to medium).

Inferring Resource Similarity

If the two players are not following similar game plans—say one is a differentiator and the other is a cost leader—their value chains will not be readily comparable. For instance, think of SIA, a full-service carrier which pursues differentiation, and IndiGo, a low-cost carrier which pursues cost leadership. SIA has in place resources and capabilities both in flight and on ground, aimed at delivering superior customer experience. Their flights are equipped with well-cushioned, broader seats with more leg room. Each seat features a dedicated entertainment system which can play content on demand. They provide menu options in economy class. Their frequent flyers and business class passengers get access to luxurious lounges and get their checked-in baggage first out in the belt.[16] The resources underlying all these are irrelevant for IndiGo's competitive strategy. They instead invest in efficiency-boosting resources such as ramps (instead of old-fashioned boarding stairs) for boarding passengers through gates not equipped with aerobridges. This ensures faster turnaround of aircrafts, as passengers tend to board faster through the ramps including those who need assistance.[17] For sure, SIA would also like to drive efficiency in its operations, but its first priority is to deliver differentiated features to its customers. That's the first priority for SIA's investments. Same way, IndiGo's first priority would be efficiency. Direct comparison of the resource configurations of SIA and IndiGo would not make sense, as their competitive

---

[16] Ramaswamy, 'Singapore International Airlines'.

[17] John Goglia, 'IndiGo Airlines Eliminates Stairs for Easy Airside Boarding', *Forbes*, 16 June 2016. Available at: https://www.forbes.com/sites/johngoglia/2013/06/16/indigo-airlines-eliminates-stairs-for-easy-airside-boarding-why-havent-other-airlines-caught-on/#7d58b7392018 (accessed 3 June 2021).

strategies dictate distinctively different resource endowments and configurations.

The alternate approach to assessing resource similarity involves comparing the output and outcomes of resource endowments of a player. We can compare two players on several dimensions such as product features and quality perception; physical resources such as supply chain, production, distribution and retail infrastructure; technology such as patent base; reputation; and human and financial resources. These dimensions would allow comparison of businesses which pursue different competitive strategies. The comparison would lead to conclusions on a relative resource position, which then tell us about the extent of resource similarity between the two players. This approach is also relevant in situations where data on type and quantity of resources which the competitor has is not readily available. Figure 4.3 provides the situations when value chain

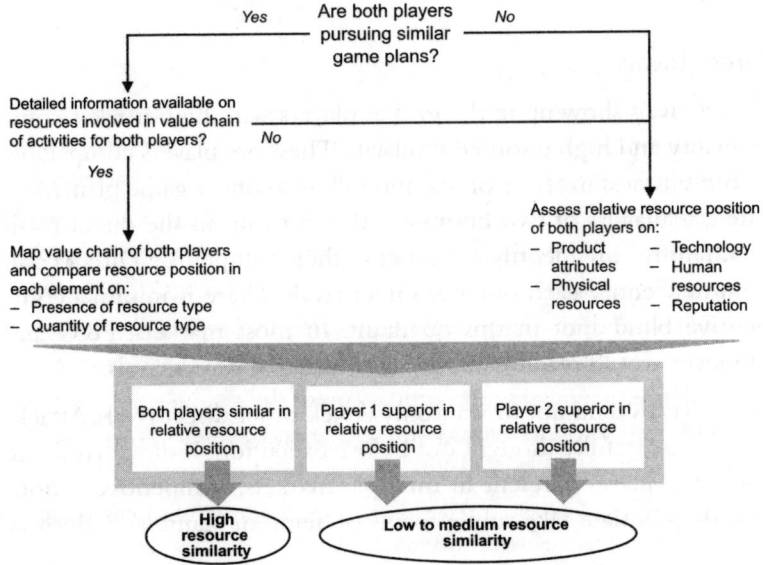

Source: The author.

Figure 4.3. Assessing Resource Similarity

mapping can be used to directly assess resource similarity and when resource similarity needs to be inferred from comparing output and outcomes of resource endowments.

Just like market commonality, resource similarity also needs to be assessed pair-wise. Having assessed both market commonality and resource similarity of our business pair-wise with those of competitors, we can place each competitor in the competitor radar.

Competitor Radar

Competitor radar—a point of view scatter plot (see Figure 4.4) from the perspective of our business—helps understand three things about competitors: what type of competitor they are for us, how easy or difficult it is for us to spot them and what their competitive behavioural traits are. It is important to remember that if we plot the competitor radar from one of our rival's points of view, the picture and insights, could be quite different than that from our point of view.

Direct Rivals

Direct rivals show up in the grid as players with high market commonality and high resource similarity. These are players comparable to our business in terms of size and follow a similar game plan. Most often, managers of two businesses that turn up in the direct rivals quadrant readily identify the other as their competitor. Direct rivals tend to identify each other as direct rivals. There is minimal competitive blind spot in this quadrant. In most markets, P&G and Unilever would readily identify each other as direct rivals.

Direct rivals tend not to wantonly attack other direct rivals. Attacks if any are carefully thought out before execution. If direct rivals are also large players present in multiple markets, competitive actions that they initiate take subtle forms of 'feint' or 'gambit'.[18] Both of

---

[18] Ian C. MacMillan, Alexander B. van Putten, and Rita Gunther McGrath, 'Global Gamesmanship', *Harvard Business Review*, May 2003, 62–71.

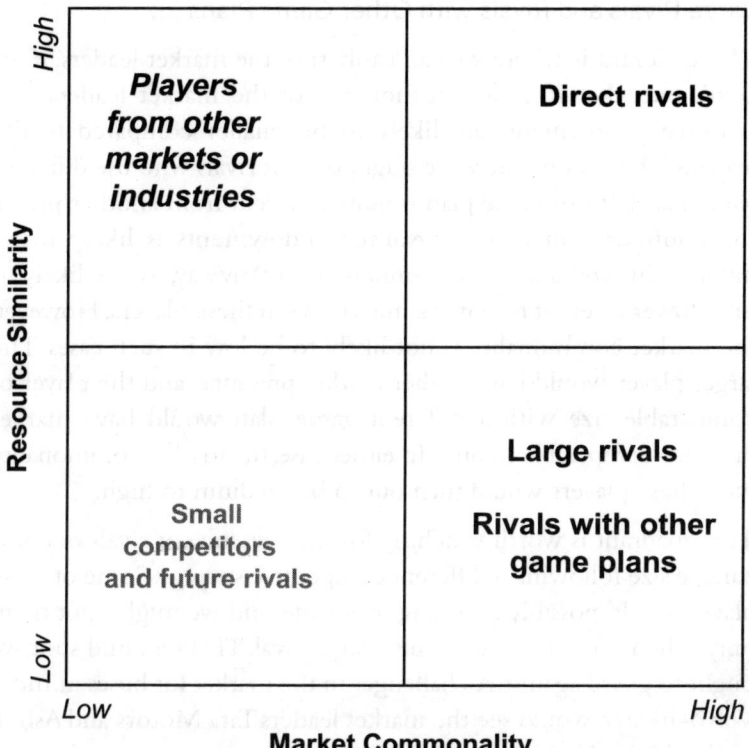

Source: Adapted from Chen, 'Competitor Analysis and Interfirm Rivalry'.

Figure 4.4. Competitor Radar: Spotting Competitors from Your Point of View

these would play out across two markets—the focal market where competitive action is initiated and the target market which is where the attacker seeks to improve its competitive position. Feint involves diverting the attention of rival away from the target market by initiating action in the focal market. Gambit involves the attacker voluntarily surrendering value in the focal market to make a larger value gain in the target market. When attacked, direct rivals respond quickly. If the direct rivals are also market leaders, their response will likely be quick and fierce.

Large Rivals and Rivals with Other Game Plans

This quadrant is where we can easily spot the market leaders, if we aren't one, that is. If we are not one of the market leaders, our resource endowments are likely to be smaller compared to the leader's. This is also where we ought to spot rivals who use different game plans. If our game plan is quite different from another player, the configuration of our resource endowments is likely to be different in type, amount or configuration. Anyway, we are likely to infer lower levels of resource similarity with these players. However, the market commonality is not likely to be low in such cases. The larger player would have higher market presence, and the player of comparable size with a different game plan would have market presence comparable to ours. In either case, the market commonality with these players would turn out to be medium to high.

This quadrant is worth watching for the presence of rivals of comparable size following a different competitive strategy. Some of these players could possibly grow big over time, and we might spot them only when they turn out to be a large rival. That's a blind spot we ought to guard against. A challenger in the market for buses in India, Volvo-Eicher, would see the market leaders Tata Motors and Ashok Leyland here. In the Indian brokerage market, mainstream players as HDFC Securities and ICICI Direct would see the native digital discount brokerage Zerodha in this quadrant.

Large rivals, if it's beneficial to attack, would go for 'onslaught'[19]—a direct attack on our markets where we have limited ability to defend our turf. The objective would be to get us to exit the market or at least make us recede to insignificance. Price wars are a common form of onslaught. Say, we are a differentiator and the rival, a cost leader and a successful one at that. Unless we are protected by being present in a niche of the market which has a distinctive job to be done, the onslaught will most likely come in the form of a price war. Large rivals, when attacked by smaller players (from their point

---

[19] Ibid.

of view), often do not react quickly because they want to wait and see if it is worth their while to respond. They may also not react because the small player is in their blind spot. If they, however, choose to respond to attacks by a small player, it is likely an onslaught.

Rivals of comparable size following different game plans are not likely to attack others of comparable size unless there are compelling reasons to do so. When they attack, they are more likely to prefer 'contests'[20]—attacks with a narrow scope in terms of product and market. They would attack where we are at a disadvantage so that we find it difficult to defend our turf. Rivals of comparable size will respond quickly when attacked. Their response will be measured and focused, befitting a contest. They can also resort to gambits and feints if there is scope for such responses.

Small Competitors and (More Dangerous) Future Rivals

We will see lower market commonality with competitors smaller than us due to their limited market presence. Their resource endowments would also be smaller in size compared to ours even if it's of similar type, resulting in lower resource similarity. Relegated to the bottom-left corner of the competitor radar, small rivals often thrive and grow unnoticed by larger players including the market leaders, only to be noticed when they are already a sizeable contender.

This quadrant is where disruptive innovators[21] would first pop up as they enter the market with innovative technologies and radically different business models. Their small market presence in initial days and their distinct configuration of resources due to different technology and business model would make them look more like a small competitor. That's if at all they are noticed. If the technology they adopt has been making buzz, we might notice them. Chances are low that we take them seriously, at least then. We will look at the

---

[20] Ibid.
[21] Clayton M. Christensen, *The Innovator's Dilemma* (Boston, MA: Harvard Business School Press, 1997).

examples of Under Armour (UA) from the perspective of Nike and Dollar Shave Club (DSC) from the point of view of Gillette in Chapter 7.

Substitutors would also appear here when they get a first taste of your market. Substitutors appearing here is an early warning that our customers' job to be done is also being fulfilled by players from another industry through a different technology. It's likely that there are specific job-to-be-done niches which we are ignoring. If this is the case, we can expect serious challenge from substitutors who are focusing on such niches. Often, it might be too late by the time we notice that a substitutor has morphed into a rival.

When managers do the competitor radar, they often find the bottom-left quadrant empty in their first-cut analysis. When asked to focus on smaller competitors, disruptors and substitutors, they find multiple future rivals popping up here. This quadrant is a critical blind spot for market leaders and well-entrenched players and is worthy of the time and effort needed to gain a deep understanding every now and then. In Chapter 9, we will discuss more about blind spots and how to overcome them.

Small competitors, disruptors (in initial days) and substitutors typically resort to 'guerilla campaigns'.[22] These attacks are aimed at narrow segments of the market which are typically not attractive to the larger players but are highly attractive to the attackers. Using this segment as a foothold, they then expand to other segments of the market. Larger players often notice these rivals only after they have grown into sizeable contenders. While small competitors can be responded to effectively through onslaught or contest, same may not work against disruptors and substitutors.

Players from Other Markets or Industries

Many of the resource endowments relevant for our market would also be relevant in other industries. Most consumer businesses would require

---

[22] MacMillan, van Putten, and McGrath, 'Global Gamesmanship'.

resources and capabilities for distribution and retailing through traditional and modern retail channels. Tool design and development is a capability which is relevant for most manufacturing-based businesses. These are generic resource endowments which find use in multiple markets and industries. To the extent resource endowments relevant for our business are not fully market specific, some players who are not (yet) playing in our market may possess the resource endowments to overcome entry barriers and execute a viable entry into our market. Players often leverage pre-existing resource endowments when considering entry into a new market. Recall how ITC was able to utilize its pre-existing resource endowment of presence in retail network in India to facilitate entry into the market for biscuits.

Again, this quadrant is a common blind spot, as managers often ignore in their competitor analysis other industries which have players with comparable or superior generic resource endowments. It is useful to remember that potential entrants who already possess many of the resource endowments to play in our market would find it easier to overcome barriers to enter our market. This quadrant is worth watching to be able to spot players from other markets or industries contemplating entry into our market.

The behavioural traits of players from other markets and industries would mirror the traits of competitors in our own market. Specifically, it would depend on how their strategy and size compare with ours. For all practical purposes, the attack and response traits of these out-siders would be like they were already in the game.

Competitor Radar for Passenger Carriers in India

I have developed illustrative competitor radar charts for two markets in the Indian commercial vehicle industry. For each market, the charts are developed from the point of view of two players—a market leader and a challenger or small rival (see Figure 4.5).

Tata Motors is the leader in both markets. It's main rivals in the two markets are different though. In buses, its main rivalry is with Ashok Leyland, while in passenger carriers, its main rivalry is with Force

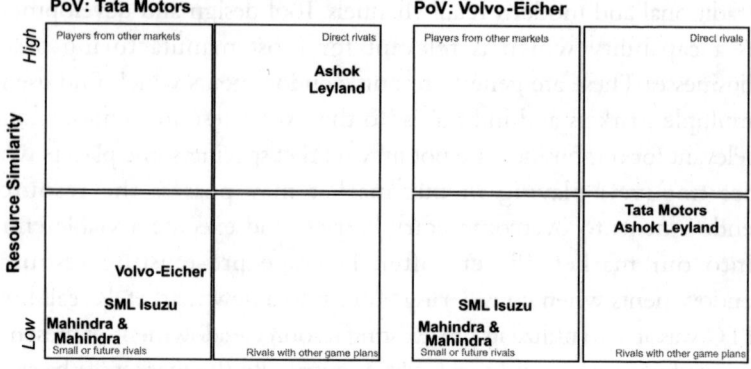

Market for Buses in India (2018–2019)

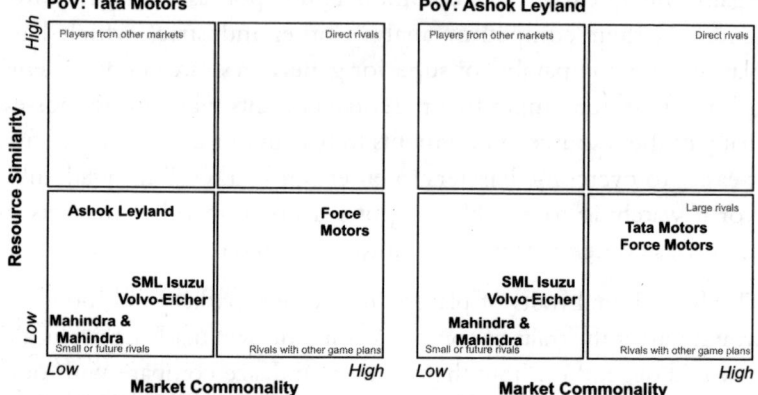

Market for Buses in Passenger Carriers (2018–2020)

Source: CMIE Industry IQ database; company websites; author's analysis.
Note: Market commonality from Table 4.1. Resource similarity was qualitatively estimated based on profiles of players available on their websites.

Figure 4.5. Competitor Radars: Selected Commercial Vehicle Markets in India

Motors. The competitive behavioural traits that Ashok Leyland is likely to exhibit in buses market against Tata Motors would be that of a market-leading direct rival—not hasty to attack but quick and fierce in response, favouring feints and gambits as modes of attack. However, in the market for passenger carriers, it would be imprudent of Ashok Leyland to try feints and gambits, and they may not have the ability to respond fiercely. Turn the tables, and we find that Tata Motors would prefer onslaught against Ashok Leyland in the market for passenger carriers, but not in the market for buses. Tata Motors and Ashok Leyland, the two gorillas in the market for buses, also face off in other commercial vehicle markets (not included in the analysis though) such as trucks and goods carriers. This provides Tata Motors (and Ashok Leyland) with multiple focal arenas to stage feints and gambits, targeting the market for buses. Tata Motors does not have this opportunity with Force Motors, which is a more focused player.

Volvo-Eicher, the challenger in the market for buses, sees main rivalry from Tata Motors and Ashok Leyland and would be expected to adopt guerrilla tactics against these biggies. On the other hand, Volvo-Eicher would find it appropriate to use direct forms of rivalry against SML Isuzu and Mahindra & Mahindra. This analysis would reveal different insights when done from the point of view of each player. More nuanced and deeper insights can be derived by doing this analysis at a more granular level, say for specific geographic markets such as sub-national regions.

In a real-life setting, the estimation of market commonality and resource similarity for the competitor radar must be done with a clear understanding of the boundaries of the arena which is relevant for our business. While it is relatively easier to find data for estimating market commonality at that level of granularity, it is a challenge to estimate resource similarity at the same granular level. Resource configurations of companies can only be observed at the company or business-unit level, which would already subsume multiple markets. Isolating the resource configurations market by market is not always feasible. Second, within a company, there would be linkages across various markets in specific activities such as sales, branding and channel policies. There would be linkages across various production units in activities such as sourcing, supply chain and production processes. The relative resource position of a company would be favourably influenced if the company is able to leverage more of these linkages. This is to say that the value of resource configurations for the game plan of a business is not merely additive. Third, there would be corporate-level resources and capabilities which would benefit various businesses but won't reside in any particular business. Given these, the best approach is to assess resource similarity at a level higher than the specific market, use judgement to figure out which resources and linkages are relevant for the market, leave out the resources which would not come into play and be conscious of any biases in the estimates.

Having understood who our rivals are, what their game plan is, how they are performing, what type of rival they are and what ought to be their competitive behavioural traits, we next move to sizing up rivals and try our hand at predicting what they would do next.

« LONG STORY » « SHORT »

To know our rivals, we need to start with figuring out their competitive strategy and how they are performing. Spotting rivals and other players is not as straightforward as we think, especially when we view competition in the arena. Market commonality helps us understand the overlap in customer base with specific rivals. Resource similarity points to the overlap in resource configuration with specific rivals. Combining these two insights about where we stand vis-à-vis each rival gives us the competitor radar. That's where we spot, in addition to rivals we already know, players with different game plans, substitutors, small players who can grow big in future and potential entrants. Each of these player-types come with certain behavioural traits. Battle-ready players keep a keen eye on the competitor radar.

CHAPTER FIVE

What's Your Move?

Some 12 minutes into the wuxia movie *Hero* (2002),[1] the nameless protagonist meets the warrior Long Sky for a death match. The two face each other, their favourite weapon in hand—a sword for the nameless warrior and a spear for Long Sky. They don't jump into the fight yet but close their eyes and mind-spar. Each warrior plays out in his mind what would be his best move and how the opponent would respond and how he would respond to that and how the opponent would respond to that and so on. For the viewers' benefit, the movie's director Zhang Yimou visualizes the fight sequence. The mind-sparring ends when the two warriors realize that they have reached the last move in the fight. Only this one move is made for real, with the nameless warrior killing Long Sky.[2]

While many managers are likely to be unfamiliar with the ways of wuxia warriors, they would have been casual chess players who typically anticipate at least the next move of the opponent. Managers could figure out the next move by a competitor, such as 'The rival is most likely to launch new product variants for value customers' or 'If I slash price, the rival is most likely going for aggressive price

---

[1] https://en.wikipedia.org/wiki/Hero_(2002_film) (accessed 3 June 2021).
[2] https://www.youtube.com/watch?v=AeeoEpmyb2Y (accessed 3 June 2021).

cuts triggering a price war.' Battle-ready players would predict the rival's actions before the event. They would pre-empt the rival's actions—initiate an action that hits the market even before competitor's action hits the market. Pre-emptive moves would make it more difficult for the rival to go ahead with the planned competitive action. It will allow the battle-ready player to deny the rival substantial benefits from their action if it's executed, while minimizing negative impact on own performance.

McKinsey & Co. surveyed managers around the world as to when they came to know about a competitive move by a rival, for two types of competitive actions—a price change and a move triggered by innovation.[3] For price change, only 12 per cent respondents claimed that they knew of the impending move well in time to take a pre-emptive action. Eighty per cent of managers came to know of price change after it hit the market, while 8 per cent knew before the event but couldn't pre-empt. For moves triggered by innovation, only 23 per cent respondents claimed that they were able to pre-empt. Another 6 per cent came to know in time but couldn't do anything, while 71 per cent of managers found out too late. The obvious conclusion is that majority of players are not battle-ready.

When I ask managers why there isn't much focus on trying to predict rivals' next likely move, the responses range from 'It's not possible, with any degree of accuracy' to 'Knowing what rivals are going to do doesn't stop them from doing it'. Such views are based on beliefs that competitors are unpredictable; trying to predict consumes too much time and effort to be beneficial; or there is nothing to be gained by predicting competitors' next move.

We will challenge these beliefs. We look at why it's not difficult to predict the competitor's actions before the event and we will figure out how to do it. In the next chapter, we will explore how we can

---

[3] McKinsey & Company, 'How Companies Respond to Competitors: A McKinsey Global Survey' (McKinsey Quarterly Survey on Competitor Behavior, April 2008), 9.

use our prediction of rival's next move to gain an upper hand over them.

WHY ARE RIVALS PREDICTABLE?

Figuring out a rival's next move involves understanding 'what', 'how' and 'when'. We need to know what specific action the rival is likely to take and how, with as much details as possible. We also need to know when the intended action is likely to hit the market. The what and how of competitor's action are interlinked and are related to the rival's game plan. The when depends on the nature of action.

Rivals announce their intention to take specific actions. Listed companies are obligated to inform shareholders about their intended strategic initiatives, and this becomes available in public domain. Where intended action requires approvals from government, the information comes into public domain. Reliance Industries, the Indian conglomerate, acquired Infotel Broadband in June 2010. This revealed their intention to enter the mobile telecommunications market in India with 4G technology, as the only claim to fame of Infotel Broadband was that it had won nationwide spectrum licence for 4G data services in India.[4] Keeping an eye on patent applications by rivals as well as companies in adjacent industries and those dealing with jobs to be done related to their products will provide insights about innovation by rivals and other participants in the competitive arena.

Battle-ready businesses keep their eyes and ears open for relevant information from outside as part of 'environment scanning'. Many a time, competitors' intentions may not be directly visible but can be inferred from triggers for action. We need to sharpen our senses

---

[4] Manu Kaushik, 'Battle Ready: Telcos Ready to Battle It Out for India's 4G Data Market Share', *Business Today*, 20 December 2015. Available at: https://www.businesstoday.in/magazine/cover-story/airtel-reliance-jio-vodafone-idea-in-the-run-to-capture-indias-mobile-data-business/story/226494.html (accessed 3 June 2021).

to pick up without delay signals which are likely to trigger our competitors into action.

Triggers for Competitive Action

In a global survey of managers on understanding competitors' moves,[5] McKinsey & Co. found that two-thirds of businesses took a competitive action as response to an external opportunity or challenge. We are familiar with the wide range of external opportunities and challenges that a business can face, such as change in customer preferences, change in demand, changes in cost and quality of inputs, and availability of innovative technology for products or processes. Battle-ready rivals spot such external opportunities and challenges quickly and often act on it first. Information about these opportunities or challenges would be observable to all in the market. If we miss picking up these triggers, or if there is a significant delay in picking up these triggers, it's a weakness in our environment-scanning capabilities which needs immediate correction.

If rivals' actions are initiated based on external triggers, we can readily anticipate that the rivals will act, as we would also pick up the triggers. Since we would also be aware of the nature of external opportunity or challenge, we can make reasonable conjectures about what the rivals are likely to do. To validate these conjectures, we need additional information about what the rivals are intending to do. We will discuss more on this soon.

In the McKinsey survey, 29 per cent businesses claimed to have acted based on internal triggers resulting from an active search for new strategic initiatives. As such, these triggers are difficult to sense by their rivals. Good news is that among these businesses, only 7 per cent undertook strategic initiatives on ad hoc basis, meaning that

---

[5] McKinsey & Company, 'How Companies Can Understand Competitors' Moves: A McKinsey Global Survey' (McKinsey Quarterly Survey on Strategic Initiatives, December 2008), 8.

the timing of action was random. About half of them decided to undertake internally triggered strategic initiatives as part of their annual planning process. The regularity with which businesses do their planning and the correlation of its timing with fiscal year make it easy to figure out when such internal triggers are likely. We need to sharpen our antennae to capture chatter about potential actions by rivals around the time of their annual planning.

Although we can anticipate the timing of intended actions driven by internal triggers, we would be blind to the nature of competitive action. For instance, the rival may have decided to increase the capacity which is not known outside the organization. We don't need to resort to getting insider information, as the decision to pursue a strategic initiative would lead to follow-on decisions such as purchase of plant equipment and other assets, hiring, and discussions with distribution and sales channels. Many of these would be observable to attentive outsiders. While our rival would like to do all these in absolute secrecy, that's not always possible.

It doesn't matter if the rivals' actions are triggered externally or internally. In both cases, our ability to predict what, how and when would require more information specific to the context of the trigger. This is where environmental scanning as a capability comes handy.

Gathering Information about Rivals

A rival that's planning to increase its sales capacity in a particular market would want to hire. They can't do this without taking some actions that can be observed by outsiders. After all, the best way for them to augment their team is to poach from rivals. I know a manager who encourages his team members to apply for job openings from rivals with the promise that he would match an offer from a rival to retain the team member. In exchange, the team members are to be transparent about job openings that come their way, including being headhunted. This turned out to be a terrific way for the manager to gather information about headhunting by rivals in the market. The cost was the occasional need to match pay for a team member about to be poached. The manager's rationale was that he would anyway have matched to retain. Now, he gets information about rival actions well ahead of time. Spotting equipment under production meant for a competitor in a supplier's manufacturing plant is another typical source of information about competitor adding capacity.

Gathering information about rivals does not have to and shouldn't involve subterfuge or morally ambiguous methods. We have to be consistently diligent about gathering and making sense of information about rivals. In gathering information, we need to go beyond the traditional sources such as news and competitor analysis reports. Most of what appears in news and analyst reports would have first popped up as chatter in the market. Reporters and analysts make it their job to pick up such chatter, follow up and dig out the stories.

In picking up chatter about rivals, timing is crucial. The whole organization should be engaged in this as part of their routine work. For instance, say a procurement executive comes by an interesting piece of information about a rival from a shared vendor, or a sales associate finds out useful information about a competitor from a retail outlet. This information is now available within the organization but sits at some corner. Often, the information meanders its way within the organization, if at all, and becomes useless over time. In a battle-ready organization, the importance of this information is appreciated by whoever picks it up from outside. They know or can find out who should get the information. They also know or can figure out how to pass on the information. The information quickly gets relayed to the team that can use it. The organization now has the ability to make sense of the information for its implications on impending action by the rival.

Making Sense of Information about Rivals

The seemingly random flow of information from outside is only part of the jigsaw puzzle of what the competitor is likely to do.

To make sense, we need to interpret this information in the context of rival's game plan. Pankaj Ghemawat observes that strategies tend to persist over time, which he calls 'commitment'.[6] He further points out that 'irreversibility ... is implicit in the concept of commitment' and 'commitment makes it costly to change one's mind'.[7] Changing the direction of strategic (commitment-intensive) choices and actions would be costly or difficult; they mostly stay the course. Henry Mintzberg defines a strategy as a *pattern in a stream of decisions*. Interestingly, he adds to this a footnote, 'Where a decision is defined as a *commitment* to action, usually a commitment of resource'.[8] A strategy manifests as a pattern of decisions and actions aligned in a certain direction, and each action reinforces past commitments in that path. Simply put, strategic decisions and actions are highly constrained to stay within the course of strategic direction.

In McKinsey's global survey on how companies understand competitors' moves,[9] 82 per cent of managers confirmed that their recent and largest strategic initiative 'was a logical extension of their existing strategy'. Only 15 per cent businesses went for a 'completely new strategy'.[10] Danny Miller and Peter Friesen found that organizations changed strategy, on average, every six years.[11] The five-year strategy cycle continues to be the de facto rhythm for businesses to carry out major reviews and updates of the competitive strategy.[12] If we

---

[6] Pankaj Ghemawat, '*Commitment: The Dynamic of Strategy* (New York, NY: The Free Press, 1991), 14.

[7] Ibid., 31.

[8] Henry Mintzberg, 'Patterns in Strategy Formation', *Management Science* 24, no. 9 (1978): 935.

[9] McKinsey & Company, 'How Companies Can Understand Competitors' Moves'.

[10] McKinsey & Company, 'How Companies Respond to Competitors'.

[11] Danny Miller and Peter Friesen, *Organizations: A Quantum View* (Englewood Cliffs, NJ: Prentice Hall, 1984), 131.

[12] The five-year strategy cycle is nowadays becoming passé, given the prominence of companies which are operating in markets and industries which see fast-paced changes. Yet the concept that a business will change the strategy on a given rhythm is not invalidated. Managers with experience in the industry will know what's relevant.

assume that the start year of a strategy cycle for any business is random, any given year will see about one-sixth (approximately 16%) of businesses going for strategy update. Remaining five-sixths of businesses are likely to be in the middle of their strategy cycle and would not be changing direction yet.[13]

It is possible for us to figure out when a competitor last went for a strategy update and what rhythm they are following for this. Listed companies would report this to their shareholders. For a privately held rival, past instances of strategy update would be discernible, as it would manifest in actions which show deviations from pattern. Data on past actions by rivals can be used to understand how often and at what rhythm they go for strategy update.

If our rival is not on a strategy update year, we can be quite sure that the range of actions they would consider would be restricted to fall along their strategic direction. If the rival is updating their strategy, we also need to figure out what likely changes they might bring to their strategic direction. Here, the tendency would be to make course corrections. Recall our discussion on game plans in Chapter 4. The successful differentiators and cost leaders would continue to reinforce their current game plans, while the stuck-in-the-middle players would try to correct past mistakes. Given enough information about a rival, it is possible to predict how their strategic direction is likely to be updated.

Actions which come from strategic decisions are commitment-intensive. They tend to persist over time and are difficult or costly to change the direction. Thus, a series of actions by any business—ours or our rivals'—cannot be a random walk but highly constrained to fall on a narrow path given by the strategic direction of the business. This is what helps us to predict what rivals are likely to do next. Once we bring together the information gleaned from

---

[13] In business landscapes which see faster pace of strategy updates, the percentage of rivals holding to their strategic direction might come down, but the shorter time span will hold for all players in that competitive arena.

environmental scanning and information about the rival including their game plan, we can identify potential competitive moves which are consistent with their strategic direction. We get a narrow set of conjectures on potential competitor moves.[14] We can predict the 'what' and 'how' of competitor actions. We now need to understand if it's possible for us to also predict when the action will hit the market.

On When the Action Hits the Market

Nobel laureate economist Jean Tirole characterizes the range of competitive actions based on the time needed to bring it to the market.[15] In the short run, a few days to a few weeks, the only competitive weapon available to managers is price. Advertising and sales effort can also be brought in, mostly to augment the primary weapon of price change by making the action visible to the target audience. During this time frame, cost structure and product attributes are difficult to adjust.

In the medium run, a few weeks to a few months, it is possible to achieve incremental improvements in cost or product attributes through changes in production process and tweaks in product design and engineering. Two new weapons can be deployed in this time frame—reduced cost supporting lower price and improved product features, albeit incremental. Advertising, sales push and pricing will augment these primary weapons.

In the long run, a few months to a few years, fundamental changes in cost and product attributes are possible through improvements in technology driven by R&D. Innovation in products and processes becomes the primary weapon in the long run, augmented by the weapons available in the short and medium runs. The range of

---

[14] The only situation when we can't predict competitor action is when their actions follow a random walk, but that's rare.

[15] Jean Tirole, 'Part II: Strategic Interaction', in *Theory of Industrial Organization*, ed. Jean Tirole (Boston, MA: MIT Press, 1988), 205–206.

weapons that a rival can bring to battle enlarges as the time frame for action lengthens.

The characterization is essentially based on the concept of 'time to build'. It takes a few months to a few years to carry out research, develop innovative ideas and deploy them through viable products or processes. If we surmise that a rival is planning to launch new products, the relevant follow-on information is what stage of new product development they are at right now. With that, we can make a reasonably sound estimate of when their new product will hit the market. Time to build for making incremental improvements in product features would be a few weeks to a few months. If the competitor is looking at adjusting prices, the time to build is only the time needed to adjust the prices in their systems and sales channels and the lead time to publicize the price change. This would be a few days to a few weeks.

Time to build acts as the constraint on the lead time needed for a player to bring an action to the market. It will be driven by the nature of competitive action. Of course, a rival might delay the action beyond the time to build, in which case the real motive may not be to execute any action, at least not immediately, but to signal to other stakeholders.[16]

It is possible to identify both external and internal triggers for competitive action. Given the game plan of a rival, it's possible to make a reasonably robust conjecture on the rival's intended actions. Once we have an idea of what and how of a competitor's action, we can estimate when that action is likely to hit the market. It's possible to predict our rivals' next move.

SIZING UP RIVALS

Profiles of our key rivals are the foundation on which we build and validate conjectures about their intended competitive moves. Doing

---

[16] Vapourware, product announcements which are meant to stall product launches by a rival are a typical example.

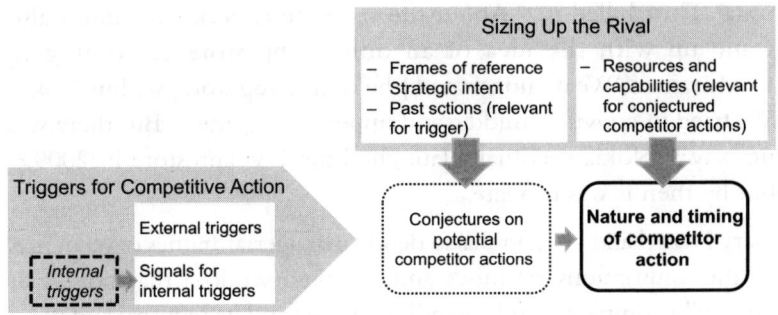

Source: The author.

Figure 5.1. Sizing Up the Rival

this is what I call 'sizing up' rivals (Figure 5.1). The profile of a competitor, or for that matter any participant in the arena, is a composite picture derived from their frames of reference, strategic intent (intent, in short), their past actions and capabilities.[17]

Frames of Reference

Three years prior to the launch of iPhone by Apple, Nokia designers came up with a prototype phone with internet connectivity and large touchscreen, somewhat like the iPhone. The company even demoed the prototype to its business customers. Ari Hakkarainen, a manager in Nokia's smartphone development team, explained, 'It was very early days, and no one really knew anything about the touchscreen's potential. And it was an expensive device to produce, so there was more risk involved for Nokia. So, management did the

---

[17] Curtis M. Grimm, Hun Lee and Ken G. Smith, *Strategy as Action: Competitive Dynamics and Competitive Advantage* (New York, NY: Oxford University Press, 2006), 208–212 discuss beliefs, intentions and past actions as determinants of future competitive behaviour. Porter, *Competitive Strategy*, 47–74 presents rival's future goals, assumptions, current strategy and capabilities as drivers of competitor's response profile.

usual. They killed it.'[18] About the same time, Nokia designers also came up with the idea of an online app store. According to Hakkarainen, 'We demonstrated [the online app store] within Nokia. We tried to convince middle and upper management. But there was no way.'[19] Nokia eventually launched the Ovi app store in 2009,[20] but by then it was too late.

Gary Hamel and C. K. Prahalad define managerial 'frames of reference' as 'the assumptions, premises and accepted wisdom that bound or "frame" a company's understanding of itself and its industry and drive its competitive strategy', analogous to the 'genetic heritage' of an individual. They identify a multitude of sources for managers' frames of reference, spanning educational and training inputs, peers, business press and, most importantly, their own experience. Frames of reference are unique to every business and reflect its evolution. They define '[the] choice of competitive stratagems … and bound a [business's] approach to competitive warfare and thus determine competitive outcomes'.[21] Frames of reference guide strategic decisions.

As early as 2004, Nokia had the prototypes for an iPhone-like product and an online app store. With hindsight, one can appreciate the importance of launching these without delay. For Nokia's managers in 2004, the primary job to be done for mobile phone would have been voice and text communication. For that, you don't need a large touchscreen or an app store. You don't even need an internet connection. Nokia managers believed that there wouldn't be many takers for a mobile phone that one can operate with fingers on

---

[18] Kevin O'Brien, 'Nokia's New Chief Faces Culture of Complacency', *The New York Times*, 26 September 2010. Available at: https://www.nytimes.com/2010/09/27/technology/27nokia.html?_r=2&partner=rss&emc=rss&pagewanted=all (accessed 3 June 2021).

[19] Ibid.

[20] Elizabeth Woyke, 'Nokia's Gigantic App Store', *Forbes*, 7 May 2009. Available at: https://www.forbes.com/2009/05/07/nokia-ovi-store-technology-wireless-nokia.html#7108c0c4513a (accessed 3 June 2021).

[21] Gary Hamel and C. K. Prahalad, 'Strategy as Stretch and Leverage', *Harvard Business Review*, May–June 1993, 63–76.

screen and that supports internet connectivity and apps. They didn't realize that an ecosystem would develop around such smartphones, driven by mobile-operating system providers, handset makers, app developers and telecom players coming together to deliver novel use cases and user experiences.[22] They also did not believe that Apple, a computer maker which was a basket case not long ago, and which recently saw success in a music player (iPod), had it in them to dethrone the undisputed leader of mobile phones.

With their frames of reference—views about evolution of technology, industry, consumer preferences, partners, competitors and themselves—Nokia's managers seem to have passed up the opportunity which came their way. They also ended up underestimating the threat posed by Apple which launched the iPhone in 2007. They didn't believe that customers will abandon them in droves. Rest, as they say, is history.

Strategic Intent

When Lee Kun-hee (aka Lee II) inherited a part of the Samsung business empire in 1987, Samsung was a low-cost manufacturer of consumer electronics and electronic components. Although it had achieved some prominence as a component maker, it was nowhere close to global majors (mostly Japanese then) in consumer electronics. Six years on, Lee II assembled his senior executives at the Kempinski Hotel Frankfurt Gravenbruch. He articulated to his team the way forward for Samsung,

> The Cold War has ended, but a more intense economic war has begun ... at Samsung, we must adhere to three credos: faulty products are our enemy, faulty products are the root of

---

[22] Nokia did launch the 7710 in 2004 which was a multimedia-capable mobile phone which featured a touchscreen and stylus with no physical keys for input. It was more a PDA (personal digital assistant, such as Palm OS or Pocket PC) and not directly comparable with the iPhone. See GSMArena specs and review of 7710 at https://www.gsmarena.com/nokia_7710-review-31.php (accessed 3 June 2021).

all evil, and if we produce a faulty product three times, we must take it upon ourselves to resign.[23]

He made achieving world-class quality—something which Sony and other Japanese players did exceedingly well—the overarching theme for Samsung. In what came to be known within Samsung as the Frankfurt Declaration, their chairman told Samsung executives to 'change everything except your wife and children'.[24]

Gary Hamel and C. K. Prahalad call this 'strategic intent'. They warn, however, that 'strategic intent is more than simply unfettered ambition'. They explain that strategic intent (intent, in short) is

> an active management process that includes: focusing the orga-
> nization's attention on the essence of winning, motivating people
> by communicating the value of the target; leaving room for
> individual and team contributions; sustaining enthusiasm by
> providing new operational definitions as circumstances changes;
> and using intent consistently to guide resource allocations.[25]

Intent, by capturing and prioritizing the 'essence of winning', becomes the touchstone for everything a business would do, including deciding on which competitive actions to take and how. Intent clarifies to decision-makers what sort of a game they would play—what would be their default mode of aggression, what they would and would not tolerate from rivals and whether they would follow rules of the game or seek to discard the current rules and define new ones. Along with frames of reference, strategic intent guides your competitive strategy. By putting quality at the top of the agenda and saying that everything about Samsung can change, Lee II provided a clear strategic intent for his team. Twelve years on, Samsung overtook Sony in brand value.[26]

---

[23] Geoffrey Cain, *Samsung Rising* (New York, NY: Currency, 2020), 90.

[24] Ibid., 91.

[25] Hamel and Prahalad, 'Strategy as Stretch and Leverage'.

[26] Interbrand estimates of brand value for Sony and Samsung in 2004: US$12.8 and US$12.6 billion; in 2005: US$14.9 and US$10.8 billion. See https://www. interbrand.com/best-brands/ (accessed 3 June 2021).

Past Actions

Earlier, we saw how the acquisition of Infotel Broadband by Reliance Industries signalled their intended entry into mobile telecom. This was the second innings for Reliance Industries and Mukesh Ambani in the Indian telecom arena. Earlier in 2002, Mukesh Ambani had entered the Indian mobile telecom market through Reliance Infocomm. The earlier entry was noteworthy for the structural shift it brought to mobile telecommunication services in India. Back in 2002, mobile telecom was an oligopoly of three players—two from the private sector and one government-owned. Mobile calls from any of them cost about ₹36 per minute (about 75 cents[27]) back then. Reliance Infocomm launched their service in December 2002 with a tariff of ₹1 per minute (about 2 cents) and later dropped this to ₹0.20 (less than half cent) per minute.[28]

Incumbent players at that time had priced mobile telecom services high, making it a luxury service which signalled affluence, and their game plan aimed for high margins. Mukesh Ambani entered the market with a different game plan, which changed the rules of the game. First, he triggered a price war which forced incumbents to drop the prices equivalent to a 97 per cent discount. Second, mobile telecom usage shot through the roof and subscriber base expanded significantly. Third, the way to profits moved from high margins to high volume.[29]

---

[27] One US dollar was about ₹48 (Indian rupee) in 2002, as per Reserve Bank of India Reference Rate Archive. See https://www.rbi.org.in/scripts/Reference RateArchive.aspx (accessed 3 June 2021).

[28] Vivek Law, 'Reliance India Mobile Service Promises to Shake Telecom Industry, Test Ambani's Ability', *India Today*, 30 December 2002. Available at: https://www.indiatoday.in/magazine/economy/story/20021230-reliance-india-mobile-service-promises-to-shake-telecom-industry-test-ambanis-ability-793863-2002-12-30 (accessed 3 June 2021).

[29] Reliance Infocomm did not perform well over time for several reasons unrelated to this, including change of hands as the venture moved to younger brother Anil Ambani as part of settlement of inheritance.

The game plan of Mukesh Ambani for Reliance Infocomm was to use a cost-efficient technology (CDMA vs GSM-2G) to offer services at a very low price which would significantly enlarge the user base. The high volumes with thin margin would help recoup investments and make profits while also scale up the business. In his second innings—Reliance Jio—what would you expect Mukesh Ambani to do? Given what Reliance did for mobile voice service back in 2002, would Jio repeat the same for mobile data a decade later?

Not surprisingly, Mukesh Ambani, in a talk addressing industry leaders in March 2016, pointed out that mobile data consumption in India was highly skewed towards affluent customers, and average data consumption per user was a measly 0.15 gigabytes (GB) per year.[30] In September 2016, Mukesh Ambani announced the launch of Jio's 4G services, which would be free for first 90 days, after which customers would be charged ₹50 (0.75 cent[31]) for 1 GB of data with unlimited free voice calls.[32] Incumbent operators were offering similar data volume for a month at about ₹250 (US$3.75) and were charging for voice calls by the minute. Within days of Jio's launch, major incumbents Airtel, Vodafone and Idea slashed data prices by 70 per cent for selected tariff plans and offered unlimited free voice calls to high-value post-paid subscribers.[33]

Past actions, in a similar context or against a similar trigger, are a window to the mind of the strategist. A dominant rival who quickly and aggressively retaliates to an incursion by a smaller player can be expected to do the same in similar situations. The value-driven player who has never worked around rules of the game can be expected

---

[30] V. Sridhar, 'Voice of Reliance', *Frontline*, 30 September 2016, 4–8.

[31] One US dollar was about ₹67 in 2016.

[32] Tech Desk, 'Reliance Jio 4G Launch: Mukesh Ambani Says All Voice Calls Will Be Free on Jio, Data at Rs 50 per GB', *The Indian Express*, 1 September 2016. Available at: https://indianexpress.com/article/technology/mobile-tabs/reliance-jio-4g-launch-ril-agm-live-3007424/ (accessed 3 June 2021).

[33] Kalyan Parbat, 'Reliance Jio's Aggressive Rates to Shake Up Industry: Experts', *The Economic Times*, 5 September 2016. Available at: https://economictimes.indiatimes.com/news/company/corporate-trends/reliance-jios-aggressive-rates-to-shake-up-industryexperts/articleshow/54009228.cms (accessed 3 June 2021).

not to bend rules. That's how reputations get built. That's how we get a better handle on what a rival is likely to do.

Capabilities

Reliance Industries invested close to US$27 billion in the Jio venture during 2010–2016. About 110 million subscribers signed up during the first seven months after Jio's launch.[34] Jio gave away SIM cards free. For much of this period, Jio provided its services free—it was ostensibly testing its network. By the time Jio started charging its customers, it had grabbed a sizeable share of smartphone users in India. It takes deep pockets to do all this.

Jio had to complete the know your customer (KYC) process and handover a SIM to each of its new customers. It facilitated the KYC process and SIM handover for 110 million customers through the nationwide network of Reliance Digital outlets, the Reliance-owned retail chain for consumer electronics products. These outlets have been selling their in-house brand of 4G-capable smartphones along with popular brands well before the launch of Jio.

Rolling out the nationwide 4G network for Jio involved a project of massive scale and complexity, involving design of the entire system, procurement, installation, testing of new equipment and integration of interfaces with third-party assets while keeping an eye on cost and time. Reliance Industries has had a track record of executing large-scale and complex projects such as the largest petrochemical refinery in Asia. The first managing director of Jio was a Reliance Industries veteran with decades of experience in petrochemical business who had also managed the nationwide fibre network roll-out for Reliance's earlier telecom venture.[35]

---

[34] Promit Mukherjee, 'Reliance Lifts Jio Investment above $30 Billion after Record Year', Reuters India, 25 April 2017. Available at: https://in.reuters.com/article/reliance-industries-results-copy/reliance-lifts-jio-investment-above-30-billion-after-record-year-idINKBN17R0J7 (accessed 3 June 2021).

[35] Joji Thomas Philip and Chaitali Chakravarty, '4G: RIL Appoints Sanjay Mashruwala as Managing Director of Reliance Jio', *The Economic Times*, 6 April

The balance sheet of Reliance Industries enabled it to fund the multi-billion-dollar investments for Jio. The nationwide retail presence through Reliance Digital allowed Jio to reach customers for KYC and distribute SIMs. The extensive project management capabilities already available within Reliance Industries made it possible for Jio to get its infrastructure up and running within time and budget. These are three instances of how Reliance Industries was able to leverage its current endowment of resources and capabilities to roll out Jio.

If critical capabilities essential for a potential competitive action are absent with a rival or difficult to acquire within a reasonable time frame, that potential action can be set aside as implausible. Frames of reference, strategic intent and past actions tell us what a rival is 'likely to do' in a given context. Capabilities tell us what the rival 'can do'.

Some conjectures of potential competitive action may not be plausible for a rival due to lack of required resources and capabilities. Rivals may engineer strategic alliances to augment their capabilities. We need to be mindful of such possibilities when sizing up rivals. Tesla, the electric car maker, acquired key resources and capabilities through alliances with the likes of Daimler, Toyota and Panasonic.[36]

By validating the range of possible competitive actions—conjectures really—against capabilities needed to viably execute the actions with a reasonable probability of success, we can eliminate several actions as implausible. We start with the competitive action which will provide the best results for the rival and ask, 'Do they have the resources and capabilities to pull it off?' If the answer is no, we set that aside as implausible and move on to the next best possible action,

2013. Available at: https://economictimes.indiatimes.com/industry/telecom/4g-ril-appoints-sanjay-mashruwala-as-managing-director-of-reliance-jio/articleshow/19408256.cms?from=mdr (accessed 3 June 2021).

[36] Paul Lienert, Norihiko Shirouzu, and Edward Taylor, 'The Musk Method: Learn from Partners Then Go It Alone', Reuters News, 17 September 2020. Available at: https://www.reuters.com/article/us-tesla-batteryday-technology-insight-idUSKBN2680K4 (accessed 3 June 2021).

repeat the question and work our way down the list. For each of the actions the answer becomes yes, we know that this is something our rival ought to do and can do, if they want to.

Table 5.1 gives the key dimensions of frames of reference, strategic intent, past actions and capabilities which we need to capture in the

Table 5.1. What We Need to Know about the Rival

Dimension	Description
Frames of Reference	
About industry and market	Player's views about the industry and market in terms of current state, outlook and future trends
About rivals	Player's beliefs about its rivals in terms of their key characteristics relevant for the market and industry
About self	Player's insights on own capabilities and weaknesses
About values	Player's beliefs about what's acceptable behaviour and what's not done in business
Intent	
About winning (and rivalry)	How the player seeks to win the competitive game
About market and self	Player's aspirations and plans for the market/industry and its presence in the market
Past Actions	
Past actions on similar trigger	How the player acted upon a similar trigger in the past
Past actions against specific rival	How the player acted on a past episode relating to a specific rival (who is part of the current trigger)
Capabilities	What resources and capabilities does the player possess, which it can bring to play to execute a conjectured competition action viably and with reasonable probability of success

Source: The author.

rival's profile. Frames of reference and intent relate to enduring characteristics of the player being sized up as well as how they play the competitive game. The frames of reference and intent relevant for a business derive from those of its promoters, key managers and decision-makers. If the business is part of a corporation, its frames of reference and intent are to a great extent shaped by those of the corporation. Often, the individual frames of reference and intent of leaders get reflected in their business. Past actions have to be filtered for relevance to a specific trigger for competitive action as well as the competitive arena. From these, we come up with conjectures on potential competitor actions.

From the endowment of resources and capabilities of a rival, we have to focus on those capabilities which are relevant to the set of conjectured competitive actions. With this, we can eliminate the implausible among conjectured actions. The result is a very small set of plausible competitive actions specific to the trigger. As the famous detective is supposed to have said, 'When you have eliminated the impossible, whatever remains, *however improbable*, must be the truth.'[37]

Nuances on Predicting Rivals' Actions

While the general arguments presented above are valid for most of the players we see in different arenas, there are nuances that influence predictability of rivals.[38] Rivals who are strategy-driven are easier to predict. Rivals who do not follow even an implicit strategy but take decisions and pursue actions on an ad hoc basis are difficult to predict, as the pattern of actions taken by them would wander off from the narrow path that a well-defined strategic direction would impose.

---

[37] Arthur Conan Doyle, 'Sherlock Holmes Gives a Demonstration', in *The Sign of the Four*, ed. Arthur Conan Doyle (Project Gutenberg ebook # 2097).

[38] These are based on findings from McKinsey & Company, 'How Companies Can Understand Competitors' Moves' and author's insights.

Larger, bureaucratic or process-driven rivals are easier to predict. Players who are less process-driven or less bureaucratic tend to be more fleet-footed and entrepreneurial and can get unpredictable. For rivals like this, your predictions are likely to be off the mark more often, and your pre-emptive actions must have built-in flexibility for you to adapt to emerging understanding of rival's intentions and actions.

Underperforming rivals are easier to predict than rivals who outperform peers. Underperformers are mostly reactive, and reactive moves are easily predicted. Persistently underperforming rivals will be subject to performance pressure, and the worst performers are practically pushed against the wall. Such players can go berserk. They cannot be trusted to act even in their long-run interest. So while underperformers can be predicted most often, there will be the once-in-a-while discontinuity when they do something that's damaging for all players in the arena. These acts would be difficult to predict.

Rivals who consistently outperform peers would do so by pre-empting competitors as well as taking proactive strategic initiatives based on internally identified opportunities and challenges. They are also typically first off the block in sensing and acting on external opportunities and challenges. To predict what they are likely to do and also pre-empt them requires that you too be as battle-ready as they are, if not better. That's to say that only battle-ready players can hope to outgun other battle-ready players, and it won't be an easy game.

The most important marker for predictability of a rival is how predictable they have been in the past, compared to predictability of other rivals. Paying attention to this dynamic is an essential feedback for the process of predicting rivals. With this feedback, you are able to calibrate the effort and approach to make sense of information about a rival in predicting their intended actions.

On When to Size Up Rivals

Any external trigger—an opportunity or a challenge which will compel a rival to act—would warrant a fresh sizing up of the rival.

Any structural change in the competitive arena, or changes in macro context that impacts the arena would require a review of rivals' profiles. Such triggers often elicit action from all who are attentive, and there would even be a race to act.

Any proactive competitive action by us should include sizing up of rivals to understand their likely response. Say, we want to launch a new product variant, or we are planning a price cut. Often, when managers assess the business case for such competitive moves, they leave out potential response from rivals. It is only when the rival reacts to our competitive action that we sit up and start thinking. We tend to ignore that a competitive action taken (or intended) by us becomes an external trigger for our rivals. Direct rivals would be compelled to act upon that trigger. Battle-ready players at least anticipate the first response of rivals to their competitive action before embarking on it. Most often they also pre-empt the best response from rivals, in their first salvo itself. We will discuss more on this in the next chapter.

There are several internal triggers which would lead to search for new initiatives by rivals. These events can be picked up through signals such as timing of annual planning and strategy update, changes in senior executive team such as appointment of CEO or top management executives, change in board composition, patent applications or announcements by the top management. These events relating to key rivals warrant an updated sizing up of the rival. This ensures that we are able to expect potential competitive moves by rivals without delay. Forewarned, we will be better placed to plan and execute our pre-emptive action, if need be.

Like the story about wuxia warriors at the beginning of this chapter, if our rivals were also battle-ready, they would have anticipated that we would pre-empt their best action or response in our first salvo itself. Which means that they would already be planning to undermine our competitive move through their pre-emptive action. Working backwards like this is useful to the extent that it helps us understand pieces of information gathered from the market that won't neatly add up otherwise, beyond which the exercise becomes a distraction.

Rivals are predictable; we too are predictable to our rivals. We can predict, with reasonable degree of accuracy, the nature and timing of competitor action. Rich and deep profiles built from sizing up of rivals are essential to predict their next move. Sizing up helps develop conjectures about a potential competitive action and check for plausibility of conjectured actions. Frames of reference, strategic intent and past actions of a player drive the conjectures about potential competitive actions the rival can take upon a trigger to act or react. Capabilities of the rival help narrow down plausible actions from the conjectured competitive actions. With these, we can predict, with reasonable accuracy, the nature and timing of intended competitive action by rivals.

CHAPTER SIX

What's Our Next Move?

In December 2015, Bharti Airtel, the then leader in the Indian mobile telecom arena, announced a buyback and upgrade offer for customers who used Wi-Fi dongles[1] of its rivals. This was before the entry of Jio. The other major incumbents were Vodafone, Idea and BSNL. For a net cost to customer of ₹300 (US$5[2]), Airtel offered to upgrade the customer's 3G dongle from one of its rivals to an Airtel 4G dongle. Airtel would destroy the rivals' dongle. A *Business Today* cover story called this the 'first salvo in the great 4G war that is in the offing'.[3]

Although Jio's 4G licence (through Infotel Broadband acquisition) allowed it to offer only data services, it went on to obtain a unified licence including for voice services three years later. Thus, by October 2013, it was clear that Jio would enter mobile voice and data services with 4G technology. Airtel had already launched its

---

[1] Wi-Fi dongles are pocket-sized devices which take a SIM (3G or 4G) and act as a Wi-Fi hotspot with which users can connect multiple devices such as smart-phones, tablets and laptops to the internet with mobile data service available through the SIM. Mobile telecom players were offering data SIMs and dongles which provided data access with 3G technology.

[2] One US$ was about ₹63 in 2015.

[3] Kaushik, 'Battle Ready'.

4G data services in Kolkata in 2012 and 4G mobile services in Bengaluru in 2014.[4] During these years, 4G-capable handsets were not widely available, and most of the customers could use 4G mobile services only through Wi-Fi dongles. Reliance Jio would eventually launch their dongles, some eight months after Airtel's offer.[5] So what was Airtel up to, with the buyback and upgrade offer? Who was it targeting through this competitive move, and what was the purpose of the competitive action?

TO ACT OR NOT TO ACT

Ming-Jer Chen identifies three drivers for rivalry among players—awareness, motivation and capabilities. According to Chen, there are 'three essential factors that underlie organizational action: the *awareness* of interfirm relationships and action implications, the *motivation* to act, and the *capability* of taking action'.[6] Awareness operates at two levels. First is the awareness about strategic interdependence with a certain player, whether they are a direct rival or a player with a different game plan, a smaller player or someone in an adjacent market and so on. The competitor radar (Chapter 4, Figure 4.4) helps us gain this awareness. Second is the awareness about specific competitive actions which rivals are intending to execute or have already executed. In some cases, rivals execute competitive actions in stealth mode, and we become aware after the event. Then there are intended actions which rivals are likely to take based on triggers. We have discussed this in Chapter 5. Having covered how to become aware, let's look at motivation to act.

Between 2010 and 2013, Jio acquired the licences needed to offer 4G mobile telecom services, positioning itself as a potential direct

---

[4] Ibid.

[5] ET Telecom, 'Reliance Jio Launches JioFi Mi-Fi Device with 90-day Preview Offer at Rs 2899', 16 August, 2016. Available at: https://telecom.economictimes.indiatimes.com/news/reliance-jio-launches-jiofi-mi-fi-device-with-90-day-preview-offer-at-rs-2899/53717635 (accessed 3 June 2021).

[6] Chen, 'Competitor Analysis and Interfirm Rivalry', 105.

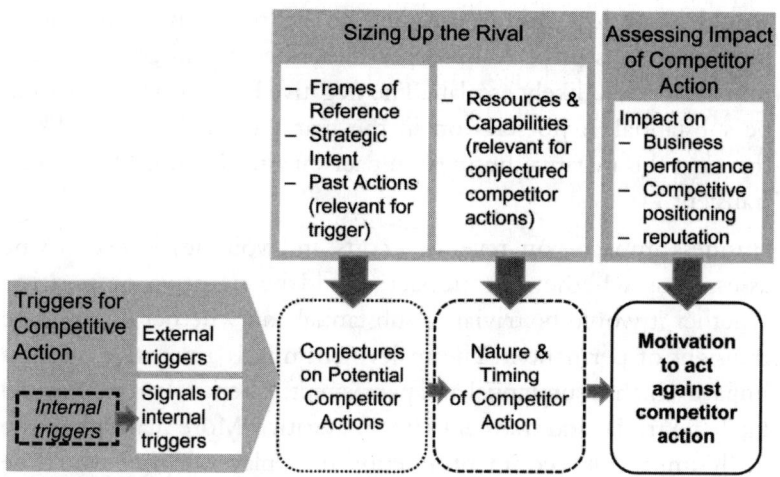

Source: The author.

Figure 6.1. Impact of Competitor Action

rival to Airtel. However, Jio would not be the only rival for Airtel. Incumbent players such as Vodafone and Idea who were active in mobile telecom services using 3G technology were preparing to adopt 4G. For instance, in 2015, Idea acquired 4G spectrum from Videocon.[7] As the market leader, should Airtel have the motivation to act? Should it pre-empt? If so, who are the players that Airtel should be motivated to pre-empt?

To understand the motivation of a player to act against a rival, we need to understand the impact that the competitive action— intended or already executed—would have on business performance, competitive positioning and reputation of the player (see Figure 6.1).

Impact on Business Performance

Jio's subscriber grab will result in loss of customers for all incumbent players. Being the market leader at the time of Jio's entry, Airtel

---

[7] Kaushik, 'Battle Ready'.

would likely lose more customers to Jio than any of the other incumbents. Its price realized per subscriber would go down and unit cost would likely escalate. The negative business impact would be substantial. If Jio stays on in the market, which is most likely the case, the negative business impact on Airtel is not likely to be transient.

Business impact—on revenues, costs and volumes—needs to be assessed as whether the impact would be negative or positive, whether it would be trivial or substantial and whether it would be transient or permanent. The malevolent mix is a negative business impact which is substantial and permanent. A benevolent mix would likely be trivial and transient even if negative. More malevolent the likely impact of a competitor action on a player, higher would be the motivation for the player to respond. For Airtel, the impending entry of Jio and others into 4G would clearly turn out to be malevolent on business impact, motivating them to act.[8] What's interesting is that Airtel's motivation to act is not just directed at Jio who is yet to enter but also at other incumbents such as Vodafone and Idea, due to their impending adoption of 4G technology.

Impact on Competitive Positioning

Recall the discussion in Chapter 4 on competitive strategy analysis (decomposing RoA into return on sales and asset turnover), the assessment of market commonality and relative resource position. Entry of Jio and adoption of 4G by other incumbents would bring changes to all these analyses for Airtel. How would the entry of Jio affect Airtel's position in the RoA scatter plot? Would Airtel continue to remain one of the best performing players? What about the market

---

[8] It is possible to arrive at quantitative estimates of size of impact in terms of loss of subscribers, impact on price/average revenue per user and cost for Airtel upon entry of Jio as well as adoption of 4G by other incumbents. Managers finding themselves in a similar situation should work out such quantitative estimates so that they can compare potential actions and the resulting change in business impact compared to the status quo.

commonality of Airtel with various rivals? Would it face more direct rivalry? How would it fare against rivals—incumbents and new entrant—in terms of relative resource position?

Again, to answer these questions, we need to look at the three dimensions of impact used earlier—negative or positive, trivial or substantial, and transient or permanent. More malevolent the impact is on Airtel's current competitive position, more motivated it would be to act. Here too, the assessment of motivation is not restricted to Jio alone but other incumbents as well.

Impact on Reputation

When a player expects or sees a competitor action, especially triggered by an external threat or opportunity which is highly visible, stakeholders are going to keenly watch the player's response. The player's chosen course of action provides important signals to stakeholders about the player. This is especially so if the player is the market leader. Reputation gets reinforced or diminished as the current action (or inaction) becomes the newest addition to the series of past actions by the player.

Jio's ambitions for aggressive growth would not have been difficult to surmise for anyone who had sized up Reliance Industries in the context of entry into telecom market. Various stakeholder groups would have been eagerly watching Airtel to see how it responded. Let's say that Airtel chose not to do anything against the impending entry of Jio and adoption of 4G by incumbent players. Both Jio and other incumbents are likely to interpret this as a weakness in the market leader—inability to respond aggressively. Afterall, Airtel has the most to lose. This will embolden some of Airtel's smaller rivals to get more aggressive in the market. Airtel employees would interpret this negatively, leading to decline in morale. Its vendors and business partners would also see this as its inability to respond. The stock market, analysts and investors would all speculate on some hidden malice within the company which is holding it back. On the whole, doing nothing would damage Airtel's reputation.

In assessing the impact on reputation, the default option is to check how stakeholders will interpret inaction. How will 'maintaining status quo' impact the player's reputation with various stakeholders—negative or positive, trivial or substantial, and transient or permanent? More malevolent the impact on reputation, more motivated the player should be to act. If the status quo is not an option, the next step is to check the impact on reputation for various potential competitive actions by the player. Thus, assessing the impact on reputation helps further narrow down potential actions. There would also be a trade-off between the impact on reputation and viability of action for the range of potential actions. This trade-off needs to be solved in choosing the appropriate action.

In the case of Airtel facing the impending entry by Jio and adoption of 4G by other incumbents, the impact on business performance, competitive position and reputation turn out to be negative, substantial and permanent. Airtel definitely needs to act, and its actions have to meet multiple objectives. It should signal to Jio that it will guard its turf aggressively. It should position itself to minimize the competitive threat from incumbents even before Jio enters, so that it stands as a more formidable rival when Jio enters. For that, it has to start clobbering incumbents right away. It should convey to its employees as well as external stakeholders such as vendors, business partners, investors and analysts that it is coming from a position of strength and it has a clear game plan to face off the external threat of a new entry coupled with technology change. The 'first salvo' of Airtel—buying off current rivals' dongles and then bulldozing them—is not aimed directly at Jio, but at current incumbents such as Vodafone and Idea. It is a clear message to all including Jio that Airtel will fight the ensuing battle head on.

Not all intended or executed competitor actions deserve a response though. If the impact on business performance, competitive position and reputation are benevolent for a trigger, it would be better for the player to wait and watch. Some effort needs to go into tracking the evolution of that trigger as well as actions and responses of other players, so as to be alerted if the motivation to act becomes more compelling over time.

WHAT'S OUR MOVE?

In the previous chapter, we focused on predicting what our rivals are likely do, either against an external trigger or on an internal trigger. We started this chapter by looking at how to figure out whether we should respond or not. Say we figure out that we need to respond. We then need to figure out what our move should be. We may be making our move before the rival's intended action hits the market—that would be pre-emption. We may be making the move after the rival acts—that would be a reactive response. Either way, we need to figure out what our next move is going to be.

Pre-empting Rivals

Robert Taylor of Minnetonka Corporation introduced a new product called Softsoap in 1978. It was born out of Taylor's idea that liquid hand soap in a bottle with a pump would be far more convenient to use than a soap bar. The launch was supported by a modest advertising outlay of US$7 million. Taylor realized that consumer products giants such as P&G, Unilever and C-P would flood the market with their own liquid soap products if the idea of liquid hand soap in a bottle finds customer acceptance.[9] This would have resulted in severe erosion of the presence of Softsoap in retail shelves and consumers' minds. Anticipating this, Taylor made a bet-the-farm move to place an order for 100 million pumps with the only two American suppliers of plastic pumps. That order tied up a year's production capacity available in the USA then. Creating new capacity to produce plastic pumps would require time to build of

---

[9] Although putting liquid soap in a bottle with a pump was Taylor's idea, he couldn't try for a patent as the liquid soap had been around for more than a century and the pump had been in use for more than two millennia.

several months. Rivals had to wait while Softsoap became a hit.[10] Softsoap successfully pre-empted consumer products majors, denying its rivals the use of their best weapons—access to shelf space and large advertising outlays—with which they could have killed Softsoap in its early days itself. But with the pre-emptive action, Softsoap revenues reached US$25 million in first six months. Seven years later, Taylor sold Softsoap to C-P.[11]

Varieties of Pre-emption

The case of Softsoap is a situation where you are planning a competitive move which has high potential to create value. However, you are apprehensive that rivals, especially those with superior relative resource position, will steal your thunder once your idea becomes apparent. Your pre-emptive action should focus on protecting your value appropriation and at the same time restrict your rival's ability to take away value or impose additional costs on you. Remember that your pre-emptive action has to prevent precisely what you would do to your rival if the tables were turned (Table 6.1).

Some external opportunities emerge, which have characteristics of high potential for durable first-mover advantage. Patent races, as witnessed in industries such as pharmaceuticals, are a classic example. You benefit from first-mover advantage when the source of advantage is a scarce resource which is controlled by you such as a patented technology or rare asset, or when the customer, once locked in with you, finds it extremely difficult to leave you—high switching costs. Such advantages, when durable, meaning that it will continue to provide an advantage over years, are extremely valuable. You should

---

[10] John Schwartz, 'Robert Taylor, Who Put Hand Soap in a Bottle, Dies at 77', *The New York Times*, 11 September 2013. Available at: https://www.nytimes.com/2013/09/12/business/robert-taylor-who-put-hand-soap-in-a-bottle-dies-at-77.html (accessed 8 June 2021).

[11] https://en.wikipedia.org/wiki/Softsoap (accessed 8 June 2021).

Table 6.1. Varieties of Pre-emption

Context for Pre-emption	Focus of Pre-emption
Action initiated by you based on internal search	• Protect your action's value • Restrict rivals' ability to impose additional costs on you
Action initiated by one of your rivals based on internal search	• Make rival's action costly • Undermine rival's value • Steal the thunder
External opportunity with potential for durable first mover advantage	• Race to be the first among incumbents to corner the opportunity, viably
Potential entry into the market where you are the leader or a close challenger	• Make entry difficult by undermining the entrant's business case • Delay entry
Potential entry into the market where you are a distant challenger	• Wait and watch

Source: The author.

race to corner the opportunity as you would be able to benefit from it and deny your rivals the benefit of it.

Awareness of a potential entry, most likely by a strong player from an adjacent arena, is serious business. If the entry succeeds, it will permanently have a substantial negative impact on our business. The best outcome of pre-emption of entry would be to get the potential entrant to abandon the plan by making their business case for entry unviable. This can be achieved by locking out the rival from accessing key inputs, denying the entrant access to these inputs or locking in customers, effectively shrinking the accessible market for the entrant. If entry can't be thwarted, locking out inputs and locking in customers would at least help delay the entry. However, it falls on the leader or close challenger to thwart entry. A distant challenger in a market is better off waiting and watching how the entry plays out.

As Jerry Wind observes, pre-emption 'is a very powerful attack that can slow or stop competitors or pin them down before they have had a chance to act'.[12] 'Locking out' rivals from access to resources and assets is one of the commonly used and powerful modes of pre-emption. Softsoap locked out incumbent consumer products majors from the supply of plastic pumps. A pharmaceutical company racing to secure a patent is seeking to lock out rivals from control of this valuable and durable asset. Once the company secures the patent, rivals are locked out of the market for that drug.[13]

Maruti Suzuki, the Indian automaker, is frequently lampooned for poor build quality of its cars visible in cheap looks and lower safety. Yet its dominance of the market for passenger cars in India has continued over years. Auto majors from Japan and America have been trying hard to get a toehold in the market but haven't been successful yet. Why would Indian car buyers stick with Maruti Suzuki? In January 2018, Team-BHP, an Indian automotive portal, ran an impromptu survey by asking its community members: Why do they 'choose Maruti Suzuki cars over others?' Within 2 days, 47 community members replied. Most of them mentioned one or more of the following reasons: excellent after-sale service available across the country, easy escalation matrix to handle issues, lower maintenance cost, and customer-centric approach. Many of the respondents claimed to own cars from other automakers as well, and their responses were based on comparing customer experience.[14] Maruti Suzuki, through its customer-centric approach to ensuring high standards of after-sale service, easy escalation, country-wide

---

[12] Jerry Wind, 'Preemptive Strategies', in *Wharton on Dynamic Competitive Strategy*, eds George S. Day and David J. Reibstein (New York, NY: John Wiley & Sons, 1997).

[13] Even if the patent holder licenses the drug to rivals, a good proportion of value appropriation would go to the patent holder. Being able to profit from patents and other IP is not that easy though, as we discuss in Chapter 10.

[14] Team-BHP, 'Why I Chose a Maruti', 14 January 2018. Available at: https://www.team-bhp.com/forum/indian-car-scene/194351-why-i-chose-maruti.html (accessed 8 June 2021).

presence of service network and lower cost of service, has created a 'lock-in' for its customers. The lock-in has effectively shrunk the market which is really accessible for automakers who have entered the market subsequently. The lock-in of customers with Maruti Suzuki, however, will only last so long as the differential customer experience persists, so Maruti Suzuki needs to be on its toes to ensure its superior customer benefits if it were to retain the customer lock-in.

Recall Airtel's Wi-Fi dongle buyback offer, primarily targeted at customers of current rivals Vodafone, Idea and BSNL? These rivals of Airtel had an existing subscriber base who used their 3G data services via dongles. Upon launching 4G, the rivals would incur much lower customer acquisition cost for upgrading their existing 3G data service customers to 4G. The 4G adoption business case for the rivals would have factored in assumptions to reflect this as well. Through its pre-emptive buyback and upgrade offer, Airtel was seeking to 'impose a higher cost' on its rivals. More the number of rivals' customers switching to Airtel through the pre-emptive offer, lower will be the existing base of data services subscribers for rivals. This will jack up their customer acquisition cost or extend the time taken to reach levels of subscriber base at which their business plan will be viable. Through its pre-emptive action, Airtel was seeking to 'weaken rivals' business case' by imposing additional costs for their 4G adoption.

Up till the 1970s, insulin for therapeutic use was a purified form of insulin extracted from animal pancreas, with Eli Lilly and Novo dominating the global insulin industry. Novo was the technology leader, the first to bring to market higher purity of insulin. By 1980, Novo's animal pancreas-based insulin had impurity of one part per million (PPM), while Eli Lilly produced insulin with 10–20 PPM impurity. Then, Eli Lilly figured out how to grow insulin in a petri dish (biotech insulin) which had 0 PPM impurity—it was 100 per cent pure. While Eli Lilly applied to drug regulators for permission to sell its biotech insulin, Novo went ahead and launched a 'semi-synthetic insulin' which was 100 per cent pure. Since Novo's product was the result of incremental changes to an already approved product, it did not require fresh approvals from drug regulators. The downside for Novo was that semi-synthetic insulin cost 20 per cent more to produce, while biotech insulin would be 15 per cent cheaper, both compared to high purity insulin already in the market.[15] Why would Novo launch a product comparable to Eli Lilly's biotech insulin which would cost 30 per cent more? Won't it result in huge losses? How good a pre-emptive action was this?

Eli Lilly would have been the first to launch a 100 per cent pure insulin which it could claim to be 'human insulin', providing a significant advantage over Novo in terms of product quality. For the first time, Eli Lilly would be able to claim technology leadership in insulin. Novo, by launching semi-synthetic insulin, was able to 'steal the thunder' from Eli Lilly. With Novo's pre-emptive move, Eli Lilly could not claim to be the first to offer 100 per cent pure human insulin. Any associated premium or market share grab was also denied to Eli Lilly. Novo had started its research on biotech insulin concurrently, and it would soon withdraw semi-synthetic insulin from the market once its biotech insulin was available for sale.

In 2017, Samsung had announced an investment of more than US$20 billion to set up their fifth-generation organic light-emitting diode (OLED) display panel manufacturing facility called A5, with a capacity to produce about 3.2 million displays a year. It had an existing capacity of 2.8 million displays in their A1 and A2 plants and was in advanced stages of completing construction of A3 and A4 plants which would bring additional capacity of 2.2 million displays. The announcement of A5 even before A3 and A4 plants went full steam in production was a signal to Chinese display manufacturers that their investments into display production capacity might end up unviable.[16] A dominant player committing credibly to

---

[15] Michael J. Enright, 'Novo Industri' (Harvard Business School Case 9-389-148, 21 January 1994).

[16] Korea IT News, 'Samsung Display to Construct World's Biggest OLED Plant', 20 June 2017. Available at: http://english.etnews.com/20170630200003 (accessed 8 June 2021).

build capacity far in excess of current demand would signal to rivals that they might be stuck with low utilization, making their intended investment in capacity addition unviable. Samsung was seeking to 'pin down' its Chinese rivals from acting.

Chasing Windmills and Reacting to Actions by Rivals

As much as pre-emption is powerful, it is also difficult to execute. Remember that pre-emption is based on an expected move by a rival. The best outcome of pre-emption is to get the rival to abandon the intended action. However, a crafty rival can signal a certain impending action tempting us to pre-empt, but with no real intention of following through. If we pre-empt, the rival abandoning the intended action would seem like we have won the round. But in reality, the rival didn't have any plan to execute and signalled the intended action just to make us spend valuable resources and effort on a fool's errand. We cannot completely disregard the rival's signals, as there is a chance that rival may follow through, seeing that we are not doing anything to pre-empt. One way to guard against such mind games is to validate whether the rival is making credible commitments to back the signals about the impending action. As long as evidence of such commitments are not available, we may want to signal back our intentions to pre-empt but waiting to make any significant commitments on pre-empting.

It is not always that we are able to pre-empt rival actions. First, we might be totally unaware of rival's impending action. If this happens often, we are definitely not battle-ready. Second, we might not be sure of the nature or timing of the rival's actions. The uncertainty would significantly influence our decision to act pre-emptively. Taking pre-emptive actions would consume resources and managerial bandwidth, for which alternate uses would always exist within organizations. Higher the uncertainty about rival's impending action, lower will be the likelihood that a pre-emptive action will find support and approval among our organization's members.

In situations where the current level of information leads to ambiguity about the rival's impending action, it is essential to focus effort and resources to gather more information. The added information can help reduce uncertainty, leading to the possibility of less risk in deciding about what to do.

Impending or actual rival actions which evaluate to substantial and permanent negative impact on our business is symptomatic of erosion of our competitive advantage over time. If our product were far more superior for its price, and if our customer experience were much better, probably our motivation to pre-empt would have been lower. High motivation to pre-empt should definitely set us thinking about how to pre-empt. At the same time, we should also start thinking and talking about how we got there, and what we can do to strengthen our moats and forts.

In general, pre-emption allows us to act with more degrees of freedom. When we are on the pre-emptive mode, there are more action choices available to us. Once the rival acts, the range of actions we can take in response would get restricted. As the time-tested adage goes, prevention is better than cure. In any case, if we fail to pre-empt, for whatever reason, we have to operate within the limited degrees of freedom available to us as a reactive player. Hopefully, we learn from this, and we do have the opportunity to get battle-ready for the next round.

Can We Pull It Off?

Inspired by how battle-ready players have successfully pre-empted grand plans of mighty rivals, we could come up with our own pre-emptive action plans to thwart our rivals. That's good news in terms of improving our battle-readiness. Such potential pre-emptive actions would be just a plan on paper. For us to execute, we need the capabilities to pull it off.

In trying to predict what our rivals would do, we first come up with a set of conjectured potential competitive moves. These are the moves which would make sense given the context. We then evaluate each of the potential moves for plausibility by asking the question: 'Does the player have the capability to viably execute the move with a reasonable degree of success?' That's when we narrow down to predicting rival's next move. Same way, for the potential pre-emptive or reactive actions which we are considering, we need to ask: 'Can we pull it off?'

More importantly, each player would have a unique configuration of resources and capabilities which will dictate different costs on each of the players for doing the same thing. Thus, the capabilities question is really an assessment of viability. This is where the feedback loop closes. Our ability to act derives from our current configuration of resources and capabilities. Our resources and capabilities are shaped over time through the actions we have taken in the past. Our past dictates the viable choices available today. By the time HMT Watches woke up to the reality of competitive annihilation at the hands of Titan (see Chapter 1), its past inactions had made it too weak to do anything meaningful by way of fighting back.

COMPETITIVE DYNAMICS

We have looked at competitive action following the emergence of triggers—external or internal (see Figure 6.1). External triggers could be common to all players in a market, such as entry of a new player or availability of a recent technology. Internal triggers could be the outcome of active search for new initiatives based on internally identified opportunities or challenges. An action initiated by an incumbent player would become an external trigger for other incumbents and players. When Airtel fired the first salvo of buyback of rivals' dongles, this action became the external trigger for incumbents such as Vodafone and Idea. They would use the same approach as detailed in this chapter to figure out how to respond. We would call it 'competitive action' by Vodafone or Idea, just that it is in response to a pre-emptive action by Airtel.

We can see the parallels with the story about two wuxia warriors which appeared in the beginning of the previous chapter. Competitive dynamics unfolds as a series of actions. Each action creates for the initiator an opportunity to benefit from the action.[17] The initiator can hope to accrue these benefits only for a while, till rivals get their act together. Once any of the rivals respond effectively, the benefit from the earlier action will change, as it now has to accommodate the response as well.

Uber Eats launched local food delivery in Mumbai, India, in May 2017. It offered its customers the feature of scheduled deliveries with which orders could be placed for deliveries to be made from one hour to one week later.[18] At the time of Uber Eats's launch, incumbents such as Swiggy and Zomato did not offer scheduling of deliveries and followed a first-in-first-out logic for fulfilment. Soon after customers placed their order, the incumbents would process and deliver the orders. Apparently, scheduled deliveries increase the operational complexity of managing the order pipeline. However, scheduling provides customers the added benefit of planning ahead, and Uber Eats was uniquely positioned to provide this at its launch. Within six months, however, Swiggy added a feature which allowed customers to schedule delivery of food up to 48 hours in advance. Swiggy promised free deliveries for customers who scheduled orders, claiming that scheduling will improve predictability of orders and deliveries, resulting in cost savings.[19]

---

[17] The premise here is that any player will initiate an action only if the action is non-trivially beneficial. If all action options for a player are detrimental, maybe doing nothing might turn out to be the best possible option. Here, the reference is to the first action and not responses to the competitive action.

[18] *Business Today*, 'Uber Launches New Food Delivery App to Directly Compete with Zomato, Swiggy and Foodpanda', 4 May 2017. Available at: https://www. businesstoday.in/technology/news/uber-launches-new-food-delivery-app-to-directly-compete-with-zomato-swiggy-and-foodpanda/story/251314.html (accessed 8 June 2021).

[19] Samreen Ahmad, 'Now, Swiggy Schedule Lets You Place Your Food Order 48 Hours in Advance', *Business Standard*, 23 February 2018. Available at: https://www.business-standard.com/article/companies/swiggy-unveils-schedule-service-customers-can-pre-order-meals-up-to-48-hrs-1180222009501.html (accessed 8 June 2021).

Before Uber Eats was launched, customers who preferred planning ahead for food deliveries did not really have an option other than to remind themselves to order about half an hour before they needed food. Uber Eats provided scheduling, and customers who valued this attribute would have flocked to them, resulting in a relative advantage in customer acquisition for Uber Eats compared to if they hadn't provided this customer benefit. This relative advantage would last only till one of the other incumbents matched the feature, which happened a few months on. Thus, Uber Eats had a narrow window of opportunity of a few months when it could benefit from the competitive advantage of scheduled delivery. Once rivals copied this feature, they were at par on this feature in the eyes of customers. The competitive advantage would diminish and eventually vanish.

Ian MacMillan characterizes the dynamics of 'strategic initiative' or competitive action[20] as playing out over three phases—launch, exploitation and counter-attack (see Figure 6.2). The first phase, 'launch', is the duration of time to build which the initiator of the competitive action takes to go from an idea to the realized advantage in the market. The duration of launch phase depends on the nature of the competitive action. A price change can go from idea to execution in a few days, while a cost-improvement initiative would take a few weeks to a few months. Capacity and capability changes would take longer to build—a few months to a few years. Innovation-driven initiatives would, in addition to having longer time to build, also involve uncertainty. During the launch period, no significant benefits in terms of performance are likely to accrue to the initiator. In fact, there would be negative impact on current performance. Financial commitments would result in negative cashflows, higher interest cost and a leveraged balance sheet. Changes in processes and operations to prepare for launch of the initiative might disrupt

---

[20] I prefer to use the term 'competitive action' as it allows us to bring within the scope of discussion initiatives which are not necessarily strategic, such as short-term pricing changes.

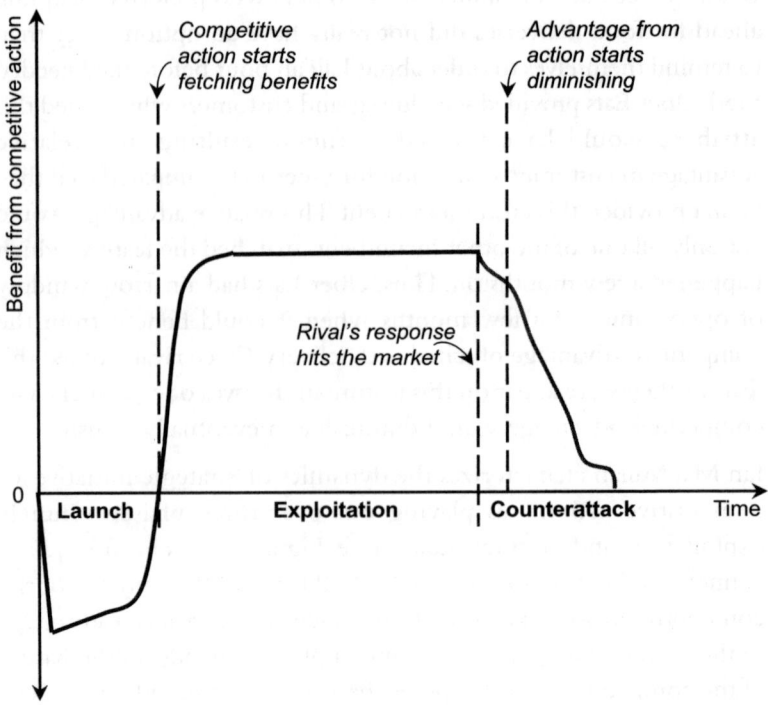

Source: Adapted from Ian C. MacMillan, 'Controlling Competitive Dynamics by Taking Strategic Initiative', *Academy of Management Executive* 2, no. 2 (1988): 111–118.

Figure 6.2. Competitive Dynamics

current rhythm of doing things within the organization, affecting current performance negatively.

Once the initiator launches the competitive action, the benefits would hopefully start to accrue—revenue increase, margin improvement, cycle time reduction, better customer experience—whatever was intended. This will continue over the 'exploitation' phase when the initiator will be uniquely positioned to offer the customer benefits from its competitive action and in turn appropriate value from offering the benefits. The duration of the exploitation phase will depend on the nature and source of advantage. A trade secret, as long as it remains valuable in the market, can last several decades. Ask the cola majors or WD-40 Company, the maker of eponymous water-displacing spray. When you can't keep it a secret, you would go for a patent which will last less than a couple of decades. Complex configurations of resources and capabilities which result in cost advantage or superior customer benefit can be difficult for rivals to imitate. They will take time to figure out how to replicate. A change in price schedule can probably be copied by rivals in a few days. More imitable or substitutable the nature and source of advantage is, more well-placed your rivals will be to shorten the duration of the exploitation phase.

It is during the exploitation phase that rivals will evaluate your action which would have become an external trigger for them. Rivals may be unaware of your move or may be in denial initially. If so, you are lucky, but you cannot pin your game plan on getting lucky. In general, rivals may choose to do nothing immediately, copy or neutralize the benefits from the action if possible, or come up with something better. In any case, rivals will take some time to assess your action and decide on their response. Once rivals decide on what to do, there will be a time to build. Thus, there will be some delay before response to your initial action will hit the market. This is the time period during which you, the initiator of the competitive action, can fully exploit the benefits of the advantage it created. The advantage and benefits from any single competitive action, however, won't last long, leave alone forever.

Rivals hitting the market with their response mark the beginning of the 'counter-attack' phase. During this phase, the benefits from the advantage to the initiator will decline as the value of the advantage in the market gets diminished by the rivals' response. Eventually, the benefits from the advantage to the initiator will become trivial, as the advantage itself gets neutralized.

The essence of competitive dynamics is its repetitive nature, like ocean waves relentlessly crashing on the shore. Competitive actions which we take, even those which come from years of toil and sizeable investments, have an expiry date. Often, it's our rivals who decide the expiry date. When we look at the business case for a competitive action, we ought to predict the expiry date which rivals would impose on the advantage we seek to build. Without that, we are likely to grossly overestimate the business case for the competitive action. Also, before the expiry date of the advantage we are currently benefiting from, we need to be ready to hit the market with the next advantage-seeking initiative. Rather than letting our rivals decide the expiry date for the sources of our competitive advantage, we can proactively make our advantage redundant by building a superior advantage. If not, our rivals may take the lead and we would be relegated to catching up.

Ian MacMillan points out, 'The challenge for today's strategist is to constantly seek the "second act"—even as the firm is benefiting from the current competitive advantage it should be laying the groundwork for the upcoming competitive advantage.'[21] Battle-ready players would ensure that they pay close attention to the three phases of competitive dynamics while developing strategic (advantage-seeking) initiatives. They would ensure that potential rival responses and their impact on competitive dynamics are factored in while validating the viability of an initiative or action. They would weave in design elements which will stretch and guard the exploitation phase. They would also build a pipeline of potential advantage-seeking initiatives for their business, a quiver of arrows from which they can draw one after the other. The mind-sparring wuxia warriors would agree.

---

[21] MacMillan, 'Controlling Competitive Dynamics', 111–118.

Motivation to act upon a trigger for a competitive action is driven by the impact on business performance, competitive position and reputation which the trigger has on our business. More negative, substantial and permanent the impact of the trigger on our business performance, competitive position and reputation, more motivated should we be to pre-empt or respond. Pre-emption helps stop or slow rivals. It pins down rivals by restricting their range of available actions. Reactive responses suffer from restricted degrees of freedom and are less preferred than pre-emption. High motivation to pre-empt or respond to the competitor's actions is symptomatic of erosion of our competitive advantage. Competitive dynamics is the continuous wave of actions by players coming up with advantage-seeking initiatives and responses by their rivals which are aimed at neutralizing the advantage or turn the table, often taking turns in the role of initiators. As we try to get and stay battle-ready, our rivals too would do so; the key to winning is to stay at least one step ahead of the rivals.

CHAPTER SEVEN

Beating the Goliaths

'Gentlemen, we are going for the gold medal. The people who win silver at the Olympic Games have trained for gold.... You are less lucky if you win silver. If you are unlucky, you end up number six. But in the chip lithography market, there isn't even room for six contenders.' That's how Gjalt Smit, first CEO of ASML, articulated the strategic intent for the newborn maker of semiconductor lithography equipment in 1984. At that time, the global market was dominated by GCA of the USA and Nikon of Japan. There were seven other smaller players—American, Japanese and German—all angling for a chance to step on to the podium. While GCA and Nikon captured most of the market and were selling several hundred machines every year, ASML was yet to sell their first machine. They were at the bottom of the list of 10 players, with zero share of installed base in chip lithography equipment.[1]

Fast forward 15 years to 2009. ASML climbed to the top of the podium with more than 40 per cent market share, with number two Nikon closely following. By 2018, ASML became the undisputed leader with 62 per cent market share. By now, numbers two and three—Canon and Nikon—were trailing at a distance. No serious

---

[1] René Raajimakers, *ASML's Architects* (Eindhoven: Techwatch Books, 2019), 252.

challenge to ASML is visible yet, as it has a monopoly on the cutting edge of chip lithography technology.[2]

The success story of ASML is driven by several internal factors— leadership by its CEOs, access to cutting-edge technology from the research labs of Philips, a distinctive culture which is surprising for its contrast with the culture at Philips and so on. But ASML did not win gold just by focusing on its internal advantages, though they are all critical. A keen interest in customers' jobs to be done, relentless search for market opportunities, deep understanding of competitors' game plans and resource configurations, unpredictability of its actions and continued attention to what customers were saying and competitors were doing turn out to be distinctive aspects of how ASML became the leader in chip lithography market.[3]

ASML's success is not a lesson in smart market moves. Rather, it highlights the dynamic nature of competition. Back in the 1980s, ASML was a David—a nobody with no visible advantages. Already since the 1970s, the market leaders of that time, GCA and PerkinElmer, both of the USA, were being challenged by Japanese players Canon and Nikon. Towards the end of the 1980s, the Japanese Davids displaced the American Goliaths. A decade on, ASML, one among the Davids of the mid-1980s, displaced the Japanese Goliaths to claim the top spot.[4] Since then, ASML has remained the Goliath in chip lithography. Who knows when and how a David will challenge ASML and succeed at that?

In this chapter, we start by exploring how Davids successfully challenge Goliaths. Ironically, successful Davids will eventually become Goliaths and will be challenged by a new breed of Davids.

---

[2] *The Economist*, 'How ASML Became Chipmaking's Biggest Monopoly', 29 February 2020. Available at: https://www.economist.com/business/2020/02/29/how-asml-became-chipmakings-biggest-monopoly (accessed 8 June 2021).

[3] Raajimakers, *ASML's Architects*.

[4] Ibid.

Yet Goliaths do have ways to guard against Davids. That's what we will explore in the subsequent two chapters.

THE KEEN EYE OF DAVID

The biblical story of David and Goliath is probably the most popular 'triumph of underdog' story. David did not win the death match against Goliath by his superior strength. He was weaker. The weapons that Goliath was bearing were far more formidable than David's sling and sword. David's victory can be attributed more to his spotting an opportunity to aim for and hit Goliath's forehead with his slingshot. Of course, he executed it to the tee.

Much the same way, challengers—the underdogs in business competition—come to the game with significantly inferior resources and capabilities. Remember that relative resource position is in comparison with the configuration and size of resources available with the dominant players. The challenger will by definition be sub-par in relative resource position compared to the dominant incumbents.

What the challenger often possesses is a keen eye. They spot market opportunities such as unmet or poorly met jobs to be done which the leaders do not see or dismiss as unimportant. Challengers spot new ways to reach customers. They spot new ways of configuring resources and capabilities, which leads to amplified impact of their resources and makes redundant the resource configurations of big rivals. They spot novel uses of available technologies in making their value chain more efficient or effective. Once in a while, they may also come up with a new technology, but that's not always the case. They spot the chance to bring in new materials and inputs, which enhances quality or reduces cost or both.

Goliaths would have been exposed to information on all these, but they tend not to pay much attention to these. They continue with their already successful game plans. The challengers however get excited about what they have spotted. They craft their game plan specifically to leverage what they have spotted, and they relentlessly pursue this game plan. Challengers bring entrepreneurial spirit into the game.

Joseph Schumpeter says that the function of entrepreneurs is

> to reform or revolutionize the pattern of production by exploiting an ... untried technological possibility for producing a new commodity or producing an old one in a new way, by opening up a new source of supply of materials or a new outlet for products, by reorganizing an industry and so on.[5]

For him, innovation can be grand enterprises such as 'motorcar'[6] or more humbler ones such as 'a particular kind of sausage or toothbrush'. Entrepreneurs spot and exploit new ways of doing things. That's what gives Davids a narrow window of opportunity to beat the Goliaths.

Battle-ready challengers adopt one or more of approaches which have proven to work in their favour in winning against dominant players. They come up with a CVP which just cannot be copied or bettered by the Goliaths. Davids take on Goliaths aggressively when it's difficult for the dominant players to wipe them out by retaliation or imitation. Otherwise, they operate below the radar. Davids orchestrate their business outside the conventional supply chains used by the industry. Once they are visible to the Goliaths, they unleash a series of advantage-seeking actions in succession, in sync with the delay in response from dominant players. Every time the Goliaths respond and neutralize their advantage, they get on to their next advantage. They act in ways unpredictable in terms of nature, timing and location, which often forces the Goliaths to wait and watch, limiting their ability to pre-empt. Battle-ready challengers focus on staying unchallenged in the 'exploitation phase' for as long

---

[5] Joseph A. Schumpeter, 'Capitalism, Socialism and Democracy' (London: George Allen & Unwin, 1943), 133.

[6] When Schumpeter wrote this, automobile industry was seeing great technical advancements and was among the hi-tech industries of that time.

as possible (see Chapter 6, Figure 6.2). They are well-prepared to move to the next advantage and its exploitation phase even as the Goliaths step in to neutralize their current advantage.[7]

Leave Luck to Heaven

When Gunpei Yokoi, an electronics engineering graduate from Doshisha University, Kyoto, Japan, applied to large Japanese electronics companies, none of them wanted to hire him. He was eventually hired as a maintenance engineer by a Kyoto-based company which used to make playing cards. His job was to maintain the machines in the assembly line. Ever a tinkerer, Yokoi put together a mechanical gripper to grab and fetch stuff without having to move. When the company's president saw this contraption, he wanted to sell it as a toy.[8] The toy—Ultra Hand—was launched in 1966 and became an instant hit in Japan, selling more than a million units.[9] Yokoi was made the company's one-man R&D team.

A decade later, when Yokoi was returning to Kyoto on the bullet train, he spotted a bored salesman playing with his electronic calculator. He saw the opportunity for handheld electronic games which could inconspicuously fit in a pocket. Thus was born 'Game & Watch' launched in 1980, the legendary handheld electronic game which would sell 43 million units spanning 60 games.[10] The company, Nintendo (roughly translates to 'leave luck to heaven'), went on to rule the global gaming industry for more than a decade till Sony and Microsoft came to the scene in the 1990s.

---

[7] Some of the approaches for challengers are from Ken G. Smith, Walter J. Ferrier, and Curtis M. Grimm, 'King of the Hill: Dethroning the Industry Leader', *Academy of Management Executive* 15, no. 2 (2001): 59–70.

[8] David Epstein, *Range: How Generalists Triumph in a Specialized World* (London: Macmillan, 2019).

[9] David Sheff, *Game Over* (New York, NY: Random House, 1993).

[10] Lara Crigger, 'The Rainmakers: Searching for Gunpei Yokoi', *The Escapist Magazine*, 6 March 2007.

Here was a poorly met job to be done. The gentleman in the bullet train wanted to kill time but did not want to read or chat with a stranger seated next to him. Walkman was a novelty in 1980, and streaming videos on to smartphones would have been stuff of science fiction then. For decades, the traditional toy and arcade game industry in Japan was dominated by the likes of Bandai, Epoch and Takara. None of them spotted the potential for games in the form of compact electronic devices which would fit in a pocket. Yokoi's keen eye spotted the opportunity. Nintendo, a small player in electronic gaming then, drove its successful commercialization.

Nintendo, thanks to Gunpei Yokoi, had another string to its bow—'lateral thinking with withered technology'.[11] That's to say that you design your products around obsolete or near-obsolete technology which minimizes uncertainties in design, performance and time to market. This also drives down costs, enables faster scaling and earns a larger profit. The product design, however, has to deliver unique and valuable customer benefits so as to ensure commercial success. The Nintendo Entertainment System (NES), which had a 95 per cent market share in the USA and Japan during the 1980s to the early 1990s, was designed with this approach. It used a previous-generation microprocessor made by Ricoh, bringing down costs drastically and allowing Nintendo to source the entire production capacity of Ricoh for the processor.[12] At the same time, Nintendo's designers squeezed in arcade quality graphics into their game consoles and cartridges.[13]

The unique and valuable customer benefits were graphics quality and the library of high quality and engaging games which Nintendo brought out for NES, both from its in-house game studio and from third-party game developers. There was one problem though. A few years prior to the launch of NES, Atari tried to collect royalty from

---

[11] https://en.wikipedia.org/wiki/Gunpei_Yokoi (accessed 8 June 2021).
[12] This wouldn't have been possible with cutting-edge processors.
[13] Adam M. Brandenburger, 'Power Play (A)' (Harvard Business School Case 5-795-167, 1995).

third-party developers for games which play on its consoles and failed. Nintendo learned from that and put a lock on the console. The key was a security chip which had to be in the game cartridge. Developers had to pay Nintendo for these chips, effectively a royalty.[14]

Nintendo also redefined the business model for game consoles and games. It started selling consoles at near cost, even below cost at launch, while extracting high margins from its in-house games. It allowed third-party game developers to publish games which work on its console for a royalty and used technology to prevent unauthorized games from running on its consoles. This ensured that Nintendo got paid for every third-party game which was sold. It also controlled quality strictly and restricted supplies to prevent price competition among games.[15] The new way of doing business, which later acquired the label of two-sided platform business,[16] has since become the de facto business model for game consoles and games. With all this, Nintendo went on to dominate the game console industry globally for a decade.[17]

However, starting the mid-1990s, Nintendo lost the top slot to Sony's PlayStation console primarily because it was unwilling to cannibalize its installed base of NES consoles.[18] Nintendo, now a challenger, took back the leadership position from Sony after

---

[14] Ibid.

[15] Ibid.

[16] Thomas Eisenmann, Geoffrey G. Parker, and Marshall W. Van Alstyne, 'Strategies for Two-sided Markets', *Harvard Business Review*, October 2006. Available at: https://hbr.org/2006/10/strategies-for-two-sided-markets (accessed 8 June 2021).

[17] Brandenburger, 'Power Play'.

[18] Video game console industry is notorious for upsetting the pecking order of players every few years, called 'generation'. Every new generation sees launch of consoles sporting new and improved capabilities matched with game titles which fully leverage these capabilities to deliver better than before game play experience. Moving to the next generation is like an arms race. Next-generation game consoles are rarely made to work with titles from previous generations as that would subdue the demand for next-generation consoles. Thus, every new generation becomes a battle between the leader from previous generation and its challengers.

a decade. Nintendo Wii, launched in November 2006, had a puny processor compared to Sony PlayStation 3 and Microsoft Xbox 360, both of which featured 10 times more powerful processors.[19] While rivals offered high-definition video and six-channel surround sound, Wii came with lower-quality standard definition video and stereo audio. Yet Wii was a runaway success and outsold rivals by a substantial margin. In first two years, Wii sold 32.4 million units, against 15.5 million units of PS3 and 20.9 million units of Xbox 360.[20] Wii overtook rivals primarily because of the novel and unique game play experience that Nintendo provided via its motion-sensing controllers that allowed gamers to play by mimicking real-life body movements involved in playing games, such as bowling or tennis. Wii could be intuitively played and became a craze across age groups, from young kids to senior citizens. Queen Elizabeth II was supposed to be a fan of Nintendo Wii.[21] The motion-sensing controllers were built from technological components such as cameras and sensors available for many years. It's just that Nintendo put it to a novel use.

Sony, a market leader for previous two console generations, was the first to respond to Wii's motion-sensing controller. PlayStation Move controller came three years after Wii, in September 2009. Microsoft followed with Kinect for its Xbox 360 in November 2010, a full four years after Wii brought motion-sensing controllers to gamers.[22] By then it was too late. Wii sold more than 100 million units by 2013, compared to 24 million Kinects and 15 PlayStation Moves.[23]

In Game & Watch, NES and Wii, Nintendo spotted unmet jobs to be done. For Game & Watch, it was the frustration of not having a fun way to kill time which could fit in a pocket. This gave Nintendo

---

[19] Andre Hagiu and Hanna Halaburda, 'Responding to the Wii?' (Harvard Business School Case 9-709.448, 2010).

[20] Ibid.

[21] Ibid.

[22] https://en.wikipedia.org/wiki/Kinect (accessed 8 June 2021).

[23] Ibid.; https://en.wikipedia.org/wiki/Wii (accessed 8 June 2021); https://en.wikipedia.org/wiki/PlayStation_Move (accessed 8 June 2021).

the opportunity to create the market and dominate it. Ten years on, Nintendo spotted the unmet job to be done—play arcade quality games at home. NES was their answer to solve this problem which made them the leader of gaming for a decade. Two decades on, Wii solved the problem of not being able to play video games the way we would play the games in real life. Older and younger people, especially those who are not adept at working with game controllers, found it intimidating to play video games. Wii broke down the barriers which restricted many from playing video games, vastly expanding the target base of gamers. While Nintendo was innovating on the fundamental game play experience, both Sony and Microsoft were busy with the arms race of game console processing power. They missed the obvious but easily overlooked insight that people would like to swing their arm while bowling.

Neither Sony nor Microsoft anticipated that Nintendo would build natural game play capability into Wii, providing Nintendo a distinctive advantage vis-à-vis rivals. The unpredictability of Nintendo's action provided it an extended 'exploitation phase' which lasted three to four years. Although the withered technology philosophy of Nintendo was well known, the rivals could not predict what Nintendo would do next with obsolete technology.

There Has To Be Something Better

'When I take this thing off and it hits the floor, it makes this big *suuup* sound. There *has* to be something better.' This is how Kevin Plank recalled his frustration with cotton T-shirts—known as shimmel shirts, worn by football players under heavy shoulder pads. Football players tend to sweat profusely during games and practice sessions. A dry T-shirt weighs about 170 g, while a sweat-soaked one would weigh 8 times at about 1.40 kg.[24] Add to that the discomfort of a heavy sweat-soaked T-shirt clinging to the body.

---

[24] Rory McDonald et al., 'Under Armour' (Harvard Business School Case 9–618–020, 2018).

Plank used to play football for his university team in the early 1990s and had been frustrated with sweat-soaked T-shirts. He observed that the inner garment worn under the team's uniform pants stays dry. The inner garment was made of moisture-wicking fabric which had the feel of lingerie and wasn't used to make base-layer T-shirts yet. Plank spotted an unmet job to be done and also spotted an opportunity to use a new input—moisture-wicking fabric—to solve the problem.

Moisture-wicking fabric, first introduced by DuPont in the 1980s under the brand name CoolMax,[25] was already used to make garments. Nike had introduced sports T-shirts for golfers using moisture-wicking fabrics way back in 1991 under the brand Dri-FIT.[26] No one thought of using this fabric to make T-shirts for football players until Plank thought of it.

Upon graduating in 1996, Plank produced a prototype of HeatGear, 'a light-weight, form-fitting, sweat-wicking, stretchy compression shirt'[27] which football players can wear under their padding. He started calling on his friends and teammates from the university to get them to try out HeatGear. Football players, who used to wear loose-fitting T-shirts made of thick cotton fabric, were reluctant to try the body-hugging T-shirt which felt like lingerie. Early adopters were often at the receiving end of jibes. However, adoption took off once the benefits of HeatGear—superior comfort and enhanced performance—became apparent. Georgia Tech became the first university team to adopt Plank's shirts in 1997, by then branded Under Armour (UA).

From there, UA grew at a fast clip to create a distinctive identity for itself. From football shirts, it diversified into apparel for other sports.

---

[25] http://dla.library.upenn.edu/dla/pacscl/ead.pdf?id=PACSCL_HML_2011320 (accessed 8 June 2021).

[26] Golf News Now, 'Nike's Dri-FIT Celebrates 20 Years', 19 October 2010. Available at: https://www.golfnewsnow.ca/soft-goods/apparel/nikes-dri-fit-celebrates-20-years/ (accessed 8 June 2021).

[27] McDonald et al., 'Under Armour'.

From sports apparel, it expanded to other products such as sports footwear and accessories. From the USA, it extended its market reach to global. To build its brand, UA used nifty movie placements and celebrity endorsements supported by advertising campaigns which celebrated the fighting spirit of the underdog; something it has been doing with Nike and others. By 2016, UA's revenue grew to US$5 billion. During 2005–2016, its revenues grew at a CAGR of 29 per cent and net income grew 26 per cent.[28] In 2015, UA overtook Reebok to become the second largest sport apparel and footwear company by revenue in the USA, next only to the market leader Nike.[29]

In its early years, UA was mostly operating below the radar. In the first year, Plank reached out to his former teammates from high school and university and got them and their teammates to try out HeatGear shirts. As some of his friends got drafted to professional football, UA entered professional football locker rooms. Through word of mouth among players, coaches and team equipment managers, UA drove adoption of its shirts by university and professional teams. It opportunistically expanded to apparels for other sports such as baseball, basketball, hockey and track, where the core benefits of its products were highly valued. In the first few years, UA generated most of its business through supply agreements with university and professional teams.

By 2002, when UA started appearing in mainstream sports retail outlets, it had already created a new category called 'performance apparel' which had grown 60 per cent over the previous year to US$130 million in revenue. It had cornered 80 per cent of this market. Market leaders, Nike and Reebok, who eventually responded with their line-up of performance apparel, were distant followers with 3.5 per cent and 1.1 per cent market share, respectively.[30]

---

[28] Ibid.

[29] Julie Creswell and Kevin Draper, 'How Under Armour Lost Its Edge', *The New York Times*, 26 January 2020. Available at: https://www.nytimes.com/2020/01/26/business/under-armour-struggles.html (accessed 8 June 2021).

[30] Charles Duhigg, 'Refusing to Sweat It', *The Washington Post*, 18 August 2003.

UA's rivals didn't respond initially. 'No one ever branded [performance apparel], and … [competitors] just sort of watched it happen,' recalls Plank.[31] By the early 2000s, leading incumbents joined the fray. Nike positioned Dri-FIT as its answer to UA. Adidas came up with ClimaLite. Reebok brought in Hydromove and PlayDry. By the time the Goliaths woke up to the idea of performance apparel, UA was the dominant player in the category it created, with a strong customer following right from high-school teams to professional players. The 'exploitation phase' for UA's innovation of performance apparel lasted about four to five years.

By 2001, even as Nike and others were taking note of UA and moving to enter performance apparel, UA had started work on its women's line. UA realized that their performance apparel was 'effectively unisex … as women were buying the same products that were being sold for men'. When Plank and team had the first look at their women's apparel designs, they weren't happy. According to Plank, the product was 'very masculine the way it looked', and 'the attempt that we made to make it feminine was creating the colour pink'. Having realized that 'shrinking and pinking does not work', Plank decided to burn the first lot of inventory worth more than a million dollars[32] and go back to the drawing board. This time, Plank brought women into the team.[33] By 2003, as Nike, Reebok and Adidas were getting serious about performance apparel, UA added an exclusive women's line of performance apparel. As the exploitation phase for unisex performance apparel was coming to an end for UA due to competitor action, it had kicked off the next advantage—seeking action—women's line, and its exploitation phase.

Even before the women's line hit the market, UA started work on entering sports footwear, a big-ticket diversification from its focus

---

[31] McDonald et al., 'Under Armour', 6.
[32] Under Armour had revenue of about US$20 million at that time.
[33] Bloomberg Quint, 'How Under Armour Took on Giants Like Nike and Adidas. In conversation with Kevin Plank', 30 March 2019. Available at: https://youtu.be/pPy-fTDnLfw (accessed 8 June 2021).

on sports apparel. Rick Anguilla, strategic advisor to the CEO of UA, advised against starting with football shoes. It's a tough product to engineer and expensive to produce. Football shoes are typically sold during a narrow window of two months a year. Unlike basketball shoes, football shoes are never worn outside the field. The market was small compared to more popular categories such as running, cross-training and basketball shoes. No one entering sports footwear would start with football shoes. Kevin Plank, however, chose to start with football shoes. Nike, the leader in the category, hadn't brought any innovations in this category for more than a decade. UA already had a solid following among football players, thanks to its performance apparel.[34]

UA launched its football shoes in April 2006 with several novel benefits to customers. UA's football shoes, which it called 'performance footwear', offered superior 'moisture management and breathability', better agility and minimized weight as well as 'progressive traction'.[35] Football players used to wrap athletic tape around their ankles to prevent injuries and had to put up with the pain of pulling the tape off the skin after every practice session or game.[36] UA's football shoes came with built-in ankle support that went up to the shin. No more 'ouch' while pulling off the tape. In the first year of launch, UA captured 23 per cent of the US$250 million US market for football shoes.[37] On the back of its success with football shoes, UA entered the market for baseball, running and basketball shoes in quick succession, directly challenging Nike which dominated the market for sports footwear for more than three decades.

UA was able to challenge dominant incumbents as its products delivered clear and tangible benefits to customers, compared to what

---

[34] McDonald et al., 'Under Armour', 8.
[35] Under Armour Press Release, 'Under Armour Unveils Performance Footwear Line', 24 April 2006.
[36] McDonald et al., 'Under Armour'.
[37] Under Armour Press Release, 'Under Armour Unveils Performance'.

the dominant incumbents offered. It had the keen eye to spot unmet jobs to be done and then come up with solutions for these problems. UA's vision captures their focus on unmet jobs to be done, maybe a bit pompously. 'Under Armour's vision is to inspire you with performance solutions *you never knew you needed* and *can't imagine living without*' (italics mine).[38]

For its first product, it had the protection of anonymity. Its subsequent product launches were in clear sight of rivals. Yet UA surprised the Goliaths by moving swiftly and in unpredictable ways. Starting the early 2000s when Nike and others launched products to counter its performance apparel, UA unleashed a series of market entries into new categories and geographies in quick succession. UA was driving its exploitation phases shorter, anticipating quick competitor response. It entered categories which were less obvious, such as football shoes within sports footwear. It continued to create new categories such as performance underwear and athlete recovery sleepwear. UA gained an upper hand by being swift and unpredictable in launching advantage-seeking actions. The dominant rivals, Nike and Reebok–Adidas were forced to wait and watch, unable to decisively pre-empt UA's growth.[39]

OUR BLADES ARE F**KING GREAT

'Do you like to spend 20 dollars a month on brand name razors? Nineteen go to Roger Federer. Do you think your razor needs a vibrating handle, a torchlight, a back scratcher and 10 blades? Your handsome-ass grandfather had one blade, and polio'. Mike Dubin's irreverently humorous YouTube video announcing the launch of a subscription service that 'for a dollar a month, [sends] high quality razors right to your door'[40] got 12,000 subscribers in the first two

---

[38] https://about.underarmour.com/about (accessed 8 June 2021).
[39] That's the story, at least up to 2016.
[40] https://youtu.be/ZUG9qYTJMsI (accessed 8 June 2021).

days[41] and more than four million views in the first month.[42] It was recognized as the 'Best Out-of-nowhere Video Campaign' in the 2012 AdAge Viral Video Awards.[43]

Ever since the US government contracted Gillette to supply razors and blades to its armed forces during the First World War, its safety razor and blade became the shaving tool for America and then the world. By 2010, more than a century after its first patent, Gillette held 70 per cent share of the global market for razors and blades.[44] Schick came a distant second with revenues less than one-fourth that of the leader.

Gillette's business was highly profitable. A four-blade pack of Gillette Fusion refills cost the company about 50 cents to produce and pack. Retailers sold it to customers for US$20–25. Gillette captured about US$13–16 per pack, leaving US$4–5 for distributors and retailers with US$3–4 as taxes to governments.[45] Gillette's gross margins covered the high fixed costs for advertising, and for R&D. Dubin's observation that 19 out of 20 dollars go to the celebrity endorser was not an exaggeration. Gillette had erected high barriers to entry by upping advertisement outlays and perfecting the art of patenting not-so-essential innovations, making it practically impossible for rivals to even have a fighting chance. Ask Schick; it has been trying for several decades.

---

[41] Jessica Naziri, 'Dollar Shave Club Co-founder Michael Dubin Had a Smooth Transition', *Los Angeles Times*, 16 August 2013. Available at: https://www.latimes.com/business/la-xpm-2013-aug-16-la-fi-himi-dubin-20130818-story.html (accessed 8 June 2021).

[42] Thomas Pardee, 'Google Takes Top Honors at Viral Video Awards', AdAge, 17 April 2012. Available at: https://adage.com/article/special-report-digital-conference/google-takes-top-honors-viral-video-awards/234155 (accessed 8 June 2021).

[43] Ibid.

[44] Kaitlyn Tiffany, 'The Absurd Quest to Make the "Best" Razor', Vox, 11 December 2018. Available at: https://www.vox.com/the-goods/2018/12/11/18134456/best-razor-gillette-harrys-dollar-shave-club (accessed 8 June 2021).

[45] Jamie Anderson, Karin Kollenz, and Nader Tavassoli, 'Dollar Shave Club: Disrupting the Shaving Industry' (London Business School Case CS-18-017, 2018).

Then entered Dollar Shave Club (DSC) Michael Dubin had been frustrated with having to deal with the 'razor fortress'—a term he uses to describe the practice of retailers, keeping razors and refills in a locked transparent case to prevent shoplifting. According to him, the customer experience of getting razors and blades was broken. 'The product was often used and often needs to be replaced … so there just had to be a better way,' observes Dubin,[46] referring to the hassle of finding someone who knows who has the key to the locked case and so on, till the case is finally opened and you add the refills to your shopping cart.

The idea for the start-up came up through a chance meeting between Dubin and Mark Levine in 2010. 'I don't know how we got on the subject of shaving, but we started talking about what a rip-off it is,' says Dubin. Levine, with experience in manufacturing, knew how to procure good-quality razors and blades from Asia at a low cost. Dubin brought branding and digital marketing skills. DSC was born a year on as an online subscription service which shipped razors and refill packs of blades to customers at regular intervals.[47] The idea was to take on the Goliath—Gillette.

Fast forward five years. US revenue of Gillette razors and blades in 2016 declined by US\$80 million over previous year. DSC revenues grew by US\$70 million in the same period[48] driven by its 2.2 million subscribers. Gillette's market share had been on a free fall, dropping by more than 15 per cent over past 6 years, from 70 per cent in 2010 to about 54 per cent in 2016.[49] Online sales of razors and blades

[46] CNBC, 'Dollar Shave Club Founder Michael Dubin on a Razor Sharp Idea | iConic Conference 2017', 28 September 2017. Available at: https://youtu.be/cCGp94leMRQ (accessed 8 June 2021).

[47] Naziri, 'Dollar Shave Club Co-founder Michael Dubin'.

[48] WSJ Video, 'Gillette Slashing Razor, Blade Prices By as Much as 20%', 4 April 2017. Available at: https://www.wsj.com/video/gillette-slashing-razor-blade-prices-by-as-much-as-20/A2F0E2D0-579F-4877-AB90-830FAB5603FF.html (accessed 8 June 2021).

[49] Sharon Terlep, 'Gillette, Bleeding Market Share, Cuts Prices of Razors', *The Wall Street Journal*, 4 April 2017. Available at: https://www.wsj.com/articles/

stood at one-twelfth of the overall market in 2016 and was doubling every three years.[50] Demand wasn't growing, but more customers were buying online. In five years, one-fourth of sales of razors and blades would go online. Already, DSC captured 52 per cent share of razors and blades sold online in the USA.[51] Gillette was forced to foray into online subscription in June 2015, which grabbed a measly 4 per cent of online sales in its first year. And then, Unilever, global arch-rival of Gillette's parent P&G, acquired DSC for a billion dollars in 2016.

Gillette announced a 20 per cent price cut in early 2017, surprising because Gillette had always come up with razors and blades with new and improved features backed by patents to justify periodic price hikes.[52] A month later, Gillette revamped its subscription club—Gillette On Demand—with new features like 'text to order refills' and 'every fourth order is free'. Towards the end of 2017, Gillette launched lower cost razors and bolstered its line-up of disposable razors. A CNN Money article called this 'Gillette's latest response to subscription competitors [who are] eating its lunch'.[53] Clearly, Gillette's approach of feature-rich products at a premium price was pushing customers towards lower-priced, functional and more convenient subscription alternatives, led by DSC. Not to be left out, distant number two Schick launched its Connect series of

gillette-bleeding-market-share-cuts-prices-of-razors-1491303601 (accessed 8 June 2021).

[50] Phil Wahba, 'Gillette Says It's Fighting Back in the Shaving Club Wars', *Fortune*. Available at: https://fortune.com/2015/10/23/gillette-shaving-club-wars/ (accessed 8 June 2021).

[51] Statista, 'Sales Share of the Leading Online Blades and Razor Brands in the United States in 2016', 2 August 2016. Available at: https://www.statista.com/statistics/670586/us-sales-share-leading-online-blades-razor-brands/ (accessed 8 June 2021).

[52] WSJ Video, 'Gillette Slashing Razor'.

[53] Nathaniel Meyersohn, 'Gillette Unveils New, Cheaper Razors to Keep Dollar Shave at Bay', CNN Money, 29 November 2017. Available at: https://money.cnn.com/2017/11/29/news/companies/gillette/index.html (accessed 8 June 2021).

razor blades that fit Gillette's razor handles, challenging Gillette's monopoly on refills for its installed base of razors.[54]

DSC offered three tiers of subscription for its customers in the USA—Humble Twin, 4X and Executive. These three subscriptions offered twin-blade, four-blade and six-blade cartridges, respectively. Every month, subscribers received a pack of four refills (five for Humble Twin) so that they could start shaving with a fresh blade every week. The subscription including the cost of shipping was US$3, 6 and 9 per month for the three plans. Customers who shave less frequently could opt for 'every other month shipping' or skip shipping for any month. Compared to Gillette, effective price per cartridge worked out to be about one-third for Humble Twin and about half for 4X and Executive. That's why the 20 per cent price cut of Gillette didn't really help much.

DSC got its razors and blades from the South Korean supplier Dorco, who also produced store-brand razors for several retail chains in the USA such as Walmart, Aldi and Lidl. Dorco ensured that razors and refill blades were compatible only within brands, avoiding commoditization of the refills market. DSC outsourced warehousing and fulfilment to a third-party logistics provider.

As it gained subscribers, DSC started offering other male grooming products such as shampoo, soap, creams and balms, which customers could add to their subscriptions. It continued to engage with customers through digital social media, often with irreverent and humorous videos. Almost all its marketing spend went to digital marketing and advertising.

Dubin spotted poorly met jobs to be done for customers looking to buy razors and blades. First, there were no functional and cost-effective options. Gillette's market dominance and strategy of

---

[54] Dennis Green, 'Gillette Is Facing a New Threat from One of Its Oldest Rivals', Business Insider, 24 May 2017. Available at: https://www.businessinsider.in/gillette-is-facing-a-new-threat-from-one-of-its-oldest-rivals/articleshow/58828160.cms (accessed 8 June 2021).

feature-rich products at a premium left a gaping hole in terms of a product which delivers functional value proposition at an affordable price. Second, it took time and effort to get a pack of refill blades into your shopping cart. Razors and blades were among sought-after categories for shoplifting. Retail industry calls this 'craved'[55] and just locks up the store inventory. Dubin's insight was that it must be possible to buy razors which give a good shave at an affordable price, and the buying experience ought to be hassle-free. On their choice of subscription model instead of an online store, Dubin says that they didn't go for subscription because it would provide steady revenues. 'You [should] launch a subscription model if the nature of subscription provides enhanced value for the customers, and it's true for razors.'[56] For DSC, subscription enhanced consumer experience as the customer didn't have to remember to get the next refill pack in time.

DSC's value chain—sourcing, production, distribution and marketing—was light on fixed assets and fixed operating expenses, resulting in a cost structure that nicely scaled with volume. It rejigged its value chain in such a way that it was impossible for Gillette to imitate and dominate. Gillette was already committed to a long-term strategy of feature-rich products protected by patents, sold at a premium and supported by high octane advertisements with celebrity endorse-ments. Gillette reached customers through the distribution and retail network, primarily relying on big box retailers as well as neighbour-hood convenience stores and drug stores. All this cost a lot of money which customers would eventually pay for. Gillette would find it difficult to change course, at least in the near future, because of the high commitments into its current business model, value chain and partners. DSC's value proposition took aim at this aspect of Gillette's game plan. This is what Dubin would have been betting on when he took Gillette head on in the first-ever video of DSC. In a humor-ous way, Dubin calls out the inanity of Gillette's needless innovations

---

[55] Concealable, removable, available, valued, enjoyed and disposable.
[56] CNBC, 'Dollar Shave Club Founder Michael Dubin'.

and high-cost advertisements, for which the customer pays. The taunt played out in DSC's favour as the video went viral.

Davids can and should go aggressive, when there's minimal risk of aggressive retaliation or imitation by the Goliath. The distinctively different business model of DSC compared to that of Gillette allowed it to taunt Gillette without the risk of getting clobbered. Gillette was tethered down by its own strategy and commitments. On the other hand, taunting the dominant player without any protection whatsoever would be quixotic and most often result in a bloody ending for the challenger.

ADVANTAGE DAVID

Challengers can overwhelm dominant players by creating for themselves distinct advantages in the market. The seeds of such advantages necessarily lie in unmet or poorly met jobs to be done. Customers, at least sections of customers, would find that the products put out by dominant players do not exactly fulfil their jobs to be done, forcing them to seek workarounds. Spotting such unmet or poorly met jobs to be done is the hallmark of a battle-ready challenger. The triggers for new products for Nintendo, UA and DSC were the identification of unmet jobs to be done.

Spotting the opportunity is only the first step. Finding a viable solution for the unmet job to be done is the next step. This takes one or more of the approaches, listed in Table 7.1—novel use of technology, new inputs and rejig of the value chain.

Novel use of technology does not necessarily mean 'new' technology. Case in point is Nintendo and its withered technology approach of product design. Security chips were already in use to control access to content such as paid television. Nintendo was the first to bring this technology to game consoles so that it could lock out unauthorized games. Online subscription-based retail was not a new technology when DSC launched its subscription club. DSC's novelty was that it offered a subscription service focused exclusively on the poorly met jobs to be done of those who wanted to shave. The

Table 7.1. Sources of Advantages for the Challenger

	Unmet/ Poorly Met Job To Be Done	Novel Use of Technology	Novel Use of Inputs	Rejig Value Chain
Nintendo	Have something in pocket to kill time in a fun way (Game & Watch)	Old/obsolete technology for new uses	–	–
	Play arcade quality games at home (NES)	Security chip to prevent unauthorized games from playing	–	Video game business model re-defined as a two-sided platform
	Play game like in real life (Wii)	Motion-sensing technology for real-life game play	–	–
Under Armour	Comfortable and performance-enhancing sports apparel	–	Moisture-wicking fabric for sport-swear	–
Dollar Shave Club	Functional and cost-effective shave with a new blade every week	Order taking through the internet	–	Redefined business model. Distribution and retail redundant
	Avoid the stress of dealing with 'razor fortress'	Subscription service	–	Digital marketing, viral videos

Source: The author.

innovation need not be ground-breaking or a global first. Battle-ready challengers find novel uses for available technologies which result in products which are more valuable for their customers compared to current offerings from dominant incumbents.

Most often, innovation involves a new configuration of things already available—technology, materials and methods. Moisture-wicking fabric was already around and was in use for a decade when Kevin Plank thought of moisture-wicking football T-shirts. Battle-ready challengers connect the dots in finding inputs already in use elsewhere to solve problems for their customers.

The solution to the unmet job to be done would most likely not be viable if the challenger were to follow the dominant player in terms of how business is done—how value is created and appropriated. Schick tried to follow the footsteps of Gillette and found that it was not possible to beat the Goliath in its game. The challenger has to come up with a distinctively different game plan—one that will make the dominant player's advantages redundant or even make it a liability. DSC bypassed the distribution and retail set-up to go direct to customers. It made expensive R&D nonessential by sourcing functional razors and blades. It provided enough refills for customers to start shaving with a new blade every week. Gillette's distribution did not solve this problem. DSC showed that funny videos produced for a few thousand dollars and distributed through social media are enough to gain attention, and celebrity endorsements are probably an overkill, at least for shaving razors and blades.

Battle-ready challengers come up with rejigs of value chain and new ways of doing business that do two things. The new ways help the challengers bypass or overcome barriers erected by the dominant players. The new ways help the challengers deliver value to customers in novel ways which enhance CVP and customer experience.

Delivering the solution for the unmet job to be done to the customer—executing the game plan—is the toughest part of being a challenger. A multitude of approaches can be adopted, depending on the context. Operating below the radar to the extent possible works well for the challenger, at least to start with. Being spotted by the Goliath is unavoidable, sooner or later. That's when the challenger needs to bank on being unpredictable and be swift in coming up with new advantage-seeking actions.

Once the dominant players spot the challenger in action, the exploitation phase for the challenger is really at its end. Anticipating that this will happen, the battle-ready challenger would have new waves of advantage-seeking actions ready to be launched into the market, kicking off waves of unchallenged exploitation phases. Being unpredictable helps the battle-ready challenger to keep the dominant player one or two steps behind. By unleashing a series of advantage-seeking actions, even incremental in nature, the challenger can sustain a lead over the dominant player over a period of time, allowing it to grow big enough to climb on to the podium and even take the gold. That's what ASML did. Sooner or later, it will face the challenge of staying there.

«LONG STORY» «SHORT»

Battle-ready challengers create advantage in the market by solving unmet or poorly met jobs to be done in offerings of dominant players. Solving the unmet or poorly met jobs to be done would involve distinctive game plans using a combination of novel use of technology, novel use of inputs and rejig of value chain. In executing the game plan, the battle-ready challenger could go head on against the dominant player if the rival cannot easily retaliate or imitate, else going below the radar makes sense. Rivals try to neutralize the advantage to the challenger through their market actions—the battle-ready challenger seeks to delay this. The battle-ready challenger unleashes waves of advantage-seeking actions as rivals start to respond, so that they move from one unchallenged advantage to another. Over time, the battle-ready challenger becomes a dominant player and eventually faces a new breed of challengers.

CHAPTER EIGHT

Chest Thumping, Moats and Forts

The year was 1991. The setting was the year-end management committee meeting of Hindustan Lever Limited[1] (HLL), the Indian subsidiary of global consumer major, Unilever. S. M. Datta, chairman of HLL, singled out the detergent business for special praise that year. In the conference room was an empty chair. Supposed to be seated in it was Karsanbhai Patel, the founder of Nirma Chemical Works. For Datta and HLL's management team, the empty chair represented a David who challenged HLL and rose to great heights.

HLL pioneered the Indian market for non-soap detergent (NSD) powder in the 1950s with its flagship product, Surf. By the late 1960s, it was the undisputed leader in this arena. In 1969, Karsanbhai Patel started Nirma, a low-cost NSD powder sold at one-third the price of Surf, supported by innovative approaches to supply chain, distribution, branding and advertising. Within a decade, Nirma drove up demand for NSD powder and became the market leader. HLL did not even realize that it had lost the top slot. By the late 1970s, Nirma was diversifying into other categories led by HLL such as NSD bars and toilet soaps.

---

[1] Now called Hindustan Unilever Limited.

It took about a decade for HLL to become aware of and then acknowledge that Nirma was indeed a rival and a seriously threatening one. Once it realized the threat, HLL assiduously worked to counter Nirma. It took another decade and couple of special projects before HLL could claim victory in its 1991 management meeting. Datta's praise for the detergent business was for having successfully fended off the threat from Nirma, and the empty chair was to thank Mr Patel for shaking HLL out of complacent stupor.[2] HLL did not kick Nirma out of the market. It copied Nirma with the launch of Wheel detergent and gained some of the ground lost to Nirma. Yet HLL saw it as a victory. It would indeed qualify as a victory for the simple reason that the Goliath survived.

For a David, the best outcome would be the clean kill of Goliath, but that's rare. Sometimes, the Goliath falls from its perch and fades away into insignificance. More often, the Goliath puts up a spirited fight to get back up and stay in the game. The likely outcome is that the David gains market presence and the Goliath is forced to accommodate, leading to a new normal in the market. And then there are the instances when David gets clobbered by Goliath.

For the Goliath, the most promising approach would be to hold the Davids at bay. Forestalling is far more beneficial than defending, as the challenger can inflict high damage on the Goliath. However, forestalling is not always possible. In this chapter, we will explore how potential challenges can be forestalled by the dominant player. In the next chapter, we will explore how Goliaths can engineer a favourable outcome when they are fighting back Davids.

To forestall or fight back successfully, the dominant player should first understand what stuff Davids are made of—what their game plans are and how they end up beating the Goliaths and morphing into Goliaths themselves. That's where we start.

---

[2] Charlotte Butler and Sumantra Ghoshal, 'Hindustan Lever Limited: Levers of Change' (INSEAD Case 302-199-1, 2002).

GAME PLANS OF CHALLENGERS

Some 40 minutes into the classic treasure hunt movie *Raiders of the Lost Ark*, the protagonist Indiana Jones aka Indy is blocked by an Arab swordsman while Indy is trying to save Marion, the lady in the story. The swordsman snickers derisively at Indy and swings his broad scimitar in fancy flourishes. It's like he is saying, 'You have met your match.' An unimpressed Indy pulls out his revolver and shoots the swordsman.[3] For the swordsman, the story ends there. Indy went on to make sequels.

We discussed the importance of knowing our rival and benefiting from predicting their next move in Chapters 5 and 6. That's straightforward when we are up against similar rivals. Davids are difficult to spot. They bring uncommon weapons to the battle. These weapons could be in the form of new technologies, new uses of existing technologies, new products or processes. Sometimes, it takes a while for the Goliath to spot Davids, figure out their weapons for what they are and realize how formidable these weapons are.

Davids come in two types. There are those who imitate the dominant players in terms of products and business models. Then there are those who add novelty to the product or business model or both.

Imitators

For much of the 20th century, Gillette dominated the market for shaving razors and blades. Two other players have been active in this market—the American player Schick and the French company Bic, which is known for disposable razors, pens and lighters. Bic has been focusing on disposable razors, which account for one-third of the wet shaving market. While Gillette was present in disposable razors, its primary growth and profit engine has been the shaving system—a reusable razor which takes blade cartridges. This accounts for

---

[3] https://youtu.be/vdnA-ESWcPs (accessed 8 June 2021).

two-thirds of the wet shaving market.[4] Gillette dominates shaving systems and makes money from the consumable—the cartridges. So much so, making profits from a proprietary consumable is commonly referred to as 'razor-and-blade pricing'.[5]

In the market for shaving systems and cartridges, Gillette enjoyed a massive lead over rivals, with a market share of about 70 per cent at the beginning of the 21st century. That's when Schick decided to mount a direct challenge.[6] In 2003, Schick launched Quattro, a shaving system which sported four blades, one blade more than Mach3 which Gillette launched in 1998. At the time of Quattro launch, Mach3 along with a new and improved Mach3 Turbo was the highest priced and top-selling shaving system from the Gillette stable.[7] Clearly, David was attacking Goliath the way Goliath would have attacked any rival.

Gillette sued Schick for patent infringement, and Schick sued Gillette back for false claims in advertising. For Gillette, the legal battle was to buy time. Three years on, in 2006, Gillette launched Fusion, a five-blade shaving system with a sixth blade on the back of the razor for trimming moustaches and sideburns. In the first two months, Gillette sold four billion Fusion razors.[8] A clear message to Schick that it can't beat Gillette at its own game of adding bells and whistles to razors and blades and taking it to customers through high-octane campaigns.

Imitators, or copycat challengers, typically come up with products which are barely distinguishable from that of the dominant player.

---

[4] Claudia H. Deutsch, 'For Mighty Gillette, These Are the Faces of War', *The New York Times*, 12 October 2003. Available at: https://www.nytimes.com/2003/10/12/business/for-mighty-gillette-these-are-the-faces-of-war.html (accessed 8 June 2021).

[5] Contrary to the popular belief, Gillette did not adopt the razor-and-blade pricing when it had the benefit of patent protection. See Randal C. Picker, 'The Razor-and-blade Myth(s)', *University of Chicago Law Review* 75 (2011): 225–255.

[6] Deutsch, 'For Mighty Gillette'.

[7] Michael D. Hartline, 'Gillette: Why Innovation May Not Be Enough', in *Marketing Strategy: Text & Cases*, 6th edition, eds O. C. Farrell and Michael D. Hartline (Mason, OH: Cengage Learning, 2014).

[8] Ibid.

Often, their business model would also be similar to that of the dominant player. Quattro could very well have come from Gillette. Schick marketed and sold Quattro exactly how Gillette would have.

When imitators attack dominant players, their product or service does not address any unmet or poorly met job to be done for the customers. Rather, it follows the well-trodden path taken by the dominant player. In terms of breadth of attack, they may focus on a specific segment or go for the mainstream market of the dominant player. Schick's launch of Quattro was a copycat attack which aimed at the broad market for shaving systems with a product very similar to Gillette's offerings. Gillette upped the ante. For the dominant players, imitators are easier to defend against compared to innovators.

Innovators

Some challengers enter the arena with a novel and distinctive solution to an unmet or poorly met job to be done for customers. This could be distinctive features in the product or in the business model. Take the case of DSC that we saw in the previous chapter. DSC's products weren't in any way superior to the razors and blades made by Gillette or Schick. DSC's distinctiveness was in the subscription model which ensured that a new pack of four blades arrived at customer's doorstep every month, and in its pricing, which did not have to cover for expensive R&D and advertising.

Back in 2006, Google was already generating revenue of US$10 billion from advertising, driven by its Search and Gmail businesses. Microsoft was the undisputed leader in office productivity[9] with 600 million users for its MS Office suite.[10] Google launched Docs (word processor in cloud) and Sheets (spreadsheet in cloud) both

---

[9] Word processing, spreadsheets, presentations, email client, calendar, to-do, notes and a few other tools.

[10] Hiten Shah, 'How Google Moved beyond Search to Reinvent Productivity with G Suite', FYI Blog, n.d. Available at: https://usefyi.com/g-suite-history/ (accessed 8 June 2021).

for its consumers and its growing base of small business customers who were already using Google's digital advertising and mail services.[11] Microsoft charged a hefty licence fee for the lifetime of a version which was a few years before the next version was released.[12] Google charged a modest annual subscription fee per user. The critical distinctiveness was that Google Docs and Sheets resided in the cloud unlike Microsoft Office which had to be installed on the user's computer. The benefits were many, such as more frequent updates, lesser need for computer resources, and easier sharing and collaboration. The distinctiveness of Google Docs and Sheets was both in the product and the business model.

That's how innovators attack. They target unmet or poorly met jobs to be done which the dominant player is not solving. Their breadth of attack could be a narrow niche or the entire customer base of the dominant player. Sometimes, innovators start with a narrow niche but grow to target the mainstream customer base over time. Battle plans of innovative challengers are likely to be full of surprises for the Goliaths. Most likely, the Goliaths haven't been in such a battle yet. Whether the challengers are imitators or innovators, to be able to counter their challenge, we have to understand how a David grows to become a Goliath.

ORIGIN STORY OF GOLIATHS

All Goliaths start off as Davids. Not all Davids would become Goliaths though. The reason why some Davids morph into Goliaths is because more and more customers buy from them, as compared to their rivals. It's tempting to view market share as the holy grail of business success, but growth in our market share is just an after-the-fact indicator that more and more customers have preferred us

---

[11] Google's Gmail service already provided calendar, to-do and notes.
[12] Microsoft has since started heavily promoting their subscription model with Microsoft365 offering, but it still maintains the old format of licensed MS Office.

over our rivals. What's important is to understand why customers prefer one business over its rivals.

The Fine Art of Customer Choice

Let's do a simple thought experiment. Biju and Bindu are looking to buy new smartphones. The choices available to them are an iPhone SE 2020 and a Samsung Galaxy M31. To make the experiment simple, let's say that these are the only two phones available to buy for either of them. Both of them can afford either of these phones. Let's also say that we are blessed with superpowers to get into their minds and observe how they choose.

Biju likes to flaunt brands and prefers the tight hardware–software integration that the iPhone and iOS provide, which he believes results in lag-free and smooth operation. He wants the convenience of wireless charging. Biju doesn't really care whether he is able to access the innards of his phone. If it keeps working well, he is happy. He likes smaller-sized phones, as most often he is just reading off the screen. Compact size also means that the phone is easier for him to carry around.

Bindu is a tinkerer and for her, root access to her phone is a must-have feature. She is an avid mobile gamer and likes large screens and faster processors. She doesn't worry if wireless charging is absent or if the phone is bulky. While Bindu is not averse to flaunting brands, she is not hung up on that.

In Figure 8.1, I have captured how both of them would evaluate the two phones. For the given attributes, Biju derives better value from iPhone SE than from Samsung M31. For the same set of attributes, Bindu sees more value in Samsung M31 than iPhone SE. In deciding which phone to buy, both of them bring one more dimension into picture—price. Even at three times the price, Biju gets better value per unit of price paid from iPhone SE. Biju will buy iPhone SE 2020. By the same logic, Bindu will go for Samsung Galaxy M31.

Attributes	Level	iPhone SE 2020 Price ₹42,500			Samsung M31 Price ₹15,999		
		Features	Value to Customer*		Features	Value to Customer	
			Biju	Bindu		Biju	Bindu
Operating system	Android or iOS	iOS	10	10	Android	1	8
Root access	Yes or No	No	NA	1	Yes	NA	10
Brand	Many	Apple	10	8	Samsung	1	8
Processor speed	10 GHz–21 GHz	12.5 GHz	6	4	16 GHz	7	5
Screen size	4.5–7 inches	4.7 inches	9	3	6.4 inches	1	6
Wireless charging	Yes or No	Yes	10	NA	No	1	NA
...:		...			...		

$$PVP = \frac{\text{Value to Customer}}{\text{Price}}$$

	Biju	Bindu	Biju	Bindu
Value to customer	9.00	5.2	2.20	7.40
PVP	212	122	138	462
Customer choice	✓	✗	✗	✓

Source: The author.

Figure 8.1. Price–Value Proposition: An Illustration

Back in 1966, Nobel laureate economist Kelvin Lancaster proposed[13] that when consumers buy something—from simple table salt to a car with thousands of components—they are essentially buying a bundle of attributes, and it is the configuration of attributes that delivers value to the buyer.[14] We can see this clearly in our thought experiment. Screen size was one among the attributes, and a large screen provided more value to Bindu but wasn't valuable to Biju who saw more value in a smaller screen. Wireless charging was of great value to Biju, but for Bindu this attribute was irrelevant.

---

[13] Kelvin J. Lancaster, 'A New Approach to Consumer Theory', *Journal of Political Economy* 74, no. 2 (1966): 132–157.

[14] Lancaster proposed a new approach to consumer demand theory as a counter to the many limitations of neo-classical microeconomic theory. Conjoint analysis, used commonly in marketing research, is conceptually similar to Lancaster's idea.

In making their purchase decisions, Biju and Bindu looked at the bundle of attributes and estimated the value they would derive from each bundle of attributes—how the product solves their job to be done. They checked the price–value proposition (PVP) for the two options. Sometimes we refer to this as 'bang for the buck'.

We have only considered a limited set of attributes of smartphones in the Biju–Bindu thought experiment. In real life, many more attributes will come into play. For maintenance- or consumable-intensive purchases like a car or printer, it's common for attributes such as durable life and those related to service needs, price of service, value and price of consumables to enter the calculus. PVP then captures lifetime value of the product in the numerator and price to be paid for the lifetime of the product, often referred to as total cost of ownership or TCO, in the denominator.

Our purchase decisions are guided by assessment of PVP for each option we are considering. Most often, the calculus of PVP happens in our mind, and we are not even conscious of it. When we have to decide on weighty purchases, we are likely to pull out the spreadsheet, as we are not sure that our mental calculus is reliable enough. Some of us pull out the spreadsheet even for monthly groceries, while the brave hearts do it for big ticket decisions, say when buying an apartment. Whether we explicitly do the comparison or not, whether we are conscious of it or not, we gravitate towards the option which makes sense, meaning higher PVP. This doesn't mean that we will always go for the cheapest option. We go for the option which gives us most benefit for the price we pay.

Davids who morph into Goliaths would have the best PVP in the market at that time, better than that of the incumbent Goliaths. Imitators, by copying the Goliaths in products and business models, don't do much to improve PVP for their potential customers. That explains why innovative challengers are far more threatening than imitators, more so when their breadth of attack covers the Goliath's mainstream customer base.

Rise of Davids

During the 1960s, the Japanese motorcycle makers invaded America. In an arena till then ruled by Harley-Davidson and BSA/Triumph, the Japanese upstarts, Honda and its ilk started from nowhere to achieve market dominance in less than a decade. Both British and American motorcycle makers saw declining sales volumes and financial loss.[15] A worried British government commissioned a study to understand reasons for the decline of British motorcycle industry and to come up with strategy alternatives. A key conclusion of the study has come to be popularly known as 'experience curve effect.'[16] That's a jargon to say that as you produce more, your unit cost will come down.

Bruce Henderson observed that the 'correlation between competitive profitability and market share was strikingly apparent' in several industries such as motorcycles, television components and semiconductors.[17] The takeaway for managers was that the business which garners the highest market share over time would also be the most profitable, by virtue of being the lowest cost producer.[18] As the report to the British Parliament observes, 'Annual production volume, both overall and at the individual model level, emerges as the key factor determining relative cost position among competitors.'[19]

---

[15] E. Tatum Christensen and Richard T. Pascale, 'Honda (A)' (Harvard Business School Case 9-384-049, 16 March 2011).

[16] The Boston Consulting Group, *Strategy Alternatives for the British Motorcycle Industry* (London: Her Majesty's Stationery Office, 30 July 1975). Available at: https://www.gov.uk/government/publications/strategy-alternatives-for-the-british-motorcycle-industry (accessed 8 June 2021).

[17] Bruce Henderson, 'The Experience Curve Reviewed: Part II', 1 January 1973. Available at: https://www.bcg.com/publications/1973/corporate-finance-strategy-portfolio-management-experience-curve-reviewed-part-ii-the-history (accessed 8 June 2021).

[18] Market share, driven by volume of production and sales, is supposed to bring forth benefits of economies of scale in the value chain of activities.

[19] The Boston Consulting Group, *Strategy Alternatives for the British Motorcycle*, xi.

To be fair, Henderson pointed out that while 'the effect itself is beyond question', 'understanding of the underlying causes of the experience curve is still imperfect'.[20] What Henderson and team observed as 'correlation between profitability and market share' was in fact a spurious correlation driven by a third unobserved variable, which resulted in superior PVP vis-à-vis rivals and also led to superior profitability sustained over time. To understand that, we need to get into another thought experiment.

You are managing a business which is one among the challengers in a market. The dominant player has a sizeable market share and is profitable. Not all the customers are happy with what's being offered by the dominant player, but they stick to buying from it, as the alternatives from other players in the arena are worse in terms of PVP. Either the attributes and quality of offerings from other players are lacking or the price is higher, or both.

You decide that following the dominant player is not going to be beneficial and look for opportunities to be distinctive. You make investments to find out how you can be distinctive and focus on broadly two areas. First, through careful observation, you identify poorly met or unmet jobs to be done among sections of customers. These are most likely to be some of the market segments and niches and related use cases ignored by the dominant player. You come up with products which better solve these jobs to be done compared to the dominant player's offering. You target your marketing campaigns to the segment of customers (or even a niche) where your product is likely to provide a superior PVP.

Second, you look for opportunities where you can reduce your cost. These would be through improved product design, better efficiency in operations and processes, higher productivity, reduced waste, savings in sourcing inputs and so on.

---

[20] Henderson, 'The Experience Curve Reviewed'.

The combination of the two focus areas for investments results in two outcomes. First, your product attributes and quality improve,[21] at least for customers in the segment or niche you are targeting. As a result, more customers perceive your products to have a superior PVP compared to the dominant player. These customers flock to you. You have gained customers who will stick with you, and at least for a while they might even pay you a premium. Even with a discount from the dominant player, these customers may not switch back, as the product they now get from you is a better fit for their job to be done, significantly upping the PVP for these customers. Your investments in the superior product give a kick to your sales volume and at the same time boost your margins.

Meanwhile, let's say your investments in lowering cost and improving efficiency bear fruit, resulting in higher margins. With margins improving from two sources—higher premium and lower cost—you are now able to lower your prices, at the same time keeping for yourself a modest improvement in profitability. The lower price further improves your PVP, which in turns brings more customers to you, all at higher profitability.

Both the number of customers and quantity sold of your products grow. Your margin per product sold grows with higher profitability. The combined effect of the two results in more profits in absolute dollar sums. That's higher surplus, part of which you now reinvest in further innovation. As your business evolves over time, PVP of your products becomes vastly superior to that of rivals, including the dominant player, driving up your quantity sold and your market share. The higher profitability with higher quantity sold drives up your profits, which in turn allows for more investments in innovation.

You are able to attract mainstream customers of the dominant player as PVP from your products tends to improve over time and becomes better than the PVP of dominant player's offering for mainstream

---

[21] Product attributes improve in the sense that now these provide better value to target customers.

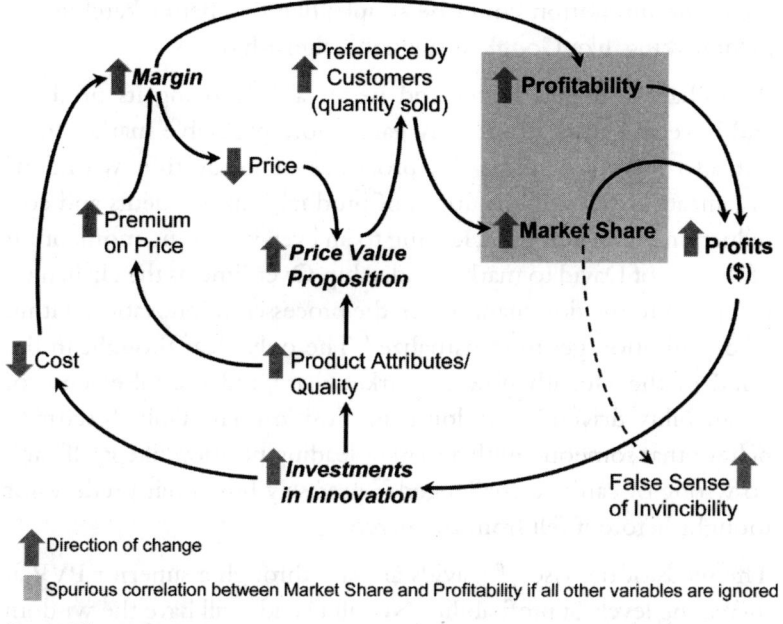

↑ Direction of change

▨ Spurious correlation between Market Share and Profitability if all other variables are ignored

Source: The author.

Figure 8.2. Evolution of David into Goliath

customers. You are now in a virtuous loop of increasing investments in innovation, driving up profitability, absolute profits and market share. As more customers flock to you, the dominant player starts losing customers, as the market size is finite. Over time, your market share becomes large enough that you are recognized as 'the' dominant player, dislodging the earlier Goliath. You have evolved from a David to the Goliath.

Henderson and colleagues looked only at market share and profitability, the two variables in the grey box in Figure 8.2, and concluded that there is a strong correlation. The only correlation they saw was spurious, as both market share and profitability are driven concurrently by 'investments in innovation'. The drivers of superior profitability and market share were superior products and lower cost, which were in turn driven by investments in innovation.

Here, the innovation could be simple, like the 'better ketchup' or pathbreaking, like Google's page rank algorithm.

As a challenger gets better and better at improving its products and lowering costs, it not only gains more profitable market share but also institutionalizes the processes of innovation within its organization. Soon the routines of product improvements and cost reduction go on autopilot, leading to an ever-increasing momentum of the rise of David to market leadership. Over time, as the challenger morphs into the dominant player, the processes of innovation within its organization get more ritualized. The only clear thought in the mind of the Goliath now is market share and the false sense of invincibility driven by its dominant position. The Goliath starts to believe that someone with a market leading position like itself can't go wrong or can't be challenged,[22] precisely how their predecessor thought before it fell from the perch.

The seeds of the rise of Davids are laid through a superior PVP at increasing levels of profitability. Not all Davids will have the wisdom to invest in distinctive product attributes or lower cost, or both. These are the superior weapons that the innovative Davids bring to the battle. Those who bring these have a higher chance of mounting a credible challenge to the reigning Goliath. Over time, some of the battle-ready Davids are able to dislodge Goliaths and take their place. It is these battle-ready Davids that the Goliaths find challenging to guard against.

Countering Davids

The dominant player's repertoire of approaches to guard against Davids can be seen as falling into two categories. The first are a set of 'deterrent actions' which are aimed at forestalling incursions by challengers. The second are a set of responses which are meant to 'drive out or thwart the rise of challengers' who managed to make

---

[22] There are examples of dominant players who did not fall victim to this hubris, but that's often an exception rather than the rule.

incursions. The second set of approaches kicks in when incursions do happen, in spite of deterrence, and we will deal with these in the next chapter. We now focus on the first set—deterrent actions.

DETERRING INCURSIONS

The best way for a Goliath to guard against Davids is to dissuade the Davids from making incursions. Deterrence is better than defence. The dominant players can build formidable moats and forts around their stronghold in the arena which Davids find impossible to cross and scale. These can dissuade potential new entrants from attempting to enter or can dissuade existing players from making incursions into the dominant player's turf. Such entry or mobility barriers erected by the dominant players would make the challengers' business case for incursion unviable by escalating the cost of entry.

Chest Thumping

Goliaths resort to 'chest thumping' from time to time, announcing to anyone who bothers to listen that they are serious about defending their turf. Davids ought to be discouraged from making incursions which would eat into Goliath's base. This is not focused on any particular challenger or any episode of incursion. This is a signal to all that the Goliath is fiercely guarding its turf and will retaliate with force to repulse any attempt at incursion.

Robert Wilson describes 'signalling' as '[an] incumbent firm reliably [conveying] information that discourages unprofitable entry or survival of competitors'.[23] The key here is credibility of the message that the Goliath is putting out. Credibility itself comes from two sources. First, the message will be more credible if it's backed by more costly and irreversible commitments. Second, the message will

---

[23] Robert Wilson, 'Strategic Models of Entry Deterrence', in *Handbook of Game Theory*, Vol. I, eds R. J. Aumann and Sergiu Hart (Amsterdam: North-Holland, 1992), 307.

be credible if it's consistent with the reputation of the dominant player.

When market leader Eli Lilly announced its intentions in the late 1970s to commercialize biotech insulin, it was a clear signal to most of the smaller incumbent players that the new technology might be too much for them to chew. Eli Lilly made initial investments in excess of US$100 million in biotech insulin. Around the same time, it also entered new geographic markets such as Western Europe, UK and Japan, which it had hitherto kept away from, indicating that it would not shy away from increased rivalry in new geographical markets so as to be profitable on its investments in new technology and related production capacity.[24] Both these actions were costly and highly irreversible, lending credibility to Eli Lilly's signal to other players in the arena that it was pursuing a new technology with which it intended to dominate the global insulin market.

Reputation is built over time, based on consistency in past actions, as we saw in Chapter 5. Thus, specific responses to incursions by challengers have two objectives. First is to respond to the incursion. Second is to add a datapoint to the pattern of actions that any potential challenger will look at, to assess the likely response of the dominant player to an incursion. Dominant players often respond forcefully and aggressively, just to set an example and discourage future challengers from making incursions.

During the early years of Android, the leading Android handset maker was the Taiwanese company HTC. As HTC started making inroads into the American market, Apple sued HTC for patent infringement. Interestingly, Apple sued HTC in the District Court for the District of Delaware and also with the US International Trade Commission. The case against HTC in the US International Trade Commission was an interesting twist. The US International Trade Commission could not award damages, but it could ban

---

[24] Michael J. Enright, 'Novo Industri' (Harvard Business School Case 9-389-148, 21 January 1994).

import of HTC's phones into the USA.[25] Thus, Apple signalled to HTC as well as to future challengers that it would aggressively guard its turf in the USA.

Chest thumping, made credible by costly and irreversible commitments as well as a strong reputation for aggressive responses, significantly dampens the interest of challengers to mount incursions. But that's not enough to keep out the determined Davids.

Moats and Forts

The US soft drinks industry was highly fragmented in the early decades of the 20 century but evolved into a duopoly by the early 1990s. By 1992, Coca-Cola and Pepsi together held 72 per cent of the market, against 54 per cent in 1966.[26] Many of the incumbents exited, and the market wasn't viable for entry. During the two intervening decades, the cola majors had built moats and forts around their soft drinks business.

Product Proliferation

The first wave of barrier building in the cola industry was in the form of new product launches. During the 15 years from the mid-1960s to the late 1970s, Coca-Cola launched 21 new brands and Pepsi launched 24.[27] Several brands which are popular today, such as Fanta, Sprite, Mountain Dew and Slice, were launched during this period. Diet or sugar-free variants of popular brands were first launched during this time. The brand launches were backed with heavy advertising.

---

[25] Eric Schonfeld, 'Apple Goes after HTC in 20 iPhone Patents', TechCrunch, 2 March, 2010. Available at: https://techcrunch.com/2010/03/02/apple-goes-after-htc-in-lawsuit-over-20-iphone-patents/ (accessed 8 June 2021).
[26] Sharon Foley and David B. Yoffie, 'Cola Wars Continue: Coke vs. Pepsi in the 1990's' (Harvard Business School Case 9-794-055, 31 March 2000).
[27] Ibid.

According to Donald Hay, 'Firms in a differentiated industry ... seek to proliferate products to fill up those parts of quality space where there could be sufficient consumer demand to attract new entry.'[28] The first wave—wide variety of new soft drinks—erected barriers primarily by ensuring that most of the profitable niches in the market were filled up by products put out by the dominant players. Pepsi wasn't yet one of the dominant players in the industry during the 1960s. Yet its relative success in establishing itself in new niches led to its evolution as one of the dominant players by the 1970s. This approach—'product proliferation'—has been adopted successfully by Apple with their range of iPods, and later by Samsung with their range of feature phones and smartphones. Once the dominant player carpet bombs the market with a wide range of products covering all possible jobs-to-be-done niches, incumbent or potential challengers find it difficult to gain a viable toehold in the arena.

Upping MVM

The second wave of barrier building by cola majors during the 1980s saw significant escalation in advertising spends through celebrity endorsements. Pepsi signed up Michael Jackson who was at the peak of his popularity then. Pepsi also roped in Michael J. Fox, the star of hit movie franchise *Back to the Future*, for a series of youth-oriented advertisements.[29] Coca-Cola responded by lining up celebrity endorsers Elton John, Paula Abdul, Whitney Houston and Selena Gomez. How does this build moats and forts?

Prior to this, the most scale-intensive activity in the soft drinks value chain was bottling. Even then, a bottler just needed about 1.2 per cent

---

[28] Donald A. Hay, 'Sequential Entry and Entry-deterring Strategies in Spatial Competition', *Oxford Economic Papers* 28, no. 2 (1976): 253.

[29] Pepsi would continue this tradition during the next decades by securing endorsement of several celebrities such as Shakira, Britney Spears, Beyoncé, Katy Perry and Ricky Martin.

market share[30] to achieve efficient scale.[31] The celebrity-endorsed television advertising which was broadcast nationally entailed significantly high fixed costs in terms of fees for celebrities, cost of production which was comparable with Hollywood movies and cost of prime-time media slots which reach national audience. To recoup these high costs at a few cents per bottle, the product had to sell in massive volumes. In short, by making celebrity-endorsed advertising a norm in the industry, Coca-Cola and Pepsi drove up the MVM, making it unviable for small or sub-national players to stay in the market.

Eli Lilly's investments in biotech insulin significantly increased the MVM from the perspective of MES for production. Earlier, when insulin was extracted from animal pancreas, a 7 per cent share of the global market would be sufficient for a player to fully utilize the benefit from economies of scale. At that MVM, an insulin maker could focus on its national market and remain profitable. Biotech insulin brought down production costs but required higher levels of investment for both R&D and setting up production facilities. This jacked up the MVM to about 40 per cent of global market.[32] Only the second largest player Novo followed Eli Lilly into biotech insulin. Innovation of new production technology for biotech insulin rendered smaller players unviable in the production of active ingredient. Most of them— Squibb, Wellcome, Continental Serum Labs and Connaught Labs— became customers of Eli Lilly and Novo for insulin active ingredient.

Gillette, as we saw in the previous chapter, engaged in aggressive innovation. Their rivals should either spend less on R&D and trail Gillette in product innovation or be less profitable with higher allocated R&D cost per unit, as the higher base of R&D spend by Gillette increases MVM. As a result, Gillette was able to maintain a lead over rival Schick in its ability to bring out new and improved products to market for several decades.[33]

---

[30] Foley and Yoffie, 'Cola Wars Continue'.

[31] This means that about 80 players can be viably active in the industry.

[32] Enright, 'Novo Industri'.

[33] Whether the extra blades and lubricating strips are really useful is a question that DSC brought in front of customers.

Increasing MVM through strategic action—advertising, innovation in production technology and aggressive product innovation—all result in heightened barriers to entry and mobility. Faced with such strategic actions by the dominant players, incumbent challengers find it tough to expand out of their current market space. Potential entrants most likely back out due to unviable business cases.

Lock-in/Lock-out

Challengers need to attract new customers, and dominant players often thwart this by locking in customers. They lock out challengers from gaining access to their customers. Microsoft, through a combination of business arrangements and technical features, locked in customers to its Windows PC operating system. Its dominance in the PC operating systems has sustained over nearly three decades.

Brand building has the potential to create strong lock-in with at least a section of customers. The Body Shop demonstrated that it's possible to lock in customers by appealing to their values.[34] Tesla has been working on building a loyal client base who believe in going green without giving up on style or performance—'people didn't need to compromise to drive electric.'[35]

Lock-in is possible not just with customers but other participants in the industry value chain as well. Suppliers and partners can be locked in to ensure that challengers have limited-to-no ability to grow. Lock-in of partners in the industry value chain is more durable and effective if it involves commitments by them. Commitments can be in the form of contractual obligations or the need to invest in assets which are specific to business with the dominant player. When Robert Taylor of Softsoap tied up the plastic pump manufacturers with a purchase order for a full year's production, he was relying on the suppliers honouring their contracts.

---

[34] https://www.thebodyshop.com/en-gb/about-us (accessed 8 June 2021).
[35] https://www.tesla.com/about (accessed 8 June 2021).

When contractual commitments require the use of specialized assets, the partner is likely to insist on reciprocal commitments, as they will need to earn a return on their investment. Bottlers of Coca-Cola or Pepsi aren't allowed to bottle competing soft drinks. Since the bottlers make the investments for the production facility and distribution, the cola majors sign multi-year contracts which grant the bottlers exclusivity to cater to demand in a geographic area.[36] All these will lock out challengers from gaining access to whatever the partner brings to the game.

Government-granted Moats and Forts

Government-granted monopolies are supposed to provide a period of competition-free business to whoever gets it. Tolled infrastructure such as roads built by private-sector players provide uncontested revenues for the duration of the toll. Patents give the innovator the right to either monopolize the market or extract value from other users of patented technology through licence fees. Patents are meant to assure a reasonable return to the inventor for the risky and often unsuccessful investments they make in R&D. Clever Goliaths create thickets of patents around their products with a view to making their monopoly better guarded. Challengers would find it extremely difficult to overcome or bypass such a moat around the dominant player's product.

Trademarks which are essential for branding protect the owners from copycats trying to undermine the brand value embodied in the trademark. Copyright prevents the use of a creative work by anyone other than those who own it. Legendary cartoonist Walt Disney released *Steamboat Willie*, featuring Mickey Mouse, in 1928.[37] The character Mickey Mouse is protected as a copyright and as a trademark, both owned by The Walt Disney Company. Disney has enjoyed its intellectual property (IP) rights over Mickey Mouse and other characters for almost a century now, allowing them to leverage

---

[36] Foley and Yoffie, 'Cola Wars Continue'.
[37] https://en.wikipedia.org/wiki/Steamboat_Willie (accessed 8 June 2021).

this monopoly through direct use in their theme parks, movies, television channels as well as third-party licensing for merchandising and other uses.

Government-granted moats and forts do not automatically assure that there won't be any challenge, as BSB found out the hard way.[38] When BSB won the licence for DSB to UK in 1986, it thought that it had an airtight monopoly. BSB was a joint venture backed by several private-sector players active in television and media industries. BSB went about the launch of its service at a sedate pace. The launch was planned for September 1989. It went through rounds of massive financing and also prioritized several activities which were not that essential for a launch.

As top managers of BSB were busy choosing the colour of carpets for their new office building—'an essay in post-modernism yet to be built in UK'—Rupert Murdoch announced that Sky would launch direct-to-home satellite service for UK. Sky's lead time from announcement to launch was a mere nine months, and it beat BSB to become the first to launch. What ensued was a vicious battle, with Sky and BSB fighting it out home by home to win customers, each losing several million sterling pounds a week. BSB eventually called quits and got acquired by Sky. The key assumption made by BSB— their licence grants them an unassailable monopoly—did not hold. Sky found loopholes to bypass the licence and provide direct-to-home television services to UK customers. The holder of mandated monopoly needs to work on making sure that their ability to appropriate value is not undermined by innovative challengers.

Stay Ahead in the Game

By far, the most promising approach to forestalling Davids is for the Goliath to stay ahead of challengers. This requires the dominant player to keep a keen eye on emerging changes in customers' jobs to be done as well as new opportunities arising from emerging changes in technology. The seeds of credible challenges lie in these. The very nature of a dominant player often handicaps their ability to spot, track and act on such changes and challenges.

---

[38] Ghemawat, 'British Satellite Broadcasting'.

It took several years before HLL realized and recognized Nirma as a rival. During that time, Nirma gained more customers and also entered other categories which HLL was dominating. Although HLL created the market for NSD powder, it hardly built any moats and forts around that market. The delay in HLL taking cognizance of the challenge by Nirma made it easier for Nirma to gain foothold and grow. It also made it more difficult for HLL to fight back Nirma. Why are Goliaths often blind to incursions by Davids? Once challengers are recognized for what they are, how can the dominant player fight back? We will focus on these questions next.

« LONG STORY » « SHORT »

Davids come in two types: imitators who copy products and business models of dominant players and innovators who come up with novel products and business models. Innovating challengers come up with products and business models which result in a superior PVP for a segment of customers, better than PVP offered by the dominant player. Innovative Davids morph into Goliaths as more and more customers prefer them due to their superior PVP. Often, Goliaths fail to notice the threat. It is easier to fight back imitators than innovating challengers. Dominant players can signal their intention to protect their turf fiercely; the signal will be credible only if backed by costly/irreversible commitments and a reputation built through past actions. Battle-ready dominant players heighten the entry and mobility barriers to discourage any potential challenge from new entry and pin down incumbent challengers.

CHAPTER NINE

Guarding against Davids

Back in 1977, Sidartha Sen, then marketing director of HLL, was on a tour of the North Indian state of Uttar Pradesh. While at a small retailer (called *kirana*) in a village, Sen observed the shopkeeper briskly selling plastic bags of yellow detergent powder, priced at one-third that of Surf, the HLL's detergent. Sen was paying careful attention to this phenomenon during this field visit. HLL had been losing a competitive battle that it did not even realize it was fighting.[1] The yellow detergent powder was Nirma, launched by Karsanbhai Patel eight years earlier.

By the time HLL realized the threat to its detergent business from Nirma, the challenger had built a high momentum for market growth and was capturing most of it. Nirma continued to consolidate its presence in the market for another decade. By 1987, Nirma sold about 250,000 tonnes of detergent, a growth of 16 times in 10 years. It captured more than 60 per cent of the market, while HLL's share dropped to less than 8 per cent.[2] The decade-long effort by HLL started to show results from 1988 onwards, when Nirma's share

---

[1] Butler and Ghoshal, 'Hindustan Lever Limited'.
[2] Ibid.

started declining. HLL had to fight inch by inch to take back some of the lost ground.

The longer it takes the Goliath to spot the incursion by David and act decisively, the more entrenched and stronger the David will get, making it more difficult for the (former) Goliath to fight back. Goliaths are better off guarding against incursions by Davids if they act early and swiftly. Unfortunately, the very nature of Goliaths makes it difficult for them to do so. We will understand the reasons why Goliaths realize too late that they are at war. We will then look at how to fight back Davids who have already made incursions.

WHY GOLIATHS FALTER?

'There's no chance that the iPhone is going to get any significant market share.'[3] This was Steve Ballmer in 2007, then CEO of Microsoft, on the launch of iPhone. He wasn't alone in dismissing Apple's foray into mobile phones. 'It's kind of one more entrant into an already very busy space with lots of choice for consumers, [but] in terms of a sort of a sea-change for BlackBerry, I would think that's overstating it,' was how Jim Bastille, co-CEO of Research In Motion (RIM), dismissed iPhone as a threat to Blackberry.[4] Padmasree Warrior, CTO of Motorola, the number two in mobile phones then, was sceptical too: 'There is nothing revolutionary or disruptive about any of the technologies [in iPhone] … [all these] are already available in products from leaders in the mobile industry—Motorola, Nokia and Samsung.'[5]

---

[3] Mark Sullivan, '10 of the Most Interesting Reactions to the First iPhone Back in 2007', Fast Company, 28 June 2017. Available at: https://www.fastcompany.com/40436054/10-of-the-most-interesting-reactions-to-the-first-iphone-back-in-2007 (accessed 8 June 2021).

[4] Wojtek Dabrowski, 'RIM Co-CEO Doesn't See Threat from Apple's iPhone', Reuters Technology News, 12 February 2007. Available at: https://www.reuters.com/article/us-rim-iphone/rim-co-ceo-doesnt-see-threat-from-apples-iphone-idUSN1236561320070212 (accessed 8 June 2021).

[5] Padmasree Warrior, 'iPhone, uPhone, We all Phone', Motorola Blog, 10 January 2007. Available at: https://web.archive.org/web/20070114215511/http://blogs.motorola.com/author/padmasree-warrior/ (accessed 8 June 2021).

With hindsight, we can say that Microsoft, Blackberry and Motorola, not to leave out market leader Nokia, did not realize iPhone for what it would be. Could any of them have seen the launch and subsequent development of iPhone differently without the benefit of hindsight? Could they have realized earlier the competitive threat from iPhone? Could they have judged how iPhone would impact their mobile phone business? Without timely insights on potential threats and the likely impact on our business, guarding against such threats is a lost cause.

Michael Porter defines 'blind spots' as 'areas where a competitor will either not see the significance of events (such as a strategic move) at all, will perceive them incorrectly, or will perceive them only very slowly'.[6] Blind spots are gaps in competition-relevant insights in the minds of managers of a business. This denies them the chance to take timely and appropriate competitive action, be it pre-emption or response.

In the normal course of business, an organization gathers competition-relevant information, processes it to gain insights, and decides and acts on competitive moves. Typically, competition-relevant information is gathered at boundary-spanning parts of the organization such as sales, procurement, logistics and customer service, where members have an opportunity to access information from external stakeholders. These members, however, are not those who are best placed to make sense of the information and come up with competition-relevant insights. The information is passed on to those parts of the organization where it can be best used. Typically, that's the job of senior managers as well as specialized units whose purpose is to process such information and gain competitive insights, such as strategy or market intelligence teams. The competitive insights gained become the basis of timely and effective competitive action or response.

Any glitch or breakdown in the process of gathering, passing on and making sense of competition-relevant information will likely result in a blind spot. The organization which carries out the business may

---

[6] Porter, *Competitive Strategy*, 59.

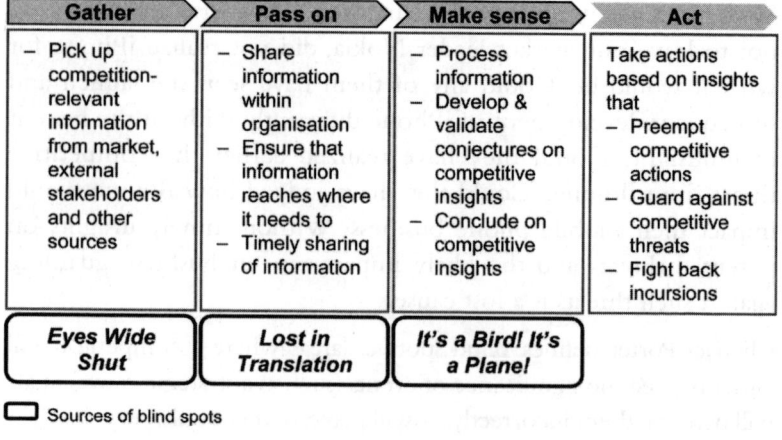

Gather	Pass on	Make sense	Act
– Pick up competition-relevant information from market, external stakeholders and other sources	– Share information within organisation – Ensure that information reaches where it needs to – Timely sharing of information	– Process information – Develop & validate conjectures on competitive insights – Conclude on competitive insights	Take actions based on insights that – Preempt competitive actions – Guard against competitive threats – Fight back incursions
Eyes Wide Shut	**Lost in Translation**	**It's a Bird! It's a Plane!**	

☐ Sources of blind spots

Source: The author.

Figure 9.1. From Competition-relevant Information to Competitive Action

not gather relevant information. The information might be gathered but might be stuck in a place where it's not used or might reach the appropriate part of organization too late. The information reaches the appropriate part of the organization in time, but the insights derived from the information may turn out to be incorrect.

Most of the mobile phone and smartphone makers did not figure out in time how iPhone would change the world of mobile devices. They were looking but 'didn't see'. Failure in any of the process stages—gather, pass on, make sense—results in blind spots (see Figure 9.1). Some organizations suffer from blind spots arising from failures in more than one of these process stages. Many of the blind spots can be corrected or compensated for. For that, we need to understand why they occur. We need to understand why information isn't picked up, why information doesn't go to the right place at the right time and why we go wrong in making sense of the information.[7]

---

[7] Even after making sense, some businesses may be unable to take appropriate action/response due to lack of capabilities. So being able to avoid blind spots is not the end of the story.

Eyes Wide Shut

BSB was the sole winner of the UK government's bid which awarded licence and spectrum for high-power direct-to-home satellite television broadcasting in the early 1990s. It assumed that it was a monopolist and didn't bother to look out for competition. It was blissfully ignorant of any competitive threat till Sky announced its entry even before BSB launched its service (see Chapters 1 and 8). It is common for top managers of businesses to assume that they have an unassailable market position, based on government-mandated monopoly privileges such as licences and patents. High market share is another key reason why managers assume that they are invincible. This self-deluding and false sense of invincibility results in break-down of the first process stage—'gathering' competition-relevant information.

Most large companies are in the habit of telling themselves and their employees that they are the best. This happens as part of new joiner orientation and is often repeated by top management in town hall meetings and internal communications. Not all employees take such messages too seriously. But there are many who would believe this message. It's natural to expect that the believers would be oblivious to the need to tune their antennae to competition-relevant information. After all, 'We are the best.'

To be fair, managers highlight challenges and what can go wrong in town halls, internal meetings and communications. But there is usually a bias towards the positive side, especially if recent performance has met or exceeded expectations. Oftentimes, a false sense of invincibility pervades the organization, all the way to the top.

Market leaders often tend to believe that they are 'the chosen one'. This belief is formed and reinforced by the prominence and deference that managers of the market-leading firm are given by industry bodies, business press and governments. Managers of the market-leading firm often consider this 'respect' to be an entitlement, not something earned through hard work. Concepts like price leadership[8] reinforce this thinking. Beliefs such as 'We are the chosen one' or 'We are the best' put managers and the whole organization in a state of 'eyes wide shut'. Their antennae, which ought to pick up competition-relevant information, are disconnected or weak at best. They remain blissfully ignorant about potential competitive threats till it's too late.

Large organizations, specifically those with several layers in their hierarchy, naturally restrict availability of information at various levels. A sizeable proportion of organizational members are exposed mostly to operational information relevant for their activities. The big picture gets more unclear as we move away from the top management. Posters of vision, mission and values which adorn corridors and shop floors are supposed to give the big picture view of business down to the last employee, but these are mostly ignored. Members of the organization who are removed from the top by several layers of management are often oblivious to an understanding of what's competition-relevant for their business. Even if such information jumps up and down in front of them in colourful costumes while banging on a pair of outsized cymbals, they won't take a second look. Providing the whole organization with a useful big picture view is an essential role of the top and senior management, but this often does not get top priority.

More than half a century ago, Theodore Levitt admonished managers not to hold a restricted view of the scope of their business.[9] For instance, he urged managers of oil companies to think about competing in energy business. Levitt's call was to broaden managers' view about competition so that they were able to spot, in time, what's going on beyond the narrow confines of their industry, direct rivals and dominant technology—avoiding tunnel vision of competition-relevant information. In a 1991 interview to *Fortune* magazine, Steve

---

[8] The market leader sets price, and all other players follow. If not, the leader punishes the erring small players in the market.

[9] Levitt, 'Marketing Myopia'.

Jobs had said, 'When IBM [leader in mainframe computers] entered the market [for PCs in 1982], we did not take it seriously enough.... We were shipping tens of thousands of machines a month—more computers than IBM [had ever sold].'[10] That was Jobs admitting that those days Apple didn't consider IBM to be a rival in their PC business, only to be proven wrong in just a few years.

Managers use classification schemes (or taxonomies) to simplify their understanding of the competitive arena.[11] They identify as competitors, those who are similar to themselves in 'form'—size, geographic presence, business model, resource endowments, goals and such. HLL would have readily acknowledged Tata Oil Mills Company (TOMCO), part of the Tata business group, as a rival in the market for soaps and detergents during the 1970s more because TOMCO conformed to HLL's conception of a competitor, someone who is similar in form. Nirma did not conform to this form, at least not in the first decade of its existence. It is not surprising that HLL had great difficulty 'recognizing' Nirma as a competitive threat even after Nirma was driving market growth and HLL had lost a sizeable share of market to Nirma. As we saw in our discussion on competitor radar in Chapter 4, it is a lot easier to spot direct rivals—those with whom we have high resource similarity and market commonality. It's tougher to spot smaller competitors, rivals with different business models, substitutors or potential entrants, as these players take 'forms' which are different from ours. Managers filter out as irrelevant any and all information about players who don't fit their conception of a rival—another driver of missing out on competition-relevant information.

Same goes for information and trends related to suppliers, customers, industries and technology. Anything that is about participants who

---

[10] Brenton R. Schlender, 'Jobs and Gates Together', *Fortune*, 26 August 1991.
[11] Joseph F. Porac and Howard Thomas, 'Taxonomic Mental Models in Competitor Definition', *Academy of Management Review* 15, no. 2 (1990): 224–240.

do not conform to the form is mostly discarded. With all this information filtered out, what's picked up, passed on and made sense of is just a narrow set of information which is already all too familiar. Anything unfamiliar, when it bites, is a total surprise. That's how businesses end up with their eyes wide shut.

Lost in Translation

Competition-relevant information is not of much use until it reaches the place within the organization where it can be processed for insights. This transportation problem is daunting for most organizations, especially large ones, which Goliaths invariably are. Three things come in the way of efficient and timely passing on of information within organizations.

Sébastien Bazin, CEO of Accor group, observes that many members of traditional, large organizations do not share information but hoard it as they believe it gives power.[12] Organizations have tried to break this behavioural trait by putting in place systems and processes which necessitate information sharing, but these fail miserably as there is no way to ascertain that useful information is indeed not hoarded. It requires a change in the worldview of members of an organization that hoarding information is harmful to the organization and, as a result, harmful to themselves.

Organizations are like a live organism which changes and evolves over time. However, in the minds of members of an organization, including its managers, there exists a fairly stable view of what the organization is and how it works. And then there is the view of the organization as depicted in the formal organization structure, job descriptions and such, which are meant to facilitate coordination and communication among different parts to work towards a common purpose. These views do not look similar, and this can be confusing. Members of the organization end up with differing views

---

[12] Sébastien Bazin at HICAP 2016. Available at: https://youtu.be/Rg7P7It0D_A (accessed 8 June 2021).

of what the organization really is, what its various parts are and how they function. Paths to communicate and coordinate get fuzzy. While the formal structure of the organization may show clear paths to communicate, many of these paths would be viewed by members as non-existent or, worse, booby-trapped, resulting in reluctance to pass on information. Gaps between as-is and should-be lines of communication and coordination mean that information just won't flow even if members are willing to share.

'Are you sure?' is a common response to information passed on from outside. 'Outside' could be anyone who is identified as not belonging to the team that receives the information. What's at work is a negative attitude towards information from external sources, held irrespective of the objective value of that information—not invented here (NIH) syndrome.[13] This bias results in organization members applying a discount to the value of information which is passed from other parts of the organization. One of the reasons why senior managers end up ignoring early warnings about competitive threats, to their peril, is this bias. Teams that are supposed to make sense of competition-relevant information ought to be free of such a bias, but in reality that's not the case.

In many instances, these three phenomena—belief that information is power, fuzziness in lines of communication and NIH bias—result in information loss or considerable delay in passing on information. The organization which is denied timely use of competition-relevant information loses the opportunity to generate competition-relevant insights to drive actions.

It's a Bird! It's a Plane!

The leading mobile phone makers in 2007—Nokia, Motorola and RIM—didn't realize how iPhone would change mobile devices.

---

[13] David Antons and Frank T. Piller, 'Opening the Black Box of "Not Invented Here": Attitudes, Decision Biases, and Behavioral Consequences', *Academy of Management Perspectives* 29, no. 2 (2015): 193–217.

Motorola dismissed it for not having any new tech. Nokia saw it as a weak product with a battery which requires charging daily, while Nokia's own phones lasted a whole week on a single charge. Blackberry believed that the touch keyboard in an iPhone was an apology to the physical keyboard in its own phones, which executives around the world adored those days.

Reviewers saw things differently. Jason Snell, reviewing iPhone for *Macworld*, was all praises for the touch screen keyboard and the software which predicted words being typed. 'With my index finger I managed to type faster than I ever have on a tiny device, physical keyboard or not.' He added that with practice, two-thumb typing on touch keyboards would be even faster.[14] John Gruber, another reviewer, was impressed with the display and the software which managed screen rendering. 'The high-resolution screen is gorgeous.... I haven't found a single element of the iPhone UI that doesn't feel super-snappy.'[15] Why is it that analysts were able to spot these seemingly innocuous but critical innovations, while the CEOs and CTOs of incumbent phone makers couldn't?

Much of the myopia that results in managers 'missing to see' what's happening out there comes from their mental models—the 'frames of reference' that we discussed in Chapter 5. For Nokia executives, long battery life was an essential feature of a mobile phone—without that, a product isn't a mobile phone. They believed that no one would buy a phone which requires daily charging. For Blackberry maker RIM, it was the keyboard. In their frames of reference, touch screen keyboards could not measure up to the physical keyboards which adorned Blackberry devices, and therefore iPhone was doomed to fail. That's what their frames of reference told them, and they believed in it.

---

[14] https://www.macworld.com/article/1058733/iphone-rev.html (accessed 8 June 2021).

[15] https://daringfireball.net/2007/06/iphone_first_impressions (accessed 8 June 2021).

As Shaker Zahra and Sherry Chaples observed, 'Well-intended dedication to a successful business concept becomes a dogma that prevents executives from seeing the connection between their existing product lines and emerging industry trends.'[16] Frames of reference are developed through experiences of the business and its managers. Over time, approaches which repeatedly yield success are adopted and ritualized, while those which do not bring success are discarded. Ritualized approaches give rise to axiomatic rules of thumb and dogma which guide sense-making and decision-making—rules which everyone in the organization follows, without much questioning. Managers start thinking alike, and alternate ways of making sense are not pursued, as they won't be beneficial or rewarding—George Orwell's 'group think'. Anything that's different, if not already ignored as irrelevant, is discounted as an anomaly or given an alternate explanation.

When Hans Rosling asked participants at the World Economic Forum, Davos—captains of industry and leaders of the world—three questions about readily verifiable facts such as level of poverty in the world, future population growth and access to primary health care, the responses for two out of three questions were wrong. Chimps picking answers randomly would have performed better, according to Rosling. He concluded that people (including those who visit Davos) tend to form their worldview based on data they were exposed to a decade or two earlier.[17] What came into the mind of the manager as an insight long ago based on facts of that day gradually morphs into a persistent idea and eventually becomes a dogma which refuses to be revalidated. Once such convictions take root in the mind of the manager, it takes existential threats to force the manager to revalidate these.

The reason why there is a need to revalidate insights which are based on past data is 'evolution'. The business environment, players,

---

[16] Shaker Zahra and Sherry Chaples, 'Blind Spots in Competitive Analysis', *Academy of Management Executive* 7, no. 2 (1993): 12.

[17] Hans Rosling, *Factfulness* (London: Hodder & Stoughton, 2018).

customers, technologies, regulatory regimes and managers, all change over time. We often ignore evolution or grossly underestimate its pace. A manager who had operated in a relatively benign market will continue to believe that the market is benign, even as it evolves over time to be far less benign. This inability to revalidate worldview has only one outcome—the manager's business gets clobbered by rivals in the now not-so-benign competitive arena.

As Davids discover new ways of doing things, be it business models, business practices or products, managers of the dominant incumbent stick to their outdated worldview of what the product means, or the business model and practices imply for competing. The Goliath fails to see the threat from David. Fact-based worldview would put emphasis on gathering data and updating insights periodically. Dr Rosling called this 'factfulness': 'the stress-reducing habit of only carrying opinions for which you have strong supporting facts'.[18] Factful managers are the exception.

In battle-ready businesses, the entire organization has a good idea of the big picture and is geared towards gathering competition-relevant information as part of their day-to-day activities. Members know who to pass on information to and how. Information reaches the right place without much delay and is not discounted by those who need to use it. Managers in battle-ready businesses are more factful, consciously trying to revalidate their frames of reference as new data emerges. They are better placed to derive appropriate insights in time and to act swiftly and decisively to their benefit.

GOLIATH'S GAME PLANS

Not all challengers are same, and not all incursions warrant a similar response from the dominant incumbent. The basis of attack by challengers varies depending on distinctiveness of challenger's solution to customers' job to be done, as well as the breadth of the challenger's attack—whether it targets a narrow market base or

---

[18] Ibid.

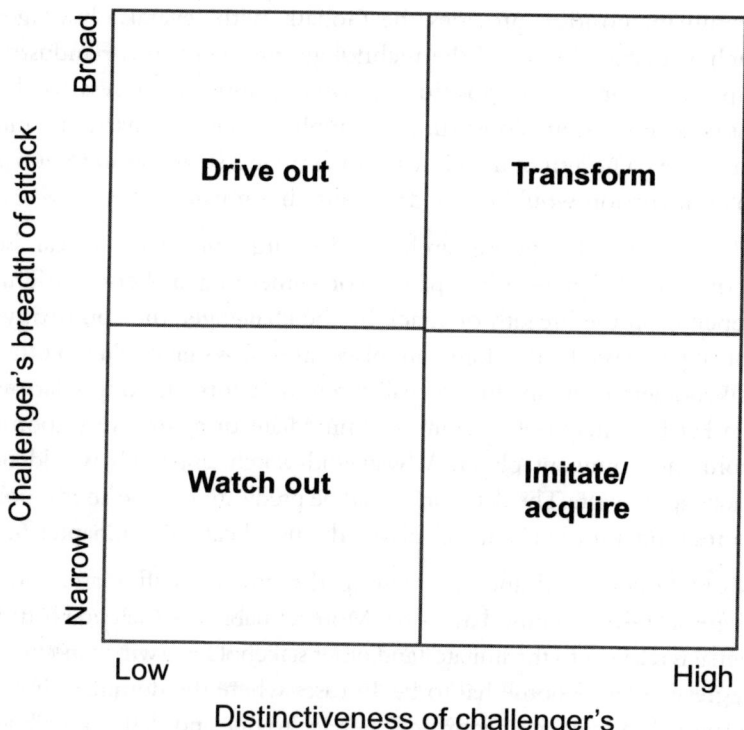

Figure 9.2. Fighting Back Challengers: Response Repertoire of Dominant Player

the entire market base of the dominant player. The response from Goliath needs to be calibrated to David's attack (see Figure 9.2).

Driving Out Imitators

Challengers impressed with the runaway success of the dominant incumbent often tend to imitate. While Goliaths face difficulty in spotting incursions, once they do spot, they can repulse imitators using a range of weapons which leverage their status quo advantage in the market. Imitation is not the smartest form of challenge.

Dominant position provides the Goliath with several advantages such as better control of the technology prevalent in the industry, superior relative cost position, as well as superior access to the business ecosystem consisting of suppliers, business partners and customers. The aim of the Goliath using these advantages in response to an incursion would be to 'drive out' the imitator.

The intensity of response can be mild—'target practice'—or can be ruthless and fierce—a 'rampage'—or something in between. This depends on the breadth of attack by the challenger, the competitive threat perceived by the dominant player as well as signal value to other stakeholders, including future challengers. Imitators attacking a narrow market base may not warrant an immediate or aggressive response from the dominant player. A 'wait-and-watch' approach would be more appropriate. The decision would be predicated by the 'motivation to respond' for the dominant player, discussed earlier in Chapter 6.

More broad-based and threatening the attack, swifter and more aggressive the response has to be. More valuable the 'defending turf' signal is relevant to the imitator and other stakeholders, swifter and more aggressive the response has to be. In cases where the dominant player wants to send out an unequivocal message to one and all that it will not even surrender an inch, the response can be disproportionately aggressive.

Leveraging Technology

Goliaths are likely to have better control over the dominant technology in their industry. This puts them at a relative advantage compared to challengers who do not have the same level of mastery in the technology or won't be in a position to invest as much in developing the technology further. The products from the challengers would mostly be similar to what the dominant player already brings out. At best, the imitating challenger's product would be marginally superior in terms of product attributes. Such superiority is likely to be temporary as the dominant player can quickly overtake the challenger, given its superior access to technology and resources.

To stay at the pole position, the dominant player has to consistently invest in technology in the form of R&D, product development as well as process upgrades. Focus of investments in technology could be wide ranging, such as exploiting scale and scope economies, enhancing product attributes and improving process efficiency across its value chain. These investments would result in capabilities which reinforce the dominant player's superior grip over the arena, as long as there is no fundamental shift in the dominant technology.

Intel's dominance of the microprocessor (processor) industry for three decades starting the early 1980s rested on the solid foundation of its mastery of dominant technology involved in design and manufacture of processors. Every time the cyclical semiconductor industry went through a downturn, players would go into hibernation, letting go of staff and reducing expenses. The first expense to be axed would typically be research, except at Intel. During downturns, Intel did let go of staff on the operational side, but it kept up its investments in research. Intel's research agenda was driven to stay true to Moore's law, named after co-founder Gordon Moore, who observed that the processing power of chips will double every 18 months, while cost will go down by half.[19] With its continued spend on research through ups and downs, Intel came out of downturns with superior next-generation products, while their rivals opened shop and dusted their old line-up. For three decades, Intel's technology dominance in processors was unmatched by rivals.[20]

Exploiting Cost Advantage

Some players ignore the cliched adage, 'Don't get into a price war.' Look carefully and you will find that these are players who have achieved the best-cost position. Having a lower cost structure vis-à-vis all rivals—being the best-cost player—is a formidable weapon

---

[19] Gordon Moore, 'Cramming More Components onto Integrated Circuits', *Electronics Magazine* 38, no. 8 (1965): 4.
[20] Michael S. Malone, *The Intel Trinity* (New York, NY: HarperCollins Publishers, 2014).

in a competitive battle. The best-cost player achieves this through persistent hard work over many years. Cost advantage should not be confused with cheap products. Cost advantage means that adjusting for differences in product attributes, the best-cost player incurs the least cost to produce, among rivals.

Best-cost players have two advantages in a competitive battle. They are able to undercut the prices of rivals in order to grab larger sales volume and market share. Their cost advantage lets them earn more profits than their rivals. The best-cost player ends up the largest and often the most profitable player.

Intel's employee number three Andrew Grove is credited with setting up the company's operations. Grove's unrelenting pursuit of operational excellence made Intel the best-cost player among makers of processors. After Grove moved on to become Intel's CEO, operations came under Craig Barrett,[21] who earned his stripes taking manufacturing efficiency of the increasingly complex Intel processors to new heights. During the three decades of its reign at the top, Intel was the best-cost player in semiconductor industry and that enabled it to dominate the market and earn superior profits.[22]

Tapping Superior Access to Business Partners

No business can survive without the support of its business partners—suppliers, customers, complementors, technology providers and others who form part of its business ecosystem. Dominant players enjoy superior access to business partners compared to their smaller rivals. Superior access to business partners allows the dominant player to influence the trajectory of change in its arena. This includes the trajectory of changes in technology, products and business model. Influence on these trends helps the dominant player reduce

---

[21] Craig Barrett later succeeded Grove as the CEO of Intel.
[22] Malone, *The Intel Trinity*.

uncertainties about future significantly. The technology would move along the lines envisioned by them. Products and business models would evolve over time in ways that reinforce their dominance. Influence on market dynamics enables the Goliath to sustain its dominance over time, by minimizing surprises from the business ecosystem.

Moore's law, the way Gordon Moore put it, was a descriptive technical statement on the evolution of the power of integrated circuits, with implications for evolution of power of processors and the cost of producing these. Moore's law enabled Intel to influence the semiconductor business ecosystem. Once Moore's law was widely accepted as an immutable law which governs the evolution of semiconductors, every player including Intel's rivals and business partners started calibrating their strategic direction along the dictates of this law.

Customers of Intel and its rivals—the PC makers—calibrated the expected increase in processing power based on Moore's law while designing their next line-up of PCs and laptops. Complementors such as independent software developers also started factoring in performance improvements in hardware, driven by Moore's law, in their product road maps. Suppliers such as Nikon, Canon and later ASML, who produced critical equipment used in manufacturing of semiconductor chips, made strategic choices on the basis of future requirements from chip makers, again driven by the trajectory aligned with Moore's law. Intel, with Moore's law, essentially aligned the evolutionary dynamics of the business of processors to a rhythm consistent with its own strategic direction. As long as Intel kept on investing in R&D to stay on Moore's law, its dominance of the market was assured.[23]

Rivals who tried to leapfrog Intel found no market and no means to bring their products to market. PC makers and software developers

---

[23] Ibid.

weren't willing to sign up for an ahead-of-time design of processor, as their product road map could accommodate this design only a few years later. Rivals who wanted to leapfrog Intel could not find equipment vendors who provided them the production technology and equipment for their ahead-of-time design. Leapfrogging Intel was just impossible. Lagging Intel meant that the rival was competing with an older-generation Intel product which was on the verge of getting commoditized. The only way to have some chance of making it was to stay on the trajectory dictated by Moore's law. But in that lane of the racetrack, Intel was ahead of all.

Combining It All

McKinsey & Company estimates that during 1996–2009, Intel captured economic profit of US$57 billion, compared to economic loss of US$47 billion by all other players in the semiconductor business ecosystem. A few others made positive economic profits. The profitable players excluding Intel made a combined profit of US$91 billion, while the loss-making players made a combined economic loss of US$138 billion. Intel made almost four times the profit of the second most profitable player.[24]

Intel's decades-long dominance of the market for processors was remarkable as it concurrently used all three approaches—leveraging technology, achieving best-cost position and influencing the business ecosystem. As Intel's designers worked to develop the next chip series in time to fit the dictates of Moore's law, the business ecosystem readied themselves to convert the design into a market-leading product. Grove and his successors developed and fine-tuned manufacturing processes which delivered the best efficiencies, aligned with the trajectory of product and production complexity predicted by

---

[24] McKinsey & Company, *McKinsey on Semiconductors* (McKinsey & Company Industry Publications, 2011). Available at: https://www.mckinsey.com/~/media/mckinsey/dotcom/client_service/semiconductors/pdfs/mosc_1_revised.ashx (accessed 8 June 2021).

Moore's law. Intel's dominance allowed little room for imitating challengers in the market.

Thwarting the Rise of Innovators

Intel's decades-long dominance in the arena for PC and server processors was the result of it being able to marginalize imitating challengers. With the advent of mobile internet devices (MIDs), Intel's dominance is being challenged by innovators now, in the second decade of the 21st century. The David is not a single business, but two—British processor designer and licensor Arm and Taiwanese semiconductor manufacturer Taiwan Semiconductor Manufacturing Company (TSMC).

Arm's designs have moved from mobile devices to challenge Intel's home turf—PCs, laptops and servers.[25] TSMC has overtaken Intel in the arms race of semiconductor manufacturing.[26] Both have been around for more than 30 years, the era of Intel's dominance. The basis of their challenge has been innovation. And that's why Intel is finding it difficult to catch up. Whether or not Intel will work its way back to its former dominant position, the arena has changed permanently. Intel can't hope to win with the old ways of doing things. Its technology, products and business model have been found inadequate, as these have been overtaken by those of Arm and TSMC. Intel needs to transform if it has to stay on.

Innovative challengers come with a distinctive solution to customers' job to be done. Their market focus—narrow or broad—is not entirely a strategic choice. It's more a function of size of the market

---

[25] Agam Shah, 'Intel Faces a Challenge in the Server Market with New ARM Chips', CIO India, 1 June 2016. Available at: https://www.cio.com/article/3077523/intel-faces-a-challenge-in-the-server-market-with-new-arm-chips.html (accessed 8 June 2021).

[26] Cheng Ting-Fang, 'Intel Falls behind Asian Rival TSMC in Chip Race', Nikkei Asia, 27 July 2020. Available at: https://asia.nikkei.com/Business/Technology/Intel-falls-behind-Asian-rival-TSMC-in-chip-race (accessed 8 June 2021).

for the unmet or poorly met job to be done which the dominant player has ignored. Whatever the breadth, innovative challengers are a tough nut to crack for the dominant player.

An innovative challenger who is targeting a narrow breadth of the Goliath's customer base is not an immediate existential threat, as the mainstream market of the Goliath is not under fire right away. Challengers who are successful with their narrow breadth of attack are likely to broaden their attack over time. Often, technological advancements including new applications of available technologies are the basis of a challenger's innovative incursion. All this can be spotted and understood well in time if the Goliath remains watchful. If spotted well before the challenger's offering goes mainstream, the dominant player has the opportunity to imitate or acquire the challenger.

Imitate and Dominate

Before deciding to acquire, Goliaths typically try their hand at imitating the David's innovation. Imitation is likely if the innovation is not protected legally, which is most often the case about business models, practices and many new product attributes. When Patanjali Ayurved's range of packaged consumer goods which emphasized herbal ingredients and traditional recipes started gaining traction in the Indian consumer packaged goods arena, Hindustan Unilever relaunched its Ayush brand, augmented with recipes from reputed Ayurveda doctors.[27]

Facebook is notoriously well-known for copying features from offerings of its rivals, most often from much smaller players. It's internal slogan when it comes to nifty features in rival offerings is 'Don't be too proud to copy.'[28] *The Wall Street Journal* reports that Facebook uses

---

[27] Saabira Chaudhuri, 'Outfoxed by Small-batch Upstarts, Unilever Decides to Imitate Them', *The Wall Street Journal*, 2 January 2018.

[28] Betsy Morris and Deepa Seetharaman, 'The New Copycats: How Facebook Squashes Competition from Startups', *The Wall Street Journal*, 7 August 2017.

an 'internal early bird warning system' which alerts its executives of the rise of smaller rivals whose offerings might pose innovative threats to its social networking offering. Using this, Facebook had identified several potential threats such as Houseparty—an upstart provider of small group video chats—which Facebook copied successfully. Facebook made overtures to Houseparty, indicating its interest to acquire, more likely to understand the rival better. When it became clear that Houseparty's offering can be copied, it went about doing just that.[29]

Acquire the Challenger

Cisco, which pioneered the market for computer networks in the 1980s, soon realized that new technologies and applications are flooding the market. Cisco keenly looks out for emerging technologies, products and applications, and quickly decides whether it can play in these with in-house capabilities. Else, they scout for and acquire smaller companies which are ahead of them in the emerging areas.[30]

Cisco's growth since the mid-1990s has been driven by an ever-enlarging portfolio of products and technologies, most of which brought within Cisco through acquisitions of smaller companies with promising technologies and products which haven't yet gone mainstream. Between 1993 and 2020, Cisco spent US$70 billion for more than 200 acquisitions—9 acquisitions per month, every month of 18 years.[31]

John Chambers, CEO of Cisco, summarizes their attitude towards innovative challengers thus, 'A lot of companies are arrogant. They're on top and they believe they belong there. We've got almost the

---

[29] Ibid.
[30] Glenn Rifkin, 'Growth by Acquisition: The Case of Cisco Systems', *Strategy+Business* Second Quarter 1997, no. 7 (1 April 1997). Available at: https://www.strategy-business.com/article/15617?gko=4dcd5 (accessed 8 June 2021).
[31] https://en.wikipedia.org/wiki/List_of_acquisitions_by_Cisco_Systems#Acquisitions (accessed 8 June 2021).

reverse attitude. We've got a tremendous fear of failing.'[32] Rather than seeing the innovative challengers as upstarts to be crushed with their might, Cisco sees them as pioneers who are shining a light on the path to new products and markets. By acquiring these upstarts, Cisco is able to combine their market presence, financial muscle and brand with the new products of the challengers to retain its dominant position.

Acquiring smaller players with promising technologies and products makes sense for the dominant player if the deal is done before the small player gets too big. How to organize the acquired business alongside the current business of dominant player would depend on the level of congruence in business model, culture, brand positioning and so on. Business history abounds with examples of Goliaths acquiring smaller players who came up with an innovative challenge, such as C-P's acquisition of Softsoap (see Chapter 6) or Facebook's acquisition of Instagram.[33] Needless to say, such acquisitions are subject to scrutiny and approval of competition regulators.

Goliaths have several advantages when it comes to imitating or acquiring. They have market access, financial clout, and many of the resources and capabilities which the innovative challengers are yet to build. All these will be more relevant if the innovation by the challenger is more incremental. That's when imitating, and failing which, acquiring, would be the Goliath's way to go.

More radical the innovation, more distinctive will be the business model and product of the challenger compared to the dominant player and less relevant will the Goliath's advantages be in imitating the challenger. It is in contexts like this that the innovative challengers who bring about radical innovations slip under the radar

[32] Rifkin, 'Growth by Acquisition'.
[33] Laurie Segall, 'Facebook Acquires Instagram for USD1 Billion', CNN Money, 9 April 2012. Available at: https://money.cnn.com/2012/04/09/technology/facebook_acquires_instagram/index.htm (accessed 8 June 2021).

of the Goliaths and grow too big before getting noticed. By then it is too late for the Goliath to imitate or acquire. The Goliath's dominant position would have seen serious decline. The only way forward for the Goliath is to transform.

Transformation of Goliath

Innovative challengers who come up with superior solutions to the job to be done for the mainstream customers offer what the Goliath failed to offer. The reason why the Goliath did not proactively bring such superior solutions to their customers' job to be done could be wide ranging. It could be a false sense of invincibility which comes with sustained success. It could be the result of hard trade-offs between cash flows from current offerings and those from moving to new offerings.[34] Or it could be anything in between.

Whatever the drivers, once the Goliath lets the innovative challenger slip through and let the customers get a taste of the superior offering from the challenger, there is no going back to the status quo for the Goliath. The only way for the Goliath to survive is to transform itself along the lines of the innovator. That's easier said than done, as the chance of succeeding in transformation tends to be low. Failure to transform simply means that the Goliath will fade into insignificance.

Superior the offering from the innovator compared to what's offered by the incumbent, tougher it will be for the Goliath to transform and survive. Broader the breadth of attack by the innovator in terms of customer base, tougher it will be for the Goliath to transform and survive. The imperative for transformation comes from the superior PVP which the challenger brings to the market. As we saw in the previous chapter, PVP goes up with superior value proposition and/ or better cost structure. The innovative challenger is likely to surpass the dominant incumbent in at least one or both of these. Customers

---

[34] Christensen, 'The Innovator's Dilemma.

would prefer the challenger's offering more than that of the incumbent, driving sales volume away from the incumbent and towards the innovative challenger.

It will take some time before the incumbent passes through ignorance and denial and reaches the point where it realizes that it has been in battle all along, against the challenger's superior PVP. By then, the challenger is likely to have grabbed a sizeable share of the market. If the challenger also offers a lower-cost product or product features which fulfil unmet jobs to be done, it is likely that the market has grown significantly and most of the new market would have gone to the challenger. This is what happened with HLL when Nirma attacked them with a lower cost and functional NSD powder. This is what happened with HMT Watches (see Chapter 1) when Titan positioned watches as a fashion accessory in the Indian market.

The incumbent under attack will not be able to adjust its value proposition or cost in the short term. As the challenger makes inroads in the market, the only way for incumbent's managers to achieve parity in PVP is to resort to price cutting. This will somewhat shore up fall in market share, but margins will drop. Since the incumbent holds a large market share, this translates into higher loss on profits in absolute dollar terms. If, instead, the incumbent holds prices, profits would still fall, as it loses more volume and would end up with higher per-unit cost.[35]

Either way, the incumbent's current business model has been called out as inadequate, and it is caught in a death trap with margins and volumes spiralling down. Unless the Goliath transforms—changes its business model—there is not much hope for survival. The longer it takes for the Goliath to realize this and make earnest efforts to transform, the deeper trouble it will get into, and more agonizing

---

[35] This mechanism, though weaker if the incumbent follows a low fixed cost business model, would still result in drop in profits.

will be the effort needed to get out of the trap. Both HLL in NSDs and HMT in watches took many years to realize that they needed to transform to stay on in business. While HLL was able to transform itself, HMT Watches couldn't.

To transform itself, the incumbent has to innovate. This often looks like copying the challenger in terms of technology, products and business model. In HLL, once the existential threat to its NSD business was recognized, its managers were able to discard their earlier worldview which came in the way of seeing Nirma as a rival. In 1987, HLL embarked on a special project—Operation STING (Strategy to Inhibit Nirma Growth).[36] HLL created a new product—Wheel—supported by a new business model which imitated Nirma all the way. Over a decade, Wheel helped HLL claw its way out of the hole.

HLL's fight against Nirma led to several new ways of doing things, especially in reaching rural customers. HLL transformed its value chain, from product design and production to advertising, marketing, distribution and sales. New capabilities developed in India during this transformation came in handy for Unilever when it later faced similar challenges in East Asia and Latin America.[37]

The focus of the Goliath caught in the trap of inferior PVP has to result in enhanced value proposition to customer or lower prices through lower costs. Through either or both, the Goliath has to enhance its PVP to match or exceed that of the challenger. There is just no other way out for the Goliath.

What's written on the topic of transforming a business could easily fill a large library. We will not go into the 'how-to' of transformation. The emphasis here is on highlighting the necessity of transformation

---

[36] Michael E. Gorman, Patricia H. Werhane, and Jenny Mead, 'Hindustan Lever Limited (HLL) and Project STING (A) to (D)' (Darden Business School Cases UVA-E-0266 to 0269, 21 October 2008).

[37] Butler and Ghoshal, 'Hindustan Lever Limited'.

as 'the only way' to overcome the competitive threat from an innovative challenger. The biggest hurdles are the incumbent's managers and their worldview which comes in the way of accepting the need to transform and at times the need to copy the innovative challenger. Once these hurdles are overcome, the rest is just hard work.

BEWARE OF WATCHDOGS

Whatever said about how the Goliath can guard against Davids can fall foul with competition regulators. Imitating innovative challengers, unless it breaks law, is possibly less likely to attract the ire of regulators. Even in this, actions of dominant incumbent in curbing the ability of the challenger to reach customers or partners can be seen as abusing their dominant position. Some regulators are more aggressive than others in ascribing intent to dominate on Goliaths. As Davids morph into Goliaths, their definition of 'evil' changes and the tendency to benefit from dominant position grows. How managers of a dominant business will behave against smaller rivals—be ruthlessly oppressive or play a fair game—depends on the values and culture of the corporation. We can easily identify examples for both camps. I will not favour one or the other but leave it to the value system which you believe in to guide you.

« LONG STORY » « SHORT »

Dominant players are often blindsided to incursions by challengers, and the delay in realizing and responding to incursions can be expensive. To realize competitive threats and respond in time requires that competition-relevant information is gathered, passed on and made sense of in time. Breakdown in any of these will result in blind spots. Imitating challengers can be driven out by dominant players using their superior access to technology, best-cost position and superior access to business ecosystem. Innovative challengers, if identified early, can be imitated, or failing which, acquired, to the benefit of the dominant player. Innovative challengers, once they grow in market presence, cannot be easily dislodged; the dominant player has to transform to survive. Battle-ready incumbents minimize blind spots, drive out imitators and imitate or acquire innovative challengers to stay on as dominant players.

CHAPTER TEN

The Pursuit of Profits

When Robert Kearns invented and patented the intermittent windshield wiper, his first stop for commercialization was the Ford Motor Company. This was in the early 1960s, when windshield wipers worked no slower than incessantly or furiously. Either of these was annoying when it wasn't raining incessantly or furiously, such as during light rain, drizzle or mist. The movement of intermittent wiper would imitate the blinking of human eye and would minimize visual fatigue for the driver. Although automakers and vendors realized this, they couldn't figure out how to make it work reliably. Kearns came up with an electronic control circuit for intermittent wiper movement which delivered variable speed as well as variable dwell at rest position—how wipers work today. This was probably the first application of semiconductor electronics in an automobile component.

Ford was keen to adopt Kearns's invention and asked him to carry out specification tests which required three million cycles of operation on his prototype. It took more than six months for Kearns to simulate this with a fish tank and share the results with Ford. Kearns believed that he would find a fair business partner in Ford, a company he admired since childhood. He had an agreement with Tann Corporation, a component vendor to Ford, to license his invention for manufacturing. He envisaged a profitable three-way deal between himself (the inventor), Tann Corporation (the component maker) and Ford (the automaker). By 1967, Kearns had the patent for his invention and Tann was in discussions with Ford to secure a contract for supply of intermittent wipers.

Automakers and their vendors had been working on a reliable technology for intermittent wiper for a while without much success, when Kearns entered the scene with his patented design which passed reliability tests. Ford introduced intermittent wipers in its 1969 Mercury line, a global first in the automobile industry. They sold it as an option at a price of US$37, while it cost them US$10 to produce. The wiper used Kearns's technology, but no royalty was paid to him.

Apparently, Ford engineers and lawyers were of the view that Kearns's patent would be deemed invalid, as they believed that it would not pass the test of non-obviousness. That's to say that the technology involved could be shown to be obvious to someone in the trade. An appalled Kearns wanted to sue Ford, but Tann backed out of the deal with Kearns. Tann Corporation did not want to jeopardize their ongoing business with Ford not related to wipers.

Kearns went ahead and sued Ford in 1978. Even before the trial started, Ford wanted to settle, but Kearns refused. He wanted to prove that his patent was valid. Twelve years later, the court ruled in favour of Kearns. His patent was indeed valid. By then, GM (in 1974) and Chrysler (in 1977) had already launched intermittent wipers using similar technology and without acknowledging Kearns's patent. European and Japanese automakers had also followed in the 1980s.

After winning the case against Ford, Kearns wanted to sue other automakers who infringed his patent, one at a time. He next sued Chrysler and won the case but was unable to sue others due to technicalities. To Kearns, Ford, Chrysler, GM and most of the European and Japanese automakers were violators of his right as the patent holder and usurpers of profits which he ought to have earned. Automakers had a different view which portrayed Kearns as a patent troll, but evidence doesn't support that.[1] Kearns's story is about the struggle of an innovator to earn the profits for his successful innovation which added value to customers. It just so happens that in this case, the innovator was an individual and his right to profits came from the monopoly granted via a patent.

Inability to earn profits which should rightfully be ours is widely prevalent across businesses, large and small. The usurpers could be other players in the value chain, including customers, suppliers, rivals and business partners. Recall our discussion on value—Keeping Scores—in the first chapter. Unless your business appropriates value corresponding to the value it adds, you are being short-changed. Shareholders and analysts are not kind to managers who let this happen.

How to be one up against rivals in fulfilling the customer's job to be done and how to positively contribute to value creation—what we have discussed so far—are meaningless if this doesn't reflect in the score—your profits. This doesn't happen by itself. 'Pursuit of profits' is the fundamental right of every for-profit business, and it needs to be engineered.

THE SOURCE OF PROFITS

Take a dollar of profit earned by any business at any time. Trace back all the way, and you will find an idea. The idea could be simple and obvious like using clear plastic bags instead of cardboard cartons to pack breakfast cereals or could be complex and not so obvious like sending pods via a vacuum channel to achieve high transportation speeds. The idea could be technical like substituting hardware with

---

[1] John Seabrook's account shows that Robert Kearns was not keen on money, and the only valuable patent to his name was that for the intermittent wiper. He is the opposite of what would be expected of a patent troll, who would typically settle fast and amass truckloads of patents in their name. See John Seabrook, *Flash of Genius* (New York, NY: St. Martin's Griffin, 2008).

software or could be commercial like deciding not to meter voice calls in an all-IP mobile telecom network. The idea could be about products like sending tourists on a trip to space and back or could be processes like ordering books online. The idea could be about the commercial potential of a new technology or the profit potential of a new business opportunity.

The idea would essentially be about doing things differently, with the purpose of delivering superior value to customers and, through that, creating and appropriating more value. The idea could lower the costs of production and delivery of a product which is already in the market, leading to higher profits. The idea could result in enhanced or new product attributes which are of value to the customers, for which they will pay more. When the increase in price is less than the cost of adding the new attribute, profits go up. The new attribute could be simple like putting a torch on the back of a mobile phone or not so simple like endowing a vacuum cleaner with the capability to navigate around your home. The idea could lead to a new product or process not yet imagined by customers or realized by competitors, creating a new market and, along with it, creating new profit streams. In all these scenarios, the idea forms the foundation of profits.

An idea alone cannot bring down costs, improve processes, enhance or add product attributes or create a new product or process. The idea has to first be implemented via technologies. The result is 'know-how'. This could be in the form of a prototype or proof of concept or any other form of knowledge such as how to bid for and win a licence from the government. The know-how then has to be embedded in a product or process and made part of a commercially viable business model. The result is an improved or new product or process which will deliver better value to customers and fetch better profits for the business. Not all ideas result in superior profits, though. Many promising ideas fail, as suitable technologies are not yet available or a viable business model is difficult to conceive. When superior profits are made, these would be based on ideas.

Recall our discussion on how Davids evolve into Goliaths in Chapter 8 (Figure 8.2). There, we said that investments will lead to superior quality or lower costs or both. Let's understand how. When an interesting idea meets focused effort to commercialize, supported by investments, there is chance for metamorphosis of the idea into know-how, and then the know-how into product or process. No guarantees though.

Edwin Land's idea of being able to see a picture soon after it's taken resulted in the know-how of Polaroid 'instant film' after many years of research to become one of the iconic innovations of the 20th century.[2] Marc Randolph's idea of having ready at hand the next movie to watch resulted in the know-how of Netflix's 'DVD queue' when implemented using a database of movies, a website to let users access the database and manage a list of movies, and supply chain to manage mail out and return of DVDs. This made its service a hit during their rental days, helping overthrow Blockbuster.[3]

Polaroid film was sold to its customers as a pack to be used in Land Cameras also sold by Polaroid. Netflix customers subscribed for one of its DVD rental plans which allowed them to create and maintain their view queues. The business model allowed customers to fulfil their job to be done. Rivals—in these cases, Kodak and Blockbuster—could not match the offering from Polaroid and Netflix. The resulting competitive superiority allowed Polaroid and Netflix to earn revenues and profits from their know-how on instant films and DVD queues.

Most businesses employ a large array of know-how drawn from diverse domains to create and deliver value to their customers. Some of the know-how would have been newly minted, while most would be of considerable vintage. Some of the know-how would be a core component of value creation, while others would be force multipliers in creating value. Each know-how contributes to the overall value

---

[2] Ronald K. Fierstein, *A Triumph of Genius: Edwin Land, Polaroid, and the Kodak Patent War* (Chicago, IL: American Bar Association, 2015).

[3] Marc Randolph, *That Will Never Work* (New York, NY: Little, Brown & Company, 2019).

created. The question is: How does the originator of know-how profit from it?

PATHS TO PROFIT

Arm Holdings, the British processor designer, has excelled in the art of profiting from know-how. Unlike Intel, the industry leader for decades, Arm does not manufacture a single chip. It does not even design the entire chip which is often more than a processor. It sells licences for using its designs of processor cores to those who need it. The licensees—Arm calls them partners—build a wide variety of systems-on-chip, often customized for specific OEMs (original equipment manufacturers), using the designs of Arm's cores alongside designs of other components including their own and that of their customers. The partners get the chips fabricated by third parties such as TSMC and sell these to their OEM customers who incorporate the chips into customer-facing products. Sometimes, the OEMs themselves are Arm partners as well.

Arm identifies itself as 'the leading technology provider of processor IP [intellectual property]' and claims that its designs are used in '180+ billion devices—from sensors to smartphones to servers'[4] and charges its partners upfront licence fee and royalty per chip of about 1–2 per cent of the cost of chip.[5] Arm has been successful in profiting from selling its know-how in the market for know-how, something that Robert Kearns tried and failed and had to litigate for decades to get his due.

In contrast, Intel has been using its know-how to design, manufacture and sell processors to makers of computers and servers. It makes profits by using its know-how in the market for products. The two paths to profit for a business—operating in the market for know-how or in the market for products—present distinctive sets of challenges.

---

[4] https://www.arm.com/ (accessed 8 June 2021).
[5] https://www.anandtech.com/show/7112/the-arm-diaries-part-1-how-arms-business-model-works/2 (accessed 8 June 2021).

Profiting from Know-how

The market for know-how suffers from what Kenneth Arrow termed the 'disclosure paradox'. The value of informational goods cannot be assessed without revealing it. Yet once revealed, the price which the buyer is likely to pay goes down, as the buyer already possesses the information.[6] Given that know-how is mostly informational, disclosure problem is acute when originators of know-how try to sell or license it, as Robert Kearns discovered.

When expected benefits from new know-how tend to be uncertain, efforts to come up with new know-how are likely to be limited, stifling the overall progress. To incentivise originators, governments grant the originator a limited-time monopoly in profits from the know-how. For instance, a patent is granted when a know-how is new, useful and not obvious to practitioners of the trade. If a know-how is granted a patent, there is some hope for the originator that her right to profit will be legally protected.

Since know-how is mostly informational, operating in the market for know-how is not going to be profitable to the owner unless the know-how comes with legally enforceable restrictions on use by others. Arm has been able to protect its profits through patents—it has been operating in a regime of 'high appropriability'. Robert Kearns found himself in a regime of 'low appropriability', where the legal protection of patent was ineffective.

Appropriability of know-how could be high or low for several reasons. Patents and other IPs are supposed to restrict imitation without consent, allowing the originator to profit from the protected know-how. Consent to use IP often requires some form of payment to the owner of IP. Government-granted monopolies and limitations in number of players via operating licences are highly valued in markets, as they are supposed to provide pricing power to those

---

[6] Kenneth J. Arrow, 'Economic Welfare and the Allocation of Resources for Invention', in *The Rate and Direction of Inventive Activity*, ed. Richard R. Nelson (Princeton, NJ: Princeton University Press, 1962), 609–626.

holding the grants or licences. Other players are legally barred from entering the arena.

By far the most promising source of high appropriability is the ability to keep the know-how a secret. That's difficult, especially when the know-how has to be revealed to use it, or when reverse engineering the know-how is not going to be expensive or time-consuming for other players. Although rare, secrecy is one of the best ways to ensure high appropriability. That's how the cola majors have milked the know-how in their cola concentrate recipes for decades.

Dominant players build formidable bases of complementary resources and capabilities over time, which puts them in an unassailable position in profiting from new know-how which is cumulative in nature. However, the effectiveness of these sources of appropriability is not always guaranteed. What's critical is to understand the nature of appropriability of a know-how and, based on that, choose the path to profit from the know-how.

Profiting from Use of Know-how

When the originator of know-how chooses to profit from use of know-how, as Intel has been doing, they have to bring together a complex configuration of complementary resources and capabilities[7] which are essential to embed the know-how into products and processes and to deliver these to customers. Right from its early days, Intel, in addition to building cutting-edge product research capabilities, has invested in world-class manufacturing and marketing capabilities. When the Japanese semiconductor makers overtook their American rivals in yield and efficiency, Intel, under the stewardship of Andrew Grove, doubled down to narrow the gap and then surpass the rivals from across the Pacific. Intel's marketing, especially its 'Intel Inside' campaign, is an acknowledged masterstroke

---

[7] Teece calls these 'complementary assets': resources and capabilities in the lingo of strategy scholars. See David Teece, 'Profiting from Technological Innovation', *Research Policy* 15 (1986): 285–305.

in cementing its position as the de facto processor among computer OEMs and driving wide adoption of Intel's processors by customers.[8]

During the 1980s, Intel had bowed out of the market for memory chips, following the onslaught from Japanese rivals, and turned its focus on processors. In the market for processors, it faced formidable rivals such as Texas Instruments, Motorola and Fairchild and an army of ambitious upstarts such as Zilog and AMD. But for the complementary resources and capabilities which Intel had built around its processors, it could not have claimed the top slot among processor makers and stayed there for decades.[9]

Ownership and control of complementary resources and capabilities become critical in profiting from use of know-how. If the relevant complementary resources and capabilities for a new know-how already exist in the market and are owned by the originator, deploying these to profit from use of know-how is straightforward. If the complementary resources and capabilities are owned by some other player in the market, it is likely that an incumbent business, possibly a large one, owns and controls these. This incumbent is likely to demand from the originator of know-how an outsized share of profits to put their resources and capabilities to use.

On the other hand, if the relevant resources and capabilities for a new know-how are novel and need to be built afresh, what's needed are financial resources and the higher-order capabilities to build the new resources and capabilities. When raising capital for sound business ideas is not that problematic, the dominant incumbent does not possess any particular advantage over the originator of know-how. Thus, in addition to appropriability of know-how, 'novelty of complementary resources and capabilities', and if these aren't novel, who 'owns or controls' these drive the originator's choice of path to profit from know-how.

---

[8] Malone, *The Intel Trinity*.
[9] Ibid.

CHOOSING THE PATH TO PROFITS

The strategic choice of path to profits for the originator of know-how depends on appropriability of know-how, as well as novelty and ownership of complementary resources and capabilities needed to profit from it (see Table 10.1). Among the potential paths to profits, use of know-how in products or processes is more prevalent than profiting by selling or licensing know-how.

Race against Rivals

During the early 2010s, several Indian start-ups created new ventures in online food delivery. Some of the more prominent ones such as TinyOwl raised millions of dollars in early-stage funding. All of them offered location-based access to menus of neighbourhood restaurants and online ordering through website or mobile app. Fulfilment was left to restaurants, resulting in highly variable customer experience. Swiggy, a late entrant to the game, chose to manage deliveries, which led to consistently high level of customer experience.

Table 10.1. Strategic Choices for Originator of Know-how

Novelty of CR&C[a]	CR&C Owned by	Low Appropriability	High Appropriability
Low	Originator	Race against rivals in the use of the know-how	Enhance PVP with the use of the know-how
Low	Other players	Depend on other players	License/sell know-how to other players
High	Not relevant	Pre-empt rivals in the use of the know-how	Build and dominate the market for the use of the know-how

Source: The author.
Note: [a] CR&C: Complementary resources and capabilities.

Swiggy's idea, which it implemented via novel policies and processes to create and manage a fleet of delivery agents on contract, was quickly imitated by many. Zomato, which was offering restaurant discovery and table booking for a decade, had earlier chosen not to enter food delivery because of its inability to ensure consistency in customer experience. Soon after Swiggy's model became well-known, Zomato entered food delivery by imitating Swiggy. It invested in delivery capabilities by acquiring last-mile delivery start-ups such as Runnr. Ride-hailing companies such as Uber and Ola followed. The only way Swiggy could stay ahead of imitating rivals was to race against them. What ensued was a fierce battle between Swiggy, Zomato, Uber Eats and Food Panda, all of them pumping investor dollars into a spiralling spree of discounts. By the time the dust settled, Swiggy and Zomato emerged as the dominant players but after taking massive hits to their bottom line.[10]

Some ideas are easy to imitate. If the idea is any good, rivals would quickly imitate, robbing the originator of profits, shortening the exploitation phase (see Chapter 6, Figure 6.2). Imitation would take away any relative advantage which the originator would have had over rivals. This is easier if the technologies which go into translating the idea into know-how are well-known or available in the market. When appropriability is low and complementary resources and capabilities exist both with the originator and rivals, the cost and time to market of imitating are alarmingly short, and that's what makes this one of the bad places to be for the originator.

Pre-emption is typically difficult in this scenario, as the essential resources and capabilities would be easily available with rivals or accessible in the market. The only way for the originator is to 'race against rivals' in winning and locking in customers. The originator can get some head-start by staying below the radar as long as possible and by making obscure the way to get to the know-how from the

---

[10] Sai Prakash R. Iyer, 'Swiggy in India: The Envelopment Challenge' (Unpublished IIM Udaipur case, 2020), 18.

idea. By the time rivals become aware of the idea and figure out how to imitate, the originator would have gained ground. Hopefully!

If the originator is one among the Goliaths, it will use the know-how to sustain its dominance and profitability. If the originator is a challenger and also possesses the complementary resources and capabilities, it will use the know-how to reduce the gap between itself and the Goliaths.

Depend on Other Players

When appropriability is low and complementary resources and capabilities are owned by other players, but not the originator, profiting from know-how is almost a lost cause. Licensing or selling the know-how to one of the other players gets tricky due to 'disclosure problem'. It's likely that the originator of the know-how is an entrepreneur or a small company, and ownership and control of relevant complementary resources and capabilities lie with a dominant incumbent who also is cognizant of the originator's limited ability to bargain or legally assert rights to profit. The Goliath has a huge advantage. The best-case scenario for the originator is a hard bargain and lower-than-expected profits from the know-how. Worst case would be being cut out of the deal.

For Robert Kearns, it turned out to be the worst-case scenario. The product improvement based on his patent for intermittent wiper had to be packaged into an automobile, and the manufacturing and marketing resources and capabilities, complementary to Kearns's know-how, were already available with Ford, its rivals and suppliers. For know-how that's cumulative in nature, complementary resources and capabilities are likely to exist and are also likely to be owned and controlled by some of the Goliaths in the relevant market.

In this scenario, the originator has to 'depend on other players' with the realization of a weaker bargaining position. The deal will likely be less than equitable for the originator. But that's yet the best way, as fighting to get fair value would result in profit share which is even less due to delays, uncertainty about ability to appropriate and high cost of going legal, if needed. For this reason, entrepreneurs and investors shun industries which are infamous for low appropriability of know-how created by outsiders.[11]

Pre-empt Rivals

Even if appropriability of know-how is low, the originator finds it more favourable to profit if complementary resources and capabilities are novel and are not yet available with other players in the arena. The originator and other players who want to imitate have to build these afresh. The originator is at an advantage for the short duration when the know-how and its deployment in a product or process are not yet revealed in the arena. It is during this time that the originator can build the needed complementary resources and capabilities. Once the know-how and its use in a product or process are revealed, rivals, especially Goliaths, would imitate. Given the head-start, the originator can and should pre-empt rivals from acquiring key resources as well as critical ingredients of capabilities which are complementary to the know-how, delaying or thwarting imitative entry.

Robert Taylor did this with his Softsoap launch. By tying up a full year's production capacity for plastic pumps, he delayed rivals' launch of liquid soap and dispenser by several months. During this time, Softsoap built its market presence much to the chagrin of Goliaths (see Chapter 6).

When complementary resources and capabilities are novel and do not exist, it is likely that the know-how is disruptive. The know-how can potentially overturn current dominant products and processes. For this very reason, Goliaths in the market are likely to be reluctant to commercialize such know-how, as it would undermine their current profits from products and business models. Dominant

---

[11] Joshua S. Gans and Scott Stern, 'The Product Market and the Market for "Ideas": Commercialization Strategies for Technology Entrepreneurs', *Research Policy* 32 (2003): 333–350.

incumbents would not be keen to invest in the novel resources and capabilities, providing a window of opportunity for the challengers to dethrone Goliaths.[12]

Oftentimes, pre-empting requires that the originator denies its rivals' access to one or a few key resources or ingredients essential to imitate. Pre-emption does not guarantee no rivalry, for long. Rivals will take more time to imitate. Before rivals can imitate, the originator has to move on to implementing the next idea. That's what UA repeatedly and successfully did in the market for performance apparel and sports accessories, outpacing Goliaths such as Nike, for several years (see Chapter 7).

Enhance PVP to Customers

When appropriability is not low, the originator has a good shot at profiting, with limited threat of imitation by rivals. In addition, complementary resources and capabilities needed to take a know-how to market might already be available with the originator. This is the case when the know-how is cumulative in nature and brings improvements to products already in the market. Without the immediate threat of imitation and in possession of the resources and capabilities needed to commercialize the know-how, the best path to profit for the originator would be to enhance the PVP to its customers.

Intel's relentless pursuit of improvements to its x86 family of processors over decades, in line with the dictates of Moore's law, was based on a stream of new know-how which was cumulative in nature. Improvements which Intel had made in processor design moved in lockstep with improvements in its manufacturing processes, enabling it to consistently improve the PVP to its core customer base—makers of computers and servers.

In this scenario, deploying already-available resources and capabilities to profit from use of know-now is an internal strategic decision for

---

[12] Christensen, *The Innovator's Dilemma.*

the originator. Most corporate R&D take this route to profits. This is how Goliaths try to sustain their dominance over time. Where there are minor gaps in complementary resources and capabilities, Goliaths bring these in through acquisitions, hiring and partnerships.

Licence or Sell Know-how

Higher appropriability means better ability of the originator of know-how to protect profits arising from the know-now. Appropriability tends to be high under strong enforcement of IP such as patents, copyrights and trademarks, or if the originator is able to maintain secrecy of the know-how. High appropriability is rather an exception, but when it is so, and when complementary resources and capabilities are available with other players, the originator of the know-how can profit by licensing or selling the know-how itself to these other players. The deal is likely to be beneficial to the originator.

Arm Holdings operates under a high appropriability context based on strong enforcement of patents in the global semiconductor industry. The complementary resources and capabilities needed to commercialize the know-how of Arm—design of systems on chip, design and manufacture of chip production equipment, fabrication of chips and marketing, and sales and service of customer-facing products—are possessed by an ecosystem of players in the semiconductor electronics industry. The different sets of players in the ecosystem—Arm, partners, OEMs, equipment makers and fabs—are locked in a mutually dependent and beneficial relationship. As long as this scenario prevails, Arm will be in a position to continue to appropriate profits by licensing its know-how.

For more than a century, Coca-Cola has operated under high appropriability derived from its ability to keep its cola concentrate formula a secret. Pepsi followed suit, keeping its cola formula a secret as well. Till the 1980s, when Coca-Cola and Pepsi got into a long-drawn brand-building war, both were appropriating profits primarily by selling their know-how to other players—the bottlers. Both

Coca-Cola and Pepsi used to sell their cola concentrates to bottlers under restrictive contractual arrangements. The investments needed to convert the concentrate into drinks such as in bottling, distribution and sales were the responsibility of the bottlers. Marketing was jointly done by the cola company and bottlers. Both Coca-Cola and Pepsi profited from selling their know-how to bottlers who owned and controlled complementary resources and capabilities in specific geographic markets. Even as large bottlers like General Cinema emerged, the cola majors did not find themselves weaker in their bargains with bottlers.[13] Such is the power of high appropriability of keeping the know-how a secret.

High appropriability gives the originator of the know-how a strong advantage over other players, especially Goliaths who have been dominating the competitive arena. The Goliaths would not have much leverage over the originator of the know-how and, as a result, would end up with limited ability to usurp profits.

Build and Dominate

If the know-how results in a new product or enables radical changes in attributes of an available product, it's more likely that complementary resources and capabilities do not exist. Even if players in the relevant competitive arena are well-endowed with resources and capabilities, what they have is not likely to be relevant or useful in the context of the new know-how. Tesla's electric cars require a host of complementary resources and capabilities in design, component manufacturing, assembly, marketing, sales and service, none of which existed among automobile players. Although global auto majors have abundant resources and capabilities in automobiles which use the technology of internal combustion (IC) engines, many of these have limited relevance for Tesla's line-up of electric cars and its business model. The service chains of auto dealers are geared to service cars

---

[13] David B. Yoffie and Renee Kim, 'Coca-Cola in 2011' (Harvard Business School Case 5-712-501, 2012), 24.

with IC engines and are not that useful in servicing electric cars. Fuel retail companies have over time carpeted highways and cities and towns with filling stations which are part of the formidable global supply chain which connects them all the way to oil fields. All of these are useless to fuel Tesla's cars, which need to be fed with electric energy.

As a result, Tesla had to build factories for production of power train, chassis, batteries and charging stations as well as car assembly facilities. It had to roll out public charging infrastructure as well as after-sales service networks in its focus markets. To tackle state-level legislation in the USA, which prevents direct sale of cars to customers, they had to create experience boutiques where customers could check out and test drive the cars and online shops where customers could place orders. Tesla has been investing considerable effort in developing its core know-how—the software which goes into its electric cars, as well as know-how related to complementary resources and capabilities such as safe batteries and fast charging.[14]

One of the reasons why electric vehicle initiatives of global auto majors had tended to be incremental was the uselessness of much of existing resources and capabilities owned by them and their partners in the context of profiting from know-how on electric cars. When the know-how is appropriable and when the complementary resources and capabilities do not exist, the best path to profit for the originator is to build the market and seek to become the dominant player. Most likely, this will disrupt Goliaths in the competitive arena who will react with force. How to pre-empt and tackle the ferocity of their response is something we have already discussed. Suffice it to say that making profits is not for the faint-hearted, especially when making profits means that you pull the rug from underneath Goliaths.

---

[14] Hamish McKenzie, *Insane Mode* (Boston, MA: Dutton, 2018).

PITFALLS IN PATH TO PROFITS

The originator of the know-how has to choose the appropriate path to profit. This itself is not sufficient to ensure that the originator profits from the know-how. The path to profits is beset with several pitfalls. The battle-ready player not only picks the appropriate path to profit but also makes sure that these pitfalls are avoided.

Misjudging Appropriability

Managers often misjudge appropriability to be high when it is indeed not so. Usurpers can undermine your ability to appropriate profits through several ways. Contrary to popular belief, patents are largely ineffective. Only a small proportion of patented know-how delivers profits to its originators. In the remaining cases, the profits not captured by the originator—spillovers—are taken by other players in the value chain such as rivals, customers and suppliers, as well as business partners.[15] Reverse engineering is a common approach to reach the same results as a patented know-how and is difficult to challenge legally. Asserting a patent is becoming an extremely expensive affair. Even obtaining a patent is tending to become expensive.

Piracy has been one of the key issues which have affected the appropriability of copyrighted content. The explosion of digital media—be it music, video or books—has made it possible for copying and distribution without loss of quality. Since the late 1990s, media corporations have been fighting a losing battle to put a stop to piracy, without much effect. Eventually, new business models have emerged around streaming music and video as well as digital subscriptions for books.

Counterfeiting of popular brands and close imitations of valuable trademarks have become routine. In some categories like luxury watches where counterfeits can never stand alongside the originals,

---

[15] Teece, 'Profiting from Technological Innovation'.

the markets are distinctive. But where the job to be done for the product is more functional and the counterfeit or imitation is almost as good a substitute, the original has a tough time retaining its customers. Profits which the owner of the original brand or trademark should have earned go to the counterfeiters and imitators.

Government-granted monopolies or restrictions in number of players via licences are often circumvented by other innovative players by exploiting loopholes. Other aggressive players enter and challenge the complacent player, who's under the delusion of protection by licence. While legal eagles fight it out in courts to establish violation of licence terms by the usurper, the battle in the competitive arena would have irreversibly undermined the profitability of the licence holder. That's what happened in the Indian mobile telecom arena during the early 2000s irreversibly paring tariffs for mobile calls by one-twentieth or less.[16]

We have seen that Goliaths who are in possession of most of the complementary resources and capabilities relevant for the cumulative know-how bite the dust when challenged with the disruptive know-how. They cannot come out of this scenario without themselves undergoing a transformation (see Chapter 9). Even then, they would never be able to go back to their glorious former self.

Living under the delusion that our IP or licence or grant is airtight and cannot be broken into by rivals and carrying on thinking that we are the only one capable of bringing new technology into the arena are signs of having fallen into the pitfall of misjudged appropriability. False sense of invincibility, a consequence of continued market dominance, often leads to overconfidence about appropriability.

---

[16] Sangeeth Varghese, *Reliance Infocomm's Strategy and Impact on the Indian Mobile Telecommunication Scenario* (London: Department of Media and Communications, London School of Economics, 2006), 20.

Misjudging Rivals

Businesses, small and large, suffer from competitive imitation. Most imitations cannot be stopped, and it just neutralizes any advantage we might have had vis-à-vis rivals. And we can reciprocate by imitating them. When we are imitated by rivals, the result is lower profits or lost opportunity to earn more profits. That's bad news.

As we saw in Chapter 6 (see Figure 6.2), the advantage for the originator which arises from a new way of doing things stays only till someone imitates or goes one step better. Originators of know-how often focus so much on themselves that they forget about the rivals who are watching and are likely to copy their successful or promising moves. We have discussed the 'why' and 'how-to' of sizing up rivals in Chapters 5 and 6. Not doing these systematically and periodically means that rivals and other players are going to take away profits which we ought to have earned.

When the underlying know-how seems to have high appropriability, such as a patent or a copyright, it is essential to assess how rivals who are left out are likely to respond. Let's say that we have a patent, and it protects our ability to appropriate value from it for many years to come. The patent also denies our rival an opportunity to get a share of the value pie. Rivals who are excluded could respond in one of the three ways—let it be, find a way around the patent to take a share of the pie or spoil the pie itself. The first approach is very unlikely. The second involves effort and investment by the rival, and we can expect them to do it if they believe that they can succeed in it within a reasonable time frame.

An excluded rival who cannot work its way around our patent is likely to spoil the pie itself. That's what happened with P&G, when it launched its Whitestrips, a teeth-whitening product, backed by a patent. This opened a new category in over-the-counter (OTC) oral care which promised to catapult P&G to market leadership as well as an outsized share of the value pie. C-P could not let P&G walk away with such a win. Three years on, they launched Simply White, a product at a much lower price but with claims of similar benefits compared to Whitestrips. P&G's tests showed that Whitestrips gave superior results, but consumers went over to C-P, and P&G was forced to drop prices. With the launch of Simply White, C-P shrunk the size of the value pie for OTC teeth whitening and also took a good bite off it[17]—a double whammy for P&G and its patented know-how. Licensing the patent to rivals could have been more profitable for P&G.

Misjudging Intent to Cooperate

Increasingly, we find rivals and business partners coming together and cooperating in a whole range of business initiatives—something unimaginable a few decades ago. Joint R&D, joint ventures for new facilities or market entry, and strategic alliances among players in a value chain including among rivals have all become more common in recent decades. Some of these have enabled the collaborating participants get richer and better placed in the arena than they would otherwise have been. Business ideas such as open innovation and value co-creation have become more common among managers talking shop.

Managers are assaulted with jargons such as 'death of competition', 'positive sum game' and 'win-win'. All these are supposed to convey the message that competing in an arena is not always about adversarial moves. In some contexts, non-adversarial moves are more beneficial. Sadly, the relentless deluge of such jargons carries the danger of lulling managers into complacency, making them believe that the current and future state of the art of competing is all about cooperative moves. Not really! Competing continues to be mostly about adversarial moves.

Cooperating with other participants in the arena is not a 'till-death-do-us-part' kind of relationship. The nature of such cooperation is opportunistic. Participants come together as they believe partnering to be more beneficial to them than not partnering. It's useful to

---

[17] Oberholzer-Gee and Yao, 'Brighter Smiles for the Masses'.

remember that deciding to cooperate is motivated by self-interest. Participants in the arena cooperate to create value, but when it comes to appropriation, the relationship is adversarial. Check out the small print in any partnership agreement, especially the clauses relating to who gets what and the sunset provisions.

Further, cooperating as a way to create value is subject to the dynamics of competition. It's essential for managers to periodically reassess, from their perspective, whether it makes sense to continue to cooperate. It's even more critical to periodically reassess whether the partner would find it beneficial to continue to cooperate. If either of these changes, the intent to cooperate will also change. The riskier scenario is when our partner realizes that the alliance with us doesn't make sense anymore, but we don't get it yet. Invariably, the partner bails out and we feel cheated. Managers ignore the dynamics of cooperation at their own peril.

THE PROFITABLE PLAYER

The profitable player pays attention to four factors. First, the profitable player pays attention to the basis for superior profits in the form of valuable know-how as well as complementary resources and capabilities. Their focus is squarely on building these more than and more often than their rivals. That's how they stay a step or two ahead of rivals and other business partners in raking up a high score.

Second, the profitable player pays attention to the paths to profit. Knowing that one size does not fit all, they are flexible in their approach to appropriating the most value out of what they have— know-how as well as complementary resources and capabilities. If it takes a partnership, they will be eager to do that. If it means keeping the know-how a secret, they will move mountains to maintain secrecy. Their approach to value appropriation is not dogmatic and is driven by the need to secure profits which are due to them.

Third, the profitable player consciously avoids the pitfalls which beset paths to profit such as not having a clear understanding of appropriability and not sizing up rivals and business partners including their intent to cooperate. Attention to the first two factors turns out to be useless if the pitfalls are not astutely avoided.

Fourth, the profitable player is conscious of dynamics. They understand that the know-how as well as complementary resources and capabilities valuable today in a certain competitive landscape might be totally useless in future or in a different arena. They know that paths to profit change over time, and sticking to old and irrelevant paths to profit is a recipe for a disaster. They are keenly aware that timely sensing of changes is of essence.

The profitable player makes focused efforts to understand what's going on in the arena, their rivals, substitutors, complementors, customers, potential entrants, as well as business partners, technology providers and other stakeholders. The acute awareness and appreciation of what drives profits, how to capture profits and how these two are changing over time are what make a player profitable. These are the characteristics of a battle-ready player.

«LONG STORY» «SHORT»

Creating value is useless if we cannot appropriate value—earn the profits which are our due. Ideas lie at the source of profits; when implemented with appropriate technologies, ideas give rise to know-how which has to be commercialized using business models. The know-how can directly generate profits through its licensing or sale in the market for the know-how. It can be used in products or processes to generate profits in the market for the use of the know-how. Managers have to choose an appropriate path to profit based on appropriability of the know-how and novelty and ownership of complementary resources and capabilities. Profiting from the use of the know-how is more prevalent than profiting from the know-how. Battle-ready managers take a nuanced view of paths to profit, which emphasizes value appropriation, and avoid pitfalls which undermine their ability to appropriate value.

CHAPTER ELEVEN

Towards Battle-readiness

Organizations, especially large and successful ones, tend to become less and less battle-ready, compared to their former selves and compared to nimbler and smaller challengers. Such a state need not be the exclusive domain of large and successful firms. Smaller businesses also suffer from similar issues. Almost all unsuccessful businesses would not be that battle-ready. What are some of the tell-tale signs which the organizations are not paying enough attention to getting and staying battle-ready?

Performance shortfalls will be explained away ingeniously with the responsibility (blame) put on factors outside the business, which are beyond our control or influence—market was on a downturn, customers suffered reversals unexpectedly, government regulations were against us and so on. At the extreme, it might sound like a conspiracy theory. In your management meetings and reviews, jot down the reasons for shortfalls in performance under three columns—'external beyond influence', 'external but within influence' and 'internal'. If the first column is long, the third is short and the second one almost empty, there is a good chance that battle-readiness is slipping. A good way to jolt managers out of this is to task them to come up with ways to move items from the first to the second column. You can't control or influence something you don't understand. That compels them to understand what's going on out there.

Information about rivals, especially challengers who are rising up, will be dismissed as a flash in the pan. During management meetings, questions about the rise of a new rival will be dismissed as not of any consequence. The next quarter is going to be fantastic for us and this so-called rising star will be gone for good. Ask your managers to pick five customers who are with or went to this rising rival. Talk to these customers and ask why the rival and not you. The answers are likely to be quite revealing. It is useful to slot in 'talk to rivals' customers' as a periodic activity, at least as part of preparations for business planning. During these conversations, if the customer gets the sense that you are not about to do a sales pitch, they are likely to offer candid and valuable insights on how you compare with the rival in terms of fulfilling their job to be done and why you are making a hash of it.

The share of revenues and volumes from new products[1] is dwindling, or the number of new product launches has gone down, or no new products have come out of your stable recently. Or worse, the rate of growth of business volume is lower than the market growth. Scratch the surface, and you will find that the product team, marketing team, sales team, production team, process planning team and any other team worth its name is playing 'passing the parcel', or worse, they don't talk to one another. Two things are likely at work here. Many of these teams haven't looked outside for a while. And they believe that the opponent is within the organization—the other team or teams which keep challenging their idea or shooting down their proposals. Bringing out new products which succeed requires close coordination among various parts of your organization and when coordination is lost, one of the first things to get hit is your ability to launch new products, make them succeed and make good money out of them. Get the teams to realize that the opponent is

---

[1] There is much con versy and debate over how to tag a product as 'new' or not new and, as a resu change the resulting 'revenue from new products'. I am assuming that you ve learnt to live with this challenge.

'out there'. A common enemy—a rival who's having you for breakfast—can bring the warring teams together, hopefully.

These are just samples. You might be familiar with more such instances which indicate decline in battle-readiness. It takes deliberate effort to stay battle-ready and stay ahead of rivals in battle-readiness. You and team need a battle-ready mindset to pull this off.

DROP YOUR TOOLS

On a dry and windy afternoon in 1994, wildland firefighters were trying to put out a forest fire in South Canyon, Colorado. 'A wall of flame raced up the hill towards the fire fighters. Failing to outrun the flames, 12 firefighters perished.... [Those] who perished *did not drop* their tools or packs while trying to escape.'[2] If they had dropped their tools like heavy backpacks and chain saws, they could have moved faster and to safety, as their surviving colleagues did. But the 12 who perished didn't, even when told to do so. Managers faced with unfamiliar or wicked challenges in their business are very much like the firefighters being chased by a wall of flame.

Karl Weick explains[3] why 'dropping our tools' is very challenging, especially when it's most needed. When you are in trouble, having your tools in hand reassures you, dropping them doesn't. You feel more in control with the tools in hand. You may feel the need to hold on to your tools due to social dynamics. You don't want to be seen as the first to drop tools, as that's a sign of accepting defeat. You may not want to give up yet. You may want to persist for a bit more, like the frog in the boiling pot. And finally, going for the tools which

---

[2] Karl E. Weick, 'Drop Your Tools: An Allegory for Organizational Studies', *Administrative Science Quarterly* 41, no. 2 (1996): 305.

[3] Karl E. Weick, 'South Canyon Revisited: Lessons from High Reliability Organizations', paper presented at Decision Workshop on Improving Wildland Firefighter Performance Under Stressful, Risky Conditions: Toward Better Decisions on the Fireline and More Resilient Organizations, Missoula, Montana, 12–16 June 1995. Available at: https://www.fs.fed.us/t-d/pubs/htmlpubs/htm95512855/page16.htm (accessed 8 June 2021).

you have relied on most is likely to be reflexive. Without thinking, you go for it. 'Pressure leads people to fall back on what they learned first and most fully',[4] what Karl Weick calls 'overlearned behaviour'.

Managers engage a wide range of tools in doing their job, such as their policies, decisions and actions about each activity which the business performs. Coming up with new products, procuring inputs, organizing production, communicating with and reaching the customers, enticing them to buy and providing after-market service—every process is in essence a tool in the manager's hands. We figure out what works and what doesn't, favour those that have yielded success in the past and discard the duds. At any time, we are likely to have a high degree of confidence about the tools in our hands. These can be as heavy as any backpack can get, simply by the conviction we carry in our minds that these tools are the basis of our success.

Our belief about the usefulness of our tools enters our worldview and gets enshrined in our approaches to solving problems. It can even become a dogma. We call it experience and expertise. All of this works wonderfully when we are trying to solve kind problems. Every time the tools prove good at tackling a problem, the overlearned behaviour just gets reinforced. That's how it becomes a reflex. All is well, till some wicked problem rears its ugly head.

When something unexpected happens, we instinctively grip the familiar tools tighter. That is overlearned behaviour at work. Faced with wicked problems, we ought to have reconsidered whether the tools we want to use will help us reach a solution. But that line of thought is blocked by overlearned behaviour, just like with the 12 firefighters who perished.

'Drop your tools' is a useful metaphor for us to think about how we handle unfamiliar challenges in business. These are situations which require us to take a step back, reassess how we want to approach a

---

[4] Karl E. Weick, 'The Vulnerable System: An Analysis of the Tenerife Air Disaster', *Journal of Management* 16, no. 3 (1990): 576.

solution to the challenge and change our approach as needed. That greatly enhances the chances that we are able to solve these wicked problems.

Take for instance a Goliath being attacked by a David with a superior solution to its mainstream customers' job to be done. This is a situation which requires the Goliath to transform and renew ourselves. 'To drop one's tools is simultaneously to accept mutation and to modernize remembered values or to believe that past as well as doubt it. These complex simultaneities are the essence of renewal.'[5] More often, we don't realize the need to change our tools until it's too late. With hindsight, most of us would conclude that we ought to have dropped old tools earlier. But in the heat of the moment? One of the key reasons why we don't drop tools is because we aren't sure if that's the right thing to do at that time. How do we tackle this challenge?

THE HEDGEHOG AND THE FOX

Greek poet Archilochus is supposed to have said, 'A fox knows many things, but a hedgehog knows one big thing.'[6] More recently, Isaiah Berlin used this obscure parable to categorize writers and thinkers. Philip Tetlock and colleagues, in their long-term study on expert judgement, found that those who self-identified with Berlin's 'fox' provided much better predictions about future than those who self-identified as 'hedgehog'. Interestingly, the foxes weren't subject matter experts in areas where their predictions were better than experts in that area. More interestingly, Tetlock observed, 'Hedgehogs and the dart-throwing chimp had equivalent forecasting skill.' That's overlearned behaviour meeting unfamiliar problems. Tetlock described hedgehogs as 'those who know one big thing ... toil devotedly within one tradition and reach for formulaic solutions to

---

[5] Weick, 'Drop Your Tools', 302.
[6] https://en.wikipedia.org/wiki/Archilochus (accessed 8 June 2021).

ill-defined problems.' The experts with their well-honed tools are great at handling familiar challenges.

The foxes 'know many little things', as Tetlock described them, 'drawn from an eclectic array of traditions, and accept ambiguity and contradiction as inevitable features of life'. David Epstein points out that while the hedgehogs—specialists in specific areas—are generally accepted as authorities in their areas, they aren't as good as foxes—generalists—in solving unfamiliar or wicked problems even in their area of specialization.

The challenge in front of us is how to know when to drop the tools. By definition, these situations are going to be unfamiliar, and the challenge of knowing whether to drop the tools or not is likely to be wicked—something that foxes are much better at handling than the hedgehogs. If our teams are full of hedgehogs, we will most likely lose the battle. Our teams will gloriously burn themselves up fully tooled and kitted. To tell us when to drop our tools, we need foxes. And the hedgehogs need to listen when the foxes are saying 'drop your tools'.

Let's not undermine the importance of hedgehogs. They are masters in their trade. Their experience and expertise are valuable. Their singular focus on the 'one big thing' is a very useful trait, especially when trying to envisage the long term. Problem is that they tend to tie themselves up in hubris, driven by their singular focus on the big thing which blinds them to changes right under their noses.

Remember Xerxes I, the Persian emperor, and his attack on Greece which we saw at the beginning of Chapter 3? Xerxes was avenging the defeat of his father Darius by the Greeks at Marathon 10 year earlier. He was driven by a singular vision of humbling the Greeks. For that, he amassed a fighting force like never before. Artabanus, his uncle and advisor, was sceptical. According to John Lewis Gaddis, 'Artabanus stresses prices to be paid—in energy expended, in supplies stretched, in communications compromised, in morale weakened, in everything else that can go wrong.'[7] Gaddis compares

---

[7] John Lewis Gaddis, *On Grand Strategy* (New York, NY: Penguin Press, 2018).

Xerxes with the hedgehog and Artabanus with the fox. Disregarding the warnings of foxy Artabanus, hedgehog-like Xerxes marched on to conquer Greece and failed. Foxes and hedgehogs can't succeed alone. We need both in our teams.

I am not talking about individuals who are either this or that. The hedgehog and the fox are in our mindset. Isaiah Berlin himself seems to think so. As Gaddis quotes Berlin, 'Some people are neither foxes not hedgehogs, some people are both.' As F. Scott Fitzgerald famously said, 'The test of a first-rate intelligence is the ability to hold two opposed ideas in the mind at the same time, and still retain the ability to function.'[8] The battle-ready mindset needs first-rate intelligence. Like a hedgehog, we need to believe in our objectives, our plans to realize the objective and the action agenda we have chalked up to get us there. We have to believe that we possess or are able to build the capabilities essential to execute our action agenda. At the same time, like a fox, we need to be alert to the possibility that our plans and action agenda can be derailed any moment, when something changes out there. Like a fox, we should be mindful of the nature of the challenge and figure out when we need to drop our tools. Like a fox, we need to adapt our way to the goal.

BATTLE-READY MINDSET

Mike Tyson was asked about his fight plan before a boxing match with Evander Holyfield. He replied, 'Everyone has a plan until they get punched in the mouth.'[9] He was echoing Prussian field marshal Helmuth von Moltke's view that 'No plan extends with any certainty beyond first contact with the [opponent].'[10] Tyson later clarified what he meant—he would trash any plan that Holyfield might have to win the match. Ironically, just the opposite happened. This was the

---

[8] F. Scott Fitzgerald, *The Crack-up* (New York, NY: New Directions Publishing, 1945).

[9] https://www.sportskeeda.com/mma/news-everybody-plan-get-punched-mouth-how-famous-mike-tyson-quote-originate (accessed 8 June 2021).

[10] Daniel J. Hughes, *Moltke on the Art of War* (Bearsville, NY: Ballantine Books, 1991).

same match in which Tyson bites off Holyfield's ear. The first punch to the mouth says that the plan is not beyond 'doubt'. If you fight without any thought of a possible punch in the mouth which wasn't in your plan, you lose the moment that punch lands. Allowing the possibility that 'the game will evolve' keeps you alert.

The not-so-battle-ready mindset would fail Fitzgerald's test of a first-rate intelligence. Managers would not be mindful that 'things will evolve'. That would make them less 'factful'. They would also not know when to drop tools. The result is a double whammy. When unfamiliar challenges come up, they don't even realize these to be so. In addition, they try to solve these with tools meant for familiar challenges. These are the very tools they ought to have dropped.

While discussing Berlin's hedgehog and fox, John Gaddis describes his experience of relating the metaphor with Abraham Lincoln as portrayed in the eponymous movie by Steven Spielberg. In the movie, Lincoln is pursuing the noble goal of enshrining civil rights in the American Constitution, but the path he takes seems far less noble. When Lincoln is asked about this contradiction by Thaddeus Stevens, Lincoln of the movie responds, 'A compass will point you true north from where you're standing, but it's got no advice about the swamps and deserts and chasm that you'll encounter along the way.' As Gaddis points out, Lincoln was being a hedgehog in aiming for his end goal but was being a fox in finding his way to it.

Steadfast as a hedgehog to the goals, and adaptive as a fox about the means, that's the battle-ready mindset. If dropping tools is what it takes to make progress, doing that and getting your team to do that is the battle-ready mindset. Like most things about business, getting battle-ready is not a one-time initiative. You need to keep at it to stay there or get better. Having a battle-ready mindset helps.

APPENDICES

APPENDIX A. ARE YOU BATTLE-READY?

The battle-readiness tool relies on your perspectives about your business, specifically your beliefs and action preferences about business and competition. The tool will help you understand where your business is currently in terms of levels of battle-readiness. The contents of this book will hopefully provide insights on how you can try and improve the battle-readiness of your business. To try out the tool, please visit the companion site https://www.battle-ready.co/.

APPENDIX B. MINIMUM VIABLE MARKET SHARE

Recall MES, which we discussed in Chapter 2. It is a descriptive concept which tells us the minimum volume of activity (for instance, quantity of production per year) at which lowest average cost per unit is achieved. The implication is that if we operate at volumes lower than the MES, our average cost per unit will go up and, as a result, profit per unit will go down. The MES typically is dictated by the technology underlying the activity. For instance, advertising on television will involve a large, fixed cost outlay, making it necessary that the advertisement should be deployed for a large market to reduce per unit cost of advertising. On the other hand, digital advertising would allow for much smaller fixed costs or make the cost of advertising mostly variable, enabling deployment to small and targeted markets.

In deciding on entering a competitive arena and in building the business case for it, one of the key considerations is at what minimum volume of activity can we be viable. This requires consideration of both MES and the quantity demanded (QD) in the market. The largest MES within the scope of activities would decide the MES. The market size would give us the QD. MVM is the ratio of MES upon QD. This is the minimum market share a potential entrant should capture to make the entry viable.

Take, for instance, QD of 100. In scenario one, the technologies used by the businesses dictate an MES of 4. This means that a new entrant would become viable by capturing just 4 per cent market share in this market. In scenario two, let's say the MES is 28. Here, the new entrant won't be viable at market shares less than 28 per cent. The implication is that higher the MVM, tougher it will be for an entrant to enter and play viably. The high MVM acts as a deterrent, dissuading potential entrants from entry, resulting in higher barriers to entry. Potential entrants can bypass this barrier by identifying which activity (production, marketing, advertising, etc.) imposes the high MVM and adopting a different technology which results in lowering of MVM for the market.

APPENDIX C. BUSINESS MODEL

A 'business model' is a clear articulation of how a business intends to create and deliver value to its customers. It is closely tied to, but distinct from, the strategy for the business, as the strategy articulates the action agenda—what's to be done and, more importantly, what's not to be done. One of the purposes of articulating a strategy is to be able to implement the business model. While there are several frameworks which seek to inform us about what a business model articulation should look like, I am partial to the one by Mark Johnson, Clay Christensen and Henning Kagermann, as it is concise and intuitively sensible and can be used in a real-life situation relatively easily. A brief description is given below. Interested readers can go to the HBR article[1] or Johnson's book.[2]

---

[1] Mark W. Johnson, Clayton M. Christensen, and Henning Kagermann, 'Reinventing Your Business Model', *Harvard Business Review*, December 2008, 51–59.

[2] Mark W. Johnson, *Seizing the White Space* (Boston, MA: Harvard Business Press, 2010).

Elements of Business Model

Johnson and others capture the articulation of the business model with four key elements, which I collapse into three. Each of these are discussed below.

Customer Value Proposition

Creating value for the customer requires a clear understanding of the customer's job to be done (discussed first in Chapter 2), coming up with offerings which meet the customer's job to be done while having clarity on who the customer is. Often, CVP goes awry when the job to be done is not clearly understood or when the target customer identification is fuzzy, leading to offerings which are neither here nor there.

Profit Formula

The profit formula consists of four components: (a) Revenue model: how is revenue generated, which covers the entire gamut of considerations about pricing and driving sales volumes, for the CVP, (b) Cost structure: what should be the approach to manage the cost of producing and delivering the CVP, (c) Margin model: how much would each unit of CVP generate as margins, closely related to the concept of unit economics and (d) Resource velocity: how much business volume and revenue to be generated from a given base of resources, a measure of efficiency in operations.

Resources and Capabilities

Johnson and colleagues identify two components—key resources and key processes—which I combine into a single component, essentially the configuration of resources and capabilities which are needed to deliver the CVP and realize the profit formula.

A more detailed explanation of business model would be, 'A business model is a design that ties resources and transactions to exploit opportunities to create value. A good business model will be viable. It will (1) meet target customer needs in a fair manner, (2) build value for the firm and all its key partners, (3) leverage valuable firm capabilities and resources, (4) be efficient in the use of its available resources, (5) differentiate the business from its competitors, (6) be sustainable beyond the short/medium term, and (7) be perceived as equitable to all key stakeholders.'[3]

---

[3] Professor Ganesh Prabhu, Indian Institute of Management, Bangalore, in correspondence with the author. Adapted from Adam J. Bock & Gerard George, *The Business Model Book* (London, UK: Pearson, 2019). Item (7) added by Professor Prabhu.

ABOUT THE AUTHOR

Sai Prakash R. Iyer is a strategy advisor to C-level executives and a passionate teacher, who brings more than 25 years of experience spanning management consulting, industry and academics with a bias towards actionable insights as the touchstone for meaningful discussions.

He earned his doctorate from the Indian Institute of Management Bangalore in corporate strategy and policy. An engineer by training, he spent the first decade of his professional life marketing industrial products and systems and later as a profit centre head with Siemens, India. He was a principal with the management consulting firm, Arthur D. Little. His client assignments took him to Southeast Asia, Middle East and West Asia, working on a wide range of topics such as competitive strategy, corporate strategy, public–sector strategy, governance, strategy implementation, capability building and transformation.

With his functional expertise in strategy and organization, he advises clients in several industries and sectors. Currently, he is Adjunct Professor of Strategy at the Indian Institute of Management Udaipur, where he teaches advanced electives on competitive strategy and multi-sided platforms.

INDEX